"CHATTER"

*Language and History
in Kierkegaard*

D1714448

MERIDIAN

Crossing Aesthetics

Werner Hamacher

& David E. Wellbery

Editors

*Stanford
University
Press*

———

*Stanford
California
1993*

"CHATTER"

*Language and History
in Kierkegaard*

Peter Fenves

Stanford University Press
Stanford, California

© 1993 by the Board of Trustees of the
Leland Stanford Junior University

Printed in the United States of America

CIP data appear at the end of the book

הַקֵץ לְדִבְרֵי־רוּחַ

(Shall windy words have an end?)

—Job 16:3

Contents

Preface   xi

Introduction:
From Conversation to "Chatter"   1
Significance 1 / The Suspension of Teleology 5 /
Kierkegaard 8 / "Chatter" 14 / The Question of
Conversation 19

§ 1 Interrupting the Conversation:
From the Papers of One Still Living   29
"The Whole Newer Development" 29 / Poul Møller,
Conversation 35 / Life-View 39 / Spilling Ink 46 /
"Sympathetic Ink" 50 / Style 55 / *Communicatio
Idiomatum* 58

§ 2 Algebra, a Rejoinder:
The Concept of Anxiety   64
Orientation in Science 64 / Kant, Conversation 68 /
Historicity, Topicality 75 / "The Speaker Is
Language" 77 / Spirit, Sexuality 85 / "Algebraic
Naming" 89 / Spirit Minus Spirit 94 /
Communicerende 99 / Crossing Communication
Out 108

§ 3 Autopsies of Faith:
Philosophical Fragments   113
The Difficulty of Thought 113 / Proposing to
Abandon the Question 117 / A Language of Names,

Absolute Difference 125 / Dispersion, Collection,
Departure 130 / "Thus" 135 / Slogans 140

§ 4 Ordeal of Autonomy:
    Fear and Trembling   145
    "Indirect Communication" 145 / Kant
    Comprehending Incomprehensibility 151 / "A
    Dangerous Standpoint" 160 / Critique, Ordeal 163 /
    Problems, Promises 170 / Abraham's Outings 174 /
    Allegory, Meaning, "Weaning" 184

§ 5 Notifying the Authorities:
    A Literary Review   191
    Fortune 191 / Occasions for *A Literary Review* 195 /
    Persuasion 199 / Surveying *Two Ages* 204 /
    Repetition 207 / Critique, Mudslinging 211 / The
    Aesthetic Validity of Revolution 214 / The Swamp
    218 / "That It Is Not" 222 / Literary Soldiers 228 /
    Prophecy, "Police" 233

    Conclusion: Negotiations   243

    REFERENCE MATTER

    Notes   253

    Bibliography   295

    Index of Names   309

Preface

"Chatter" deserves to be placed in quotation marks to the extent that it eludes conceptualization. The word seems to spurn the dignity of the concept to such a degree that all talk of "chatter" threatens to turn into the phenomenon itself, and it is against this threat that "scare quotes" were erected in the first place. "Chatter" exists, if it can be said to exist at all, only in quotation, citation, and recitation. The word cannot free itself of these marks and rise to an independent concept—on the one hand because its field of demarcation is far too wide, its various usages are too diffuse, and its scope tends to lose focus; on the other because the ambiguity of this word, as involuntary movement of the teeth, as the noise of certain animals, as insubstantial talk, brings into question, if only in a playful manner, the ability of speech to distinguish itself from, say, involuntary movements of the mouth and the noise of certain animals.

Since everything in communication and everything communicated can lay claim under certain conditions to being "chatter," the word can hardly be used to describe anything determinate, not even a mode of language in which things somehow become insubstantial, unimportant, weightless. Such indeterminacy implies conceptual emptiness, which could then turn out to be the meaning and subject matter of "chatter" itself, if only, after a methodical process of clarification, "chatter" was indeed shown to be unambiguously linguistic. But insofar as "chatter" can communicate everything and nothing, insofar as everything and nothing can fall into the subject matter of "chatter," it impedes unambiguous clarification every step of the way. For this reason, it demands careful reading. Its conceptual emptiness does not imply, however, that it belongs to the unconceptualizable, as long as the latter is understood in terms of comprehension and incomprehensibility; nor does this emptiness then take refuge in the wordless and the ineffable. The emptiness of "chatter" brings a specifically linguistic "nothingness" and a specifically linguistic "insubstantiality" into view and, in doing so, removes the assurance that a specific language—or language at all—is being spoken. The structure of this historical situation is the topic of this book; it traverses this topic by reading certain Kierkegaardian texts in which the situation is determined for the first time with precision.

~

As one could expect, numerous conversations have contributed to the development of an interest in "chatter." For reasons that will, I hope, emerge in the course of the presentation, this book cannot, however, claim the status of a dialogue. Nevertheless, it has emerged from the many discussions I have had with teachers, students, colleagues, and friends. To name them in the context of "chatter" would perhaps do each of them an injustice, so I leave them unnamed but not unacknowledged.

I thank Julia Watkin for sending me her fine translation of Kierkegaard's *From the Papers of One Still Living* before it had been published, and I thank Howard Hong for sending me copies of essays by Poul Møller and Johan Ludvig Heiberg. Chapter 3 is an altered version of "Autopsies of Faith in Kierkegaard's *Philosophiske Smuler,*" *Modern Language Notes* 102 (1987): 162–89. Chapter 4, "Ordeal of Autonomy," was prepared in 1990–91 and is scheduled to appear in a collection of essays on literature and philosophy yet to be published. The other chapters were written for this volume.

"CHATTER"

*Language and History
in Kierkegaard*

Introduction:
From Conversation to "Chatter"

Das rechte Gespräch ist ein bloßes Wortspiel.
—Novalis, "Monolog"

Ein Mittel des Bösen ist das Zwiespräch.
—Franz Kafka, a note to himself

Significance

Perhaps nothing is more difficult to bring into conceptual clarity than "chatter." Garbled speech, undecipherable script, and even the phenomenon of meaninglessness itself have been delimited and brought into definitive forms according to the canons of meaning and the rules of meaning-formation that make themselves known during the laborious process of conceptual analysis and elucidation. The efforts of philosophers and linguists have never ceased to be directed toward defining the conditions under which languages, irrespective of the "content" communicated and the "circumstances" of communication, can act as vehicles of meaning. Bringing into view the conditions of meaning—the forms, that is, in which things make sense and by means of which statements can be judged to be true—is no easier and yet no more difficult an occupation than determining the conditions under which speech can be said to be meaningful, since the clarification of these conditions is itself a meaningful linguistic enterprise. Difficulties of an entirely different order arise when language no longer carries anything substantial. Utterances are neither garbled nor indecipherable nor meaningless; rather, they have become, for all their clarity, idle vehicles, vehicles without content, vehicles in which "nothing" is said. Since neither this lack of content nor this "nothingness" amounts to a *nihil negativum* and since neither can be said to constitute an absence of language—whether it is called silence, stupidity, or brutality—something has to be added to these phrases for them to be understood, and so it is said that nothing of substance, nothing of value, nothing of significance, or nothing of interest is carried in utterances consigned to the category of "chatter." The vehicles of communication carry nothing of *weight.* Communication continues to take place, and its pace may very well accelerate, but everything is still somehow idle. In such non-movement—or incessant movement at a standstill—empty and idle talk finds its point of departure: the vehicle of communication, language as structure and act, remains in operation, but it no longer *works*, for whatever it carries is somehow "nothing."

"Somehow nothing": emphasis falls on both words. Somehow an utterance is nonsense, even though it fulfills every canon of meaning within a given language and a given group of speakers. This "somehow" is a clear indication that the judgment whether an utterance is nonsensical or not is "subjective," a matter of a particular perspective. As a judgment on value, it proceeds from the interests of a particular recipient, so all talk of an utterance being "of no significance" can be traced back to the desires and values of the listener or reader, and neither desire nor value constitutes an essential aspect of the sentences themselves. For this reason, traditional conceptions of the difference between subjectivity and objectivity, as well as those between fact and value, seem to shed light on the phenomenon of "idle talk": already constituted subjects declare that certain comprehensible utterances within a given language fail to move them and are therefore, if not sheer "nonsense," at least mere "chatter."

But this clarification will hardly suffice, for it is against the establishment of subjectivity and the givenness of language that idle talk bears witness. The idleness of the ones who talk and the meaningfulness of their idioms serve to challenge the very concepts of a *given* language and *already* constituted subjects to such an extent that the operations of both given languages and already constituted subjects are suspended—in idleness. And this suspension expresses a possibility that no effort at clarification can ignore: the idiom, namely, may be working in another direction; it may be on its way toward another language—or toward something other than language as it has been hitherto conceived—so the speech of its "idiots" may be the something other than *their* speech, speech over which they could claim ownership and whose results could justly be called their own work. In this way, "chatter" joins a long line of challenges to the pillars on which human subjectivity has been understood to rest.

The image of rambling or anguished words uttered by idiots who unwittingly speak the truth does not belong simply to a traditional rhetorical topos; it designates a site in which conflicts over the relation of language to subjectivity have been staged again and again. Religious orthodoxy and secular enlightenment have joined forces to dispose of "enthusiasts" whose tongues appeared to move without effective control by the soul or the mind. New methods have been invented to show that certain idiomatic modes of speaking did indeed make sense, that they had a "logic" of their own and could therefore be shown to have significance. Psychoanalysis, along with many other disciplines, has been enlisted in the effort to demonstrate the scope and legitimacy of speech hitherto deemed "babble," but insofar as these disciplines, including certain schools of psychoanalysis, have assigned themselves the task of making this speech meaningful and showing how it does work after all, they have left a highly ambiguous legacy. For they deprive "babble" of what is perhaps its most daunting characteristic: its idleness, its peculiar emptiness, its privative—but by no means private—character.

Keys to disclosing the significance of apparently insignificant objects and idiolects have generally been sought in the practices through which communities express themselves and tell themselves of their origin. Armed with such keys, the very notion of subjectivity alters; it no longer serves to designate the essence of an accidentally "individuated" human being and becomes the function of a community in which abstractions like "individuation" could first take place. Collective functionality opens up apparently insignificant, but not altogether meaningless, objects and idiolects to clarifying examination. No other concept is more often invoked in the investigation of "chatter," since this concept allows the investigator to understand the speech of a determinate "group" as coded action, as group-speak in which certain functions necessary for the genesis and maintenance of the group are carried out. Whereas the concept of collective functionality overthrows conventional notions of subjective constitution, it cannot do without the presupposition that the language under investigation is in fact *given*; it is inconceivable that the various functions a particular collective carries out should miss their mark and indeed that these functions could not be carried out at all. Conceptions of collective functionality, like those drawn from certain quarters of psychoanalysis, require that apparently empty and idle speech be understood to carry out definable functions; they assume, in short, that this speech *is* speech and that it belongs ultimately to a *given* language.

The function of the word "collectivity" in the concept of collective functionality is to gather the subject into a whole, even when the speech of the collective is somehow uncollected, indeed distracted and dissipated, neither able nor willing to function at all. Nothing characterizes "chatter" so much as this distraction and this dissipation. Doubtless psychoanalysis and concepts of collective functionality would be useful for the decipherment of any significant cargo carried in communication. But chatter "itself" can be clarified only if emptiness and idleness command respect, if they are treated as traits of language in its retreat from the task of fulfilling functions and contributing to already established operations, if the very concepts of emptiness and idleness disengage themselves from symmetrical opposition to fullness and proper functioning. Such a disengagement—and the concomitant dissociation of each word from its opposite and each judgment from disjunction—doubtless runs the risk of "chatter," but this risk can be avoided only if the functions and telos of language have been secured in advance. Once teleology releases its grip, however, the thought of language cannot escape the threat of a nonelevating and indeed leveling negativity, the indeterminate negativity of "chatter."[1]

The Suspension of Teleology

However difficult it may be to clarify the concept of chatter, it is nevertheless a category in the original sense of the word: a *katēgorein*, an accusation raised against someone, an act whereby someone is exposed to the *agora*, the "public" space. Even if the accusatory character is mitigated to the point of mirth, it persists in determining the sense of every judgment and every discourse in which the word plays a part. For it implies that the immanent telos of language is somehow not fulfilled. The multiplicity of situations in which this "category" tends to occur already indicates the extraordinary polysemy of the word and likewise shows how ill suited it is for conceptual elucidation. Not only is the word "chatter" difficult to translate; each of its many translations—*lēros, phluaros, mataiologos, garrulitas, Geschwätz, Gerede, bavardage, snak, sladder,* to name only a few—says something about the very act of translating. For "chatter" cannot be even understood as *human* language unless it is clarified by other categories and other accusations: "idle talk," "empty talk," "prattle," and so forth.[2] This apparently onomatopoetic word challenges the specificity of the much discussed definition of the human being as *zōon echōn logon*.[3] The animality of language, if not of the logos, is suggested in the very word "chatter," and this suggestion—that the functions of the logos are not fulfilled, that the logos does not give fulfillment, that the promises of its plenitude are broken from the start—perhaps underlies the vehemence with which accusations of chatter have been voiced among those for whom the logos still and yet again promises fulfillment.

Thus one finds, to cite a familiar example almost at random, the resolutely anticlerical Voltaire incensed at the impious "chatter" that takes place in lecture halls, on the streets, and in the salons, indeed everywhere in the world. Even if, as in *Candide*, all talk of cosmic functions and divine teloi is shown to be empty, the emptiness of talk itself is all but blasphemous: accusations of "chatter" replace those of "sin." The vacuousness of speech is an even more powerful vacuum than that created by the absence of recognizable divine ends, and since nature cannot tolerate a vacuum, this vacuousness has to be replaced with *work*: the cultivation of the fields in which the idle culture of empty talk is finally vanquished. The telos of language remains secure, even as every grand telos and every telos of a divine Logos has been lost. Cultivation, which is nothing other than the fulfillment of natural functions, excludes speech, since the latter cannot *not* fall into empty phrases, including the one that assigns idle speakers the prelapsarian task of "cultivating the garden."

The recognition that language has gone "on a holiday"[4] generates a command: the ethical demand to cultivate the earth or, inversely, the aesthetic command that the world abandon itself not to insubstantial talk but to a "pure" and "free" play. Ethics and aesthetics join hands to condemn empty talk; the basis of this condemnation and therefore the very category of "chatter" is an implicit teleological conception of language. The crisis of chatter arises when teleological conceptions not only cease to be acceptable in the clarification of nature but are positively unacceptable in ethics and aesthetics. At that moment the emptiness and idleness of "chatter" disrupt the conception of language as a facility determined to fulfill certain functions. Its naturalness is no longer decidable according to the schema, already formulated in Plato's *Cratylus*, of *physis-nomos*; the accusations of *lēros* (small talk) that occasionally break up Plato's shorter dialogues and interrupt their *logoi* (arguments) tend to suspend the distinctions through which the relation of nature and culture are explicated, including the distinction of *lēros* and *logos*.[5] Without an ability to decide on the naturalness of linguistic functions, however, it becomes difficult to speak of a natural language and impossible to escape endless discussions of the origin of language.

The age in which teleological conceptions of both nature and "culture"—whether the latter be placed under the rubric of "ethics," "aesthetics," or some other term—were systematically discredited is not difficult to name. It would be the age of Spinoza, but an epoch was spent discrediting him instead of the teleological conceptions of the world he had systematically shown to be groundless. Spinoza's effort could be appreciated only after Kant had, in his own way, subjected teleological conceptions of nature, ethics, and aesthetics to thoroughgoing critiques. By conceding the validity of teleology under the rubric of "culture," Kant also staked out a place for its revival. The first determination of the present inquiry is therefore in place. Its point of departure will be "chatter" after Kant.

After Kant, "conversation" and "dialectics," if these two are in fact distinguishable, become ever more intensive topics of discussion. Both hermeneutical inquiries and systems of speculative reason rely on the model of dialogue to generate their methods and axioms: the self-division of the subject is seen as a division into a living whole whose liveliness consists for the most part in the dialogue and dialectical sentences engendered by and in the division itself. Romantic urbanity, the "friendly" conversation from which Schleiermacher delineates the art of hermeneutics, the dialectical development of the concept as it realizes itself in the Idea— each of these motifs takes dialogue as the movement that radicalizes and brings to fruition the Kantian revolution in thought. No longer is a revolutionary turn taken by human reason so that it can criticize itself; it is undertaken instead as a turn in which speech learns to speak about speaking. In these turns and turnabouts, each of which is performed by a differently conceived subject, teleological conceptions are no longer tied to a stable and independent substance that, absolved of all relations, puts each thing in its proper order; teleology is rather the immanent movement of the *logos* itself, the movement of language—of dialogue, dialectics, conversation—as it speaks about itself, criticizes itself, and brings about its own immanent fulfillment.

"Chatter" would then be the interruption of this conversation about conversation: an interruption and disruption in which the

conversation does not conclude in a gesture of silent consumma-
tion or defiance but continues on, altered, indeed so altered by this
altercation that its continuation cannot be distinguished from a
break. "Chatter" is recognized after the conversation about conversation founders, and it is recognized as its alteration into a discourse, never a dialogue, that cannot speak of "itself." No discourse
on "chatter" can turn away from a recurrent demand for the
dialectic of selfhood and alteration; none can help but posit an
authenticity in which the self, unperturbed by its effects, speaks,
and the proper form of such speech is understood as silence.

Kierkegaard

An accusation of "chatter" does not presuppose a speaking
subject but posits instead a self whose speech is altogether its own.
The suspicion that the self is a function of language and therefore
cannot own its speech but is itself always only on loan inhabits and
propels the development of romantic urbanity, hermeneutics, and
speculative dialectics. Schleiermacher's discovery of a null-point in
language makes this suspicion palpable, but his conception of such
a null-point as the "null-value," or pointlessness, of certain discourses for the enactment of the art of interpretation[6] makes it into
a function of this art, not a challenge to its effectiveness. As the
limit to hermeneutical exercises, conversations of no value, null-
discourses—the supreme example of which is, for Schleiermacher,
talk of the weather, *Wettergespräche*—deserve as much attention as
discourses of "absolute" value, which for Schleiermacher, defines
"the classical."[7] Schleiermacher, however, kept his attention geared
toward the classical, as did those who would again and again revive
his teaching. By contrast, the most far-reaching scholarship in the
areas of hermeneutics, romanticism, and Hegelian dialectics has
explored, if not the catastrophes that take place in talking of the
weather, whatever the meteorological conditions may be, then the
catastrophes to which the subject is exposed when its speech,
including the statement "I think," can no longer be said to shelter
it from an ungraspable and unappropriable, always altering out-

side. Such catastrophes—the eruption of irony, the interruption of hermeneutics, the caesura of speculative dialectics, the exposure of dialectics to an unmasterable difference from itself—are neither accidental occurrences nor natural revolutions but are ineluctable altercations in which different linguistic functions are set against each other and in turn set against whatever, as singular, recedes from functionality in general.[8]

Nowhere are these catastrophes more concentrated than in Kierkegaard. For they are indissociable from his most persistent trope: the "leap," the interruption and disruption of a continuum in whose movement the ground of a particular domain of discourse gives way, exposing every discourse and every conversation that does not leap in turn to the category of "chatter." It is therefore on the corpus of writings associated with the name Kierkegaard that this study will concentrate. In his writings the suspension of teleology is itself suspended, but this "teleological suspension" not only does not rescue teleology but carries the suspension of teleology to its limit.[9] As a thinker whose explorations of ethics and aesthetics are everywhere indebted to Kant, as a careful reader of romantic writing and hermeneutic theology, and of course as a fragmented philosophical writer who relentlessly attacked Hegel and Hegelianism, Kierkegaard offers an incomparable point of departure for an investigation into the category of "chatter."

But his writings are even more alluring in this context, for they played no small part in the development of philosophemes in which authenticity and silence—these two indissociable motifs—are presented as the highest axioms and values: the philosophemes, in other words, that at one time went under the rubric "existentialism." If the category of "chatter" posits a self whose speech is altogether its own when this self no longer speaks at all, it is inseparable from the founding gesture and promulgation of "existentialism." From this perspective, "chatter" indicates an emptiness whose "existential" fulfillment is supposed to be decided in silence. Perhaps no statement is more prone to parody than this thesis, for its very enunciation makes it into a parody of itself. And it has no choice but to parody itself, to demonstrate its own inauthenticity, because "chatter" already undermines its basic presupposition: the assumption, namely, not only that language does have a function and a specifiable telos but that we already know what that function and what the telos is supposed to be. Once this presupposition is suspended, Kierkegaard's discussion of "chatter" sets itself apart from the philosophemes of "existentialism," however revised, and can even emerge as a topic of study in its own right, not a locus of evaluation, invective, or recuperative amusement.

If "chatter" is understood simply as speech unable to live up to its assigned functions and these functions are known in advance, clarification of the phenomenon would be an uncomplicated affair. But since this inquiry into the nature of "chatter" cannot begin with these premises, it cannot set out to elucidate the phenomenon; it cannot even determine that "chatter" *is* a phenomenon in the first place. In the first place, it is a *word*, but even this determination is under dispute, since the English word collects several Danish words in the text of Kierkegaard. Reading these words— *snak, passier, sladder, vrøvl, nonsens*—is the preliminary task of any inquiry. If, however, these words turn out to be unreadable, if no context can stabilize their meaning, if they suspend the modes of reading and decipherment grounded in the concept of a given language intended for already constituted subjects, then reading is not only the preliminary task; it is the only one. Accomplishing any other task, fulfilling any other function—including, for instance, stating without equivocation the constituent elements and the possible modalities of the phenomenon in question—would not constitute an advance over reading but a falling back into the naive view that "chatter" would be fully visible if only our eyes functioned properly. The advance "beyond" that constitutes a retreat "before" was a constant source of amusement for Kierkegaard. The incessant demand that "one must go further, one must go further"[10] cannot be annulled, but its authority can nevertheless be disputed, and the places of this dispute are the limit-points of the concept, the limits within which certain concepts operate, the limits to the Hegelian *Begriff*, and thus the limitations on conceptuality in general. To the extent that "chatter" eludes conceptualization, it disputes the demand to go further, and the locus of this dispute is the exhaustive reading of the word "itself."

The reading of the words in the Kierkegaardian text translated under the rubric of "chatter" is to this extent implicated in Kierkegaard's procedure: the procedure in which the demand to "go further" and conceive of a more extensive and intensive concept is thwarted. But the reading of Kierkegaard's words for "chatter" is implicated in his procedure in other, less obvious ways as well. Each of Kierkegaard's discussions of "chatter" delves into, and comes out of, a mode of reading, until in a review of a novel he discovers the "secret mode of reading" to which "chatter" owes its amplification if not its source.[11] These discussions are not simply appendixes to the representation of various—aesthetic, ethical, religious—"lifespheres" in which "the existing subject" acts out the scenes of its "inwardness." Nor are these discussions undertaken solely in order to distinguish his most well known "technique" of presentation, "indirect communication," from the apparent directness of those who by continuing to prattle and prate preclude the possibility of the incomparable and the incommensurable. For Kierkegaard's discussions of "chatter" are implicated in the critical readings of texts: in *book reviews*, the communicative character of which escapes the opposition of direct to indirect and to this extent disorients the customary guides to the interpretation of Kierkegaard's writings.

Two lengthy book reviews, each of which makes "chatter" into the matter of reading, frame Kierkegaard's "authorship" and therefore serve as the opening and closing chapters of this book. The first of these reviews takes its point of departure from a novelist's capitulation to "chatter," whereas the second celebrates a novelist's ability to represent its effects in "the present age" and by representing them, to keep her distance from "chatter" itself. Since the reviewer of such representations of the present cannot maintain this distance from "the present age," each review becomes an exposition of its historicity; each expounds the presence of "the present age" without the customary categories of ground and consequence, cause and effect, succession, or even development.

Nothing further from *parousia* could be found than "the present age," so each "literary review" Kierkegaard undertakes makes this emptiness into a topic from which it could never sufficiently distance itself. The topicality of these reviews consists in making public the specter of "chatter," and its method is reading "the times," whether as newspapers, journals, or other periodicals, including particularly unoriginal novels. In the central chapters of this book, the discussion is less of the ways Kierkegaard reads "the times" than historical talk itself. For the talk of history—and above all, so-called world history—amounts to another capitulation to "chatter," since it assumes that history *can* be comprehended and once comprehended, constructed in the form of a compendium. The conceptuality and inconceivability of history is examined in a reading of *The Concept of Anxiety*; the possibility of decisive significance in history organizes a reading of *Philosophical Fragments*; and the necessity of communicating a "poem" of coming-into-being, which would constitute the historical literary text par excellence, serves as the point of departure for an examination of *Fear and Trembling* in relation to a metaphysics of morals that by leaving the legacy of language aside, seeks to secure ethics from repetitive exposition.

The topical and historical dimensions of "chatter" are inexhaustible. Every conception of insignificant speech implies the priority of significance. The concept of "chatter" thus includes the representation of a loss of significance and in the end a fall into insignificance. Kierkegaard's *Concept of Anxiety*, as a treatise on the dogmatic "problem" of original sin, sets out the terms in which the discontinuity marked by the fall into sin and sensuousness—into history, in sum—makes every historical representation into an image of falling, of decline and decay. But "chatter" is not an expression of this falling; its very lack of "inwardness" makes it incapable of expression, so it cannot be simply counted among the phenomena of fallenness. On the contrary, nowhere is "chatter" more at home than in the prelapsarian condition, the only condition in which language, and not a determinate subject, can be said to speak on its own. Like anxiety, therefore, "chatter" traverses the distinction between the prelapsarian and the lapsarian, the pre-historical and the cultural. And again like anxiety, its mode of existence is *anticipation*: "Chatter anticipates essential speaking."[12] Not only does chatter refer back to the discovery of loss; it also anticipates recovery while at each interval displacing and reinscribing the terms in which "discovery" and "recovery" are cast. The historical character of "chatter" thus corresponds to nothing so much as *fate*. Just as fate refers back to a fault in its anticipation of a future, "chatter" implies a discovery of having fallen as it at the same time gives a preliminary indication of the world to come. And just as fate culminates in a fatality, "chatter" culminates in its very own intensification: in more widespread, more extensive, more empty talk. These two comparisons do not exhaust the inner relation between modern "chatter" and ancient *fatum*; indeed, "chatter" takes over the function of *fatum*—"having been addressed"— insofar as they are both implicated in self-fulfilling prophecies. The very announcement of *fatum* draws the fated ones into the crimes for which their death is expiation, just as the accusation of "chatter" draws the accuser into an emptier and more insubstantial talk whose expiation is supposed to be nontalk, muteness, or silence. In the first case, "life" is lost; in the second, "language."[13] Silence would then correspond to freedom, just as fate does to chatter.

But silence is not unambiguously freedom; silence is just as well "demonic" and thus implicated, again and again, in fate. The abrogation of fate cannot take place in speech or silence but in the suspension of this very opposition, in "chatter": "Chatter suspends the passionate disjunction between silence and speaking."[14] This suspension yields its anticipatory character. Nothing could be more contrary to the conception of freedom as ground of autonomy or immanent telos of reason than this determination of its relation to fate and "chatter." For this reason, inquiry into the category and concept of "chatter" cannot accept the set of oppositions usually associated with the terms "empty talk" and "idle chitchat." The suspension of disjunctive judgment is the preliminary method-ological requirement, and it is one that denies every discourse its ability to secure itself against "chatter." No reading of this word, as the preliminary task of the inquiry, can bypass this cycle, a cycle into which language and history are drawn together.

"Chatter"

Speaking without saying anything, saying things without making sense of what one says, making sense in speech but not having any sense to what one says—these are not uncommon accusations, but every accusation of this sort has something in common with what it denounces: the only ground and the sole reason for speaking reside in speech itself. The structure of hearsay repeats itself in the denunciation of hearsay, not because the denunciation necessarily repeats the rumor spread through hearsay but because both hearsay and its denunciation consist in speaking about nothing but speaking. Hearsay speaks about things that have only been heard, not adequately experienced; the denunciation of hearsay speaks about the mode of speaking that no longer speaks about things but only about speaking. Once it is no longer possible to refer to a foundational discourse through which denunciations of hearsay, gossip, and "loose talk" in general gain their authority and rigor, denunciations of such talk cannot escape the looseness and the laxity they denounce.[15] The fate of "chatter," which includes hearsay, gossip, and loose talk, is thus to spread itself out as the moorings of discourse in revered myths, authoritative pronouncements, and sacred texts are loosened.

The loosening of talk not only gives rise to more extensive and more intensive forms of hearsay, it also makes possible modes of belief and articles of faith that no longer seek the status of knowledge and no longer find legitimation in the canonical procedures through which cognition is ascertained and secured. A discourse is believed against all evidence simply because it has been said; one has faith in a saying although no evidence supports it—neither situation could take place if it were not for something like rumor, hearsay, or loose talk, as long as the word "evidence" means the appearance of the thing itself in the presence of self-conscious subjectivity. Only when "evidence" no longer implies such univocal appearance can belief and faith be saved from loose talk, rumor, and hearsay. The only means of making "evidence" mean something else lies in the alteration of the meaning of "presence," the significance of subjectivity, and the structure of temporality in general. Once standing in the presence of the thing itself takes place in language alone, once the thing before which one takes a stand is utterly linguistic, once language has thus become the unique territory on which to stand when speaking, belief and faith can be rescued from hearsay, loose talk, and "chatter."

Yet this rescue operation amounts to a total capitulation, for belief and faith are declared to have no other home than hearsay, and the sense of "presence" in the phrase "standing in the presence of the thing itself" can only mean what is commonly called, with good reason, "absence." The absence of the thing about which one speaks and the absence of the speakers to themselves—their distraction, inattention, absent-mindedness—not only continue to define hearsay but come to determine the sense of any creed that removes itself from the norms of knowledge and the canonical procedures through which it is established. The fate of "chatter" thus encircles the spread of faith.

If the discourse of salvation cannot save itself from "chatter," saving discourse itself from "chatter" cannot be a simple affair. Each strategy deployed in this rescue operation, regardless of its ultimate goal, tends to end in idleness. Employing the referential function of language, which seems the most obvious defense against "chatter," is of no lasting help, since reference to particular, palpable things involves a naive faith in their permanence, reality, independence, and significance. Referring to oneself may be less naive, and it is the critique of this naivety that dominates every philosophical project after Kant, but self-reference by its very nature cannot do without reference to things from which the self is distinguished. As a result, the self about which one speaks can never sufficiently secure its distinctness, its significance, its uniqueness. Constant reference to one's own exalted status not only does not escape the accusation of "chatter," but under certain circumstances—circumstances Kierkegaard will place under the rubric of "leveling"—invites this accusation with renewed vigor. Speaking about the one who speaks empties the referential character of "about" to such an extent that language no longer refers to the things brought to light and determined in speech but, instead, to this very emptiness, this suspension of the referential function, this discursive idleness. The resources of the referential function are thus exhausted.

Yet the prospects of a pure conceptual discourse are no more promising, since such a discourse falls prey to the loss of significance that every denial of the immediacy of reference, hence every discourse of mediation, risks. Even if the single, comprehensive concept discussed in purely conceptual discourse is the concept of the self in the process of self-division—and this defines Hegelianism—the risk has not been averted, for the very comprehensiveness of the concept precludes a distinct self, an outstanding individuality, the "existing" self that, as Kierkegaard insists, alone lets any discourse stand out. However much Hegelianism may be conceived in an effort to secure language from "chatter," its inability to speak about anything in particular, or better stated, to conceive of the uniqueness of "existence," makes it into the discourse most given over to hearsay, rumor, and the recitation of formulas. By dissolving singularities into the totality of the self-conceiving concept, purely conceptual discourse has nothing left to speak of, and without saying so it makes this "nothing" into the point of departure for its endless elaborations of a conceptual system.

If reference to things, self-reference and purely conceptual discourse are all equally incapable of keeping language free of "chatter," then it seems as though there is only one chance for speech to avert this fate: it must rid itself of reference and concept alike. Speech must henceforth transform itself into *action* and thus annul the very possibility of *idleness*. Yet the thoroughgoing deployment of this strategy demands a speech act so wholly distinguished from those that rely on self-reference to legitimize their operation—"I hereby pledge," "I herewith promise," and so forth—that the very notions of speech and action would have to alter in turn. Reference to an ascertainable self who acts in speaking would be as inappropriate as reference to anything that the action is said to have accomplished.[16] Indeed, agency itself becomes impossible as long as it presupposes a teleological continuum of intention and fulfillment. If, however, action cannot be carried out, no speech act can take place.[17] Action in turn becomes indistinguishable from idleness, and speech acts can no longer be distinguished from inactive, inert, and thus idle talk.

Since the unique speech act that is absolutely active—the act of creating things, not merely debts or obligations, in speaking of them, hence the original speech act in which reference and creation are one and the same—cannot be accomplished but only cited, the strategy of dissolving speech into action does not do what it first promised: it does not secure language from "chatter." But an answer to this insecurity can be found in a specific form of discourse. The speaker replaces the act of promising, or any other self-referential speech act, with a compromise: the subject matter about which one speaks has not yet been secured, and the subjects who speak are not yet sure of themselves. Rather, the subject matter is defined through a *question*, the subject is a *questioner*, and a decisive response to the question becomes the telos of speaking. Interrogative discourse thus appears to answer the threat of "chatter" by submitting itself to provisional insecurity.

A question does not refer to something in particular but to a delimited indeterminacy—the subject matter in question. Such indeterminacy not only does not condemn interrogative discourse to idleness, it sets the stage for the enactment of something: the commencement of a dialogue. But a question enacts something *only* insofar as it prompts a dialogue, and it can do the latter only as long as the question is posed in all seriousness. Otherwise, the dialogue is not a genuine dialogue, and the inertness of the ensuing discourse sends it in the direction of idle talk. The posing of a question in all seriousness thus presents itself as a decisive strategy whereby language shelters itself from idleness, emptiness, vanity. By deploying this strategy, Plato was able to distinguish dialectics from eristics and to demonstrate the difference between philosophy, sophistry, and rhetoric. From its inception in Socratic dialogues, then, the distinctive trait of philosophical discourse has been the posing of questions in all seriousness, while the ground and guarantor of this seriousness has been from the beginning the "ironic" comportment of the questioner. The impossibility of securing seriousness in speech makes irony all the more appealing and all the more assuring. Each ironic speech, when properly presented and recognized, gives evidence that not *every* word is in vain, since the very speech that seeks to show the vanity of speaking makes possible a presentation and recognition of the emptiness, idleness, and vacuity of language.

Thus conceived, irony achieves a vertiginous ambiguity: as the seriousness of a discourse comes into question, the seriousness of the questioner becomes more and more certain, and as the seriousness of the questioner is no longer incontrovertible, the seriousness of the question, however it has been posed, is less and less subject to doubt. By facilitating this transference of seriousness between question and questioner, or more generally between discourse and "existence," irony supports the strategy whereby philosophy defends language from "chatter." But irony is a most unfaithful point of support, for irony turns against its champions as soon as—no longer subservient to a particular strategy or subsumable under a determinate goal—it shuts down the transference between discourse and "existence" with the alacrity and deftness that it otherwise facilitates this very transference. However unfaithfully it might serve the causes for which it is deployed, irony nevertheless names a strategic move, perhaps even *the* strategic move by virtue of which philosophical discourse has been able to defend itself against the threats of idleness, indolence, and emptiness. By declaring in advance that nothing serious takes place in language, this discourse can reserve for itself the possibility of activity, fullness, significance. Because irony has so often occupied an exalted position in the "apologies" philosophy offers for its immersion of logos into language, it cannot be called on to comprehend the scope and character of hearsay, idle talk, or empty prattle. On the contrary, the fate of "chatter," which includes all these, absorbs the eruption of irony with the same motion that it encompasses the spread of faith.

The Question of Conversation

Without so much as saying so, Hans-Georg Gadamer, who has played no small part in bringing the concept of conversation to the forefront of contemporary philosophical and critical debates, indicates the fateful character of historical language. A preliminary discussion of Gadamer's concept of *Gespräch* (conversation, dialogue, the gathering of speech) can therefore serve as a point of orientation for a reading of "chatter" that acknowledges a difference between its peculiar emptiness and the subject matter of all genuine conversation: the subject matter, that is, according to which the judgment on the genuineness and authenticity of a conversation is measured. Gadamer's hermeneutic endeavor is an auspicious but by no means unique point of orientation. Other and perhaps more fruitful orientations would turn in different directions—toward dialogical theologians, toward certain literary critics whose efforts at comprehension begin with a comprehensive theory of dialogics, toward political theorists who conceive of a "conversation of mankind," toward philosophers who champion "conversation" as they adopt a conversational style of writing, or toward literary critics who conceive of literary history in terms of questions and answers.[18] The list could be vastly expanded and endlessly discussed. But Gadamer has a special significance for the study of "chatter," since his concept of conversation is a complex response to romanticism, Schleiermacher's hermeneutics, and Hegelian speculative dialectics; in addition, Gadamer often appeals to Kierkegaard for support in his explication of the temporal dimension of aesthetic and hermeneutic experience. Out of this explication emerges an understanding of the fateful character of historical language. The emergency and urgency of such an understanding impart the demands on "conversation" to which hermeneutics is then supposed to respond: "Understanding or its failure is like an event that happens to us. Thus we can say that something was a good conversation or that it did not stand under a favorable star [*es unter keinem günstigen Stern stand*]. All this shows that a conversation has a spirit of its own, and that the language in which it is conducted [*geführt*] bears its own truth within it—i.e., that it allows something to "emerge" [*entbirgt*] which henceforth exists."[19]

Unfortunately, Gadamer nowhere clarifies the relation of favorable stars, indices of fortune itself, to the course of conversation; rather, every unfavorable star recedes into the background as the conversation brings to light its telos, understanding or agreement (*Verständigung*). Here it is understood that an unfortunate "conversation," as the dialogue on which our fortunes rest, stands in no essential relation to the stars and therefore appears to be able to do without "fate," without contingency, and thus without historicity. The telos of understanding establishes the horizon from which speech is granted its exalted status. The question therefore arises: is a dialogue in which nothing "emerges" a dialogue? Is a misbegotten conversation whose emptiness precludes effectivity and thus "actuality" a conversation at all? If a conversation no longer lives up to its aim—the emergence of understanding or agreement—does it then lose all right to this title? Does it not as a result cease to be exposed to fate and thus cease to be historical in the first place? Is not the exposure to utter misfortune precisely that which gives conversation its historical, if not its "historically effective," dimension? Does the effectiveness attributed to history deny history of perhaps its most disturbing characteristics, idleness and emptiness? Each of these questions is absorbed into, and therefore set aside from, the question that Gadamer explicitly does address: the question of the question as the sum and substance of conversation. For the presence of a "real" question is supposed to distinguish the "genuine" conversation from its "inauthentic" (*unecht*) derivative, that is, from everything that would be carried along in the vacuous vehicle of "chatter." Nothing is more essential to Gadamer's universal hermeneutics than the ability by its practitioners to decide on the reality and genuineness of the question. For in the posing of a question, according to Gadamer, lies the *fatum* of conversation itself.

"The priority of the question" in conversation,[20] as both a logical and temporal determination of discourse, dictates the terms in which every conversation takes place and the terms at which it finally terminates—in another question: "To conduct a conversation requires first of all that the partners do not talk at cross purposes. Hence it necessarily has the structure of question and answer."[21] Cross-purposes undermine conversation just as surely as crossed stars doom love. But purposes can be kept straight only to the extent that the very conduct of the conversation be the end held in common. And yet this conduct, Gadamer insists, is not up to the partners in conversation; it does not rest on a subjective conductor who would be, as it were, a pedagogical leader; only the subject matter itself (*die Sache selbst*) can lead the conversation, and only when things are left up to the subject matter is the ground-laying, "fundamental" question unearthed. The question on which the matter depends is moreover not precisely posed but rather imposed as a task: "Questioning too is more a passion than an action. A question presses itself on us; we can no longer avoid it and persist in our accustomed opinion."[22]

The original question on which all decisions over genuineness are made is supposed to give conversation its "passionate" character: submitting oneself to the question constitutes the heroism, if not the martyrdom, of the questioner who on the basis of passionate submission is led into the heart of the subject matter, into the conversation constitutive of impassioned selfhood: in a word, into authentic existence. The subject matter posed in every authentic questioning turns into the very matter of the subject, its "existential" substance. From this substance "we" are made, so Gadamer can adopt as his motto a phrase that Friedrich Hölderlin doubtless wrote but perhaps deflected in a different direction: *Seit ein Gespräch wir sind* (since a conversation we are).[23] Participation in this conversation gives rise to the humanistic tradition, and the attitude of questioning, this attunement to the question as the "substance" of our being, discloses the depths of its historical dimension. Such an attitude is, for Gadamer, incontrovertible. The historical dimension it discloses is therefore anything but contingent; not only is it not open to chance, to fate and fortune, but it is ordered according to the immanent telos of the question, the answer.

However open the "horizon of understanding" may be and however much Gadamer may distance himself from categorial and predicative interpretations of being, a final answer, conceived on the model of a responsive sentence, is nevertheless inscribed in the movement of understanding as its telos. For according to Gadamer, the question must be *real*: it must be a real question, a question posed in all seriousness, and therefore a question awaiting a definitive answer; it cannot be merely an apparent question, nor can it be a question undertaken under the guise of a different telos or perhaps no telos at all. On no other condition can history, for Gadamer, be *effective*; its power lies in the "actuality" (*Wirklichkeit*) of the question and the authenticity of the questioner. At the foundation of the claims universal hermeneutics makes on its subject matter and on those who, "since a conversation," come into being is the incontrovertibility of the question. The reality of *its* subject matter is beyond dispute. To question the question—Is this really a question?—is to cast history adrift, which for Gadamer can only mean to "close" its horizons. To question the question—But what is not a question?—is to condemn the hermeneutic order dominated by the schema of question and answer to vacuity to the degree that the supposed subject matter can no longer impose itself as a task, much less as a positive fact, but sinks into an unavoidable void from which it would be impossible to secure a place of possible fulfillment. Nothing would be spoken in the conversation from which we measure our existence, so it would be questionable whether "we"—and all that we are—have ever existed in a past we can "retrieve."

So unquestionable is the question in the discussion of hermeneutics and its projection of history that the simplest question to which one can submit it—Is it a question or not?—is excluded from discussion. Dialogue is thus saved from eristics. The unity of the subject matter, to say nothing of the newly retrieved subject, depends upon the "actuality" of a question whose emergence generates "the conversation that we are." The answer to the question, to be sure, has not been determined, but the very indeterminacy of the answer rests on a "passionate" determination of the questioner, who in turn can see only indeterminacy in the *answer*, never in the question itself: "Every genuine question requires the openness [of provisional indeterminacy]. Without it, it is basically no more than an apparent question [*Scheinfrage*]. We are familiar with this from the example of the pedagogical question, whose difficulties and paradoxical nature consists in the fact that it is a question without a questioner. Or from the rhetorical question, which not only has no questioner but no object."[24] Pedagogy disengages itself from the universality of hermeneutics to the extent that its aim, "leading children," no longer takes its lead from the indeterminacy of the *answer* and therefore opens the question itself to an indeterminacy that cannot be reduced to the simple disjunction, "real" or "illusory." Since leading children precludes the possibility of being led by the subject matter, the subject matter, according to Gadamer, assumes the illusory (*scheinhaft*) character of the question it poses, and this illusory character is supposed to be altogether removed from the domain of truth.

For a text as heavily indebted to Heidegger as *Truth and Method*, its lack of concern for the "positive phenomenon" of *Gerede*[25] and its corresponding complacency with regard to untruth as illusion is truly remarkable, even if one leaves aside the massive association of *Schein* (illusion, shining) with *das Schöne* (the beautiful) from which Heidegger himself is not exempted.[26] For this *Schein* could very well be "truth": the site where something new breaks into the open, the ineluctable place of disclosure. In lieu of such a site, Gadamer cannot help but maintain that *someone,* who will of course be the pedagogue par excellence, can decide whether a question is "real" or "illusory." This pedagogue would not be troubled with certain questions: For instance, does the very possibility of a pedagogical question have something to do with the matter of questioning? Is it, once again, a mere misfortune, an accident that befalls an otherwise authentically oriented discussion? The incontrovertible presence of an authority who can decide when a "real" question has been posed allows one to call a conversation a conversation in the first place. The ghostly presence of an unnamed pedagogue so completely traverses the paths on which

Truth and Method travels that the drift of the tradition shows itself
to have been led according to this invisible but not for that reason
ineffective decision maker. Since, however, the very presence of this
ghost suspends the distinction between "reality" and "illusion," it
undoes the distinction into which the question has been cast: either
"real" or "illusory," never neither or both at the same time.

   With the assurance that the "reality" of question can be ascertained, the tradition can guard its authenticity and genuineness
against the threat momentarily envisaged under the rubric now of
pedagogy and now of rhetoric. These two titles are chosen to
indicate an improper manipulation of a primordial situation, but
they lead elsewhere: to the possibility of a question without the
potential presence of the questioner, to a question that can be
questioned as a question, which is supposed to be different from
and opposed to an answer. But a question without even the potential presence of the questioner—what is that? Nothing but a mode
of language without foundation in the "reality" or "effectiveness" of
the subject matter on the one hand and in the "existence" of the
speaking subject on the other. Such a question in turn is no longer
indisputably a question but is already as groundless and distracted
as every speech no longer oriented toward an "illusory" subject
matter: in other words, it is "chatter," the effectiveness of which is
in no way commensurate with the "historical effectivity" (*Wirk-
ungsgeschichte*) through which the tradition, according to Gadamer, is activated.

   At the precise moment Gadamer lays the basis for the thesis that
in conversation nothing is presupposed other than language, he
withdraws from language a constitutive characteristic: its ability to
generate "illusions," to make errors, to be aberrant. That such
aberrations are generated in the course of straightening children
out only emphasizes the altercations into which different functions
of language tend to fall. In the *Schein* of the so-called rhetorical
question—but there is no need to single out questions here—a
specifically linguistic mode of negativity is named and then quickly
consigned to "illusion": it has no place, in other words, on the
horizon of understanding. No, it erases this horizon, and without a

horizon, there is neither understanding nor incomprehensibility; instead of a horizon, a fata morgana, always from a distance, suspends the simple opposition of "illusion" to "reality." Faced with the threat of this erasure, Gadamer turns away: the "difficulties and paradoxical nature" of rhetorical and pedagogical questions are not impasses on the path of hermeneutics or its nonmethodical truth. With the bypassing of these difficulties and this paradoxy, it ought to become all the more difficult to appeal to Kierkegaard and to find in him—and especially in his difficult, paradoxical undoing of "effective" time in the temporality of contemporaneity—an impetus to modern hermeneutical endeavors.[27]

A Kierkegaardian heritage that turns its back on "difficulties" and "paradoxical natures" will also want nothing to do with the pedagogue, the rhetor, the sophists—in short, the pseudonyms—who populate the Kierkegaardian text. Only a "real" Kierkegaard could undergo and in turn pose a "real" question. To insist on the *absence* of any questions, which could then be interpreted as the essence of "faith" and thereafter seen as the source of all "secrecy," would doubtless run counter to the spirit of hermeneutics that Gadamer promotes, but the very certainty of absence, and the negativity envisaged in "negative theology," is only the mirror image of ascertained presence and easily gives rise to a negative hermeneutics. The absence of any question is as little certain as the presence of a single one. For this reason, it is impossible to substitute a reading of Kierkegaard's texts for a deployment of particular themes, including the ones that are developed and broadcast in *Truth and Method,* according to a model of communication that resembles nothing so much as conversing with a friend ex cathedra.

The specific character of "illusory" questions whose illusoriness suspends the distinction between reality and illusion is as worthy of study as the "conversation" supposedly founded on the imposition of a real question. That it has been studied under the rubrics of pedagogy and rhetoric goes without saying. But the dignity of these titles tends to conceal their more or less hopeless point of departure: in "illusory" questions, in questions without a questioner, in questioners without a question, in language no longer bound up with the existential decision of the speaker to pose a question and throw himself into the already imposed questions of the "tradition," in language exposed to linguistic *Schein*. Since the historical dimension of "chatter," moreover, does not orient itself towards an immanent goal—understanding, agreement, *Verständigung*—and cannot therefore accommodate in its "tradition" the unity of an effect, its conceptual presentation is prone to a certain disintegration. Dialogue and monologue, conceived according to a tradition that "chatter" neither sustains nor opposes, are equally misleading terms through which the disintegrative and disorienting dimensions of speech are brought into focus; dialectic and dialogism are in turn unable to capture its peculiarity. And every conversation, like every question, is prone to fall into the hands of "chatter" once its immanent telos—answering a question posed and imposed in turns—no longer finds its security in incontrovertible seriousness, authenticity, and reality—or, inversely, in mere irony, playfulness, and humor.

However often hermeneutical enterprises may define their object through the concept of play, the questions posed and imposed are one and all "serious," indeed the very definition of seriousness. Suspending this seriousness, which is not the same as simply "playing," opens up the magic circle of "chatter": the circle, that is, produced by the "categorical" character of this word by virtue of which one accusation leads to a counteraccusation without end and without goal. In the course of his very first work, which was a text of literary criticism, Kierkegaard throws himself into *this* circle, not the one named in honor of the immanent movement of interpretation toward the telos of full understanding. Starting from the magic circle of "chatter," where accusation follows upon accusation without succession and without development, Kierkegaard sets out to expose the intimate relation of language to history. The motto appropriate for the clarification of "chatter" could never be "since a conversation we are," for it would bar "us" access to a mode of reading that would turn around and inform "us" who we were. But another motto could perhaps be sought in a less straightforward, less celebratory, more resigned, and far clearer elucidation of us, "our land," and its history:

offen die Fenster des Himmels
Und freigelassen der Nachtgeist,
Der himmelstürmende, der hat unser Land
Beschwätzet, mit Sprachen viel, unbändigen, und
den Schutt gewälzet
Bis diese Stunde.

open the windows of the sky
And the night-spirit is let free,
The one who storms the sky, who has made our land
Chatter, with many languages, unruly, and
rolled the rubble
Until this hour.

(Hölderlin, "The Next Best")

§ 1 Interrupting the Conversation:
From the Papers of One Still Living

> I like to consider myself a *reader* of my books, not
> their *author*.
>
> —Kierkegaard, a note to himself

"The Whole Newer Development"

Talking about nothing at all—this phrase summarizes Kierkegaard's evaluation of his first literary production, *From the Papers of
One Still Living* (1837). As a negative evaluation, it does not stem
from the distant reflection of an aged author on a youthful trifle;
this evaluation is integral to *Papers* itself. For not only is the object
to which this work makes "constant reference"—a poor and vain
novel by Hans Christian Andersen about an equally poor and vain
"artist"—devoid of significance; both the procedure and the results
of Kierkegaard's lengthy review of Andersen "as a novelist" are just
as insignificant, just as thoroughly condemned to constant poverty
as Andersen's hapless work and perhaps even more hapless hero.
Nothing but this general condemnation to insignificance can be
gathered from the interleaf instructions to the reader of the review,
and the judgment it announces, as the review sets out to demonstrate, is valid for the reader of the novel as well: "*Postscript* for
the readers who possibly could be harmed by reading the preface:
they could skip over it, and if they skipped far enough so that
they skipped over [*sprang over*] the treatise as well, it is of no
consequence."[1]
But these papers, which constitute neither a book nor even an
essay, do not simply wear their insignificance on their sleeves; their

29

thematic point of departure is the "nothingness," or the thorough-going "negativity," in whose space something like Andersen's novel on the one hand and Kierkegaard's review on the other could take place. And this "negativity" circumscribes the precise historical moment of their joint composition. If negativity so thoroughly vitiates and in the end determines every new phenomenon that newness itself, and therefore the announcement of a new literary phenomenon within the framework of a "review" devoted to the judgment on something "novel," is presentable only in its terms, it is not so easy a matter to skip over these papers. For such a movement, as a continual procession of leaps, would amount to nothing less than an overstepping of what Kierkegaard will call "the present age." Not reading *Papers* cannot be accomplished simply by neglecting to look at it; even if the reader leaves these papers "unread," which is more than likely, the multitude of negativities in whose matrix the novel and its review are composed and deposited before a "public" are not overcome, not "skipped over," so the papers, disorganized to the point where any "paper" of anyone who "is still alive" could be included in their company, will nevertheless have been read. In the end, therefore, this reading must be an explicit one whose ultimate, although not continual point of refer-ence is an empty and vain literary production, the insignificance of which doubles in its review and redoubles in reading the review all the way through. Talking about nothing at all is the great accom-plishment of these papers, and it is an accomplishment of a de-structive reading: a reading whose aim is anything but agreement and whose procedure has nothing in common with the friendly dialogue. Each moment in the movement of this text—and here "the text" could perhaps include all of Kierkegaard's scattered papers—determines in ever more precise terms the history and structure of the "nothing" about which "no one," not even Kierke-gaard himself, speaks.

At the very beginning of Kierkegaard's review, "negativity" emerges as that which defines the "whole newer development" (61). To this extent, the accomplishment of Kierkegaard's review, speak-ing of nothing at all, belongs to this novel development, the underlying tendency of which is to promote active amnesia: "The whole newer development—in order to begin again from the beginning—has a great tendency even to forget, if possible, the results this development has gained in the sweat of its brow" (61). Everything positive in the past must be forgotten, actively and with an uneasy awareness that "posterity could treat it in the same way" (61). It is on account of this awareness, which is inseparable from the activation of such forgetting, that anything positive—the positing, namely, of something new—can arise out of recent developments. But whatever positions do arise are so deeply traversed by the negativity of their origin that they can only present themselves in a negative manner—as ironic "positivities" and therefore as positions that on account of their irony evade the all-encompassing explanatory power of the Hegelian conceptual system.

Hegel is, as one would expect, the first of the "newer" developments to whom Kierkegaard pays his respects, and he is the one who lets the active amnesia of modernity appear "in its most respectable form" (61). But Hegelianism is not only *not* the only form; it is not even the dominant one through which all the others could be conceived; on the contrary, there is no dominant instance, no domineering concept, and this lack of domination is itself made manifest in the political "development" whose contours the young Kierkegaard, already the author of various open letters on current political questions,[2] seeks to outline. At bottom, both the "respectable" negativity characteristic of recent philosophy and the disrespectable force of negation develop into a politics of precisely that—*disrespect* for tradition and authority; in the end, "distrust" (64) with regard to every phenomenon, no matter how much trust the past has invested in it.

The "watchword" for recent political developments is therefore "Forget the actual (and this is already an attack), and insofar as the grandiose forms of government developed through the centuries do not let themselves be ignored, so must they, like primeval forests of old, retreat before the plough of culture at the dawn of enlightenment, in order that on the cleared plains there cannot now be the slightest poetic shelter" (64). Continuity and tradition are uprooted at the moment this watchword not only summarizes the underlying maxim of "the whole newer development" but in its authoritarian pronouncement also establishes the obligatory point of view from which to watch this development in the first place; the loss of continuity is in turn the destruction of the organic, the "primeval forests," in favor of a now artificial, dead and entirely open field. The agent of this leveling, "culture," does not rest content with undermining everything living; it goes on to destroy the very place in which its highest achievements are enshrined: "poetic shelter." Culture—and here one must note that culture and agriculture are so closely linked that the "culture" of which Kierkegaard writes eludes both the category of *physis* and that of *thesis*, both "nature" and "artifice"—obliterates every significant and long-standing phenomenon and goes so far as to obliterate *itself.* Active forgetfulness leaves nothing but an entirely open space in which all points of shelter, all guiding points, and indeed all horizons finally vanish.[3]

The expansion of "culture" into primeval lands is at the same time the destruction of the shelters that "culture" sets up. Poetic shelter is no longer possible when natural fields yield to the "poetic" in the broadest sense: to the domain, that is, of everything "made." But Kierkegaard does not abandon the ambiguity of "culture" to an ahistorical paradox; this ambiguity takes on a precise historical and geographic location, and this localization takes place in an "illustration" of the oblivion, as the vanishing horizon, that characterizes "the whole newer development" and sets it apart from the past. Revolutionary France invades feudal Russia and there succumbs to vertigo: "Or what, indeed, could there be for poetry to do in a time when the younger person who is striving after something higher must feel in a spiritual sense the same symptoms as the Frenchmen on their march across the Russian steppes, where the eye seeks a point on which it can rest, in a time when the older men, who still know what they want, with pain must see individuals trickle like dry sand through the fingers?" (72).

Kierkegaard is not in a position to answer this question. Every answer to the question What is to be done? is already subject to global distrust, since the march of enlightenment, figured in the movement of the French soldier, not only falls victim to the disease but becomes at the same time its unwitting agent. The young soldiers, and therefore the "youth" who are committed to poetry, are levelers, however much they may wish to build a shelter for themselves. Oblivion and leveling meet on the vast, snow-filled Russian plain: it is an illustration of vanishing horizons, an image of the disappearance of imagination, a figure for a negativity that characterizes "the whole newer development" and in turn sets out the limits not only of "the present age" but even the West. With the appearance of this figure Kierkegaard first gives shape to his talk of "nothing."

If the negativity of "the whole newer development" cannot be grasped through the concepts of oblivion and leveling, it is because conceptual operations do not exhaust the processions of *life* on the one hand and *language* on the other. Since neither Hegelianism nor the politics of modernity put a halt to the negativity of "the whole newer development," Kierkegaard finds them wanting. It is easy to show this failure with regard to "life" or, to use the term he will later favor and will in turn gain favor with his fame, with regard to "existence." Hegelian negativity consists, according to Kierkegaard, in letting all previous existence (*Tilværelse*) appear as a "life of serfdom" (62), if serfdom can be said to be "life" at all, and Hegel's respectability consists above all in trying to show how nothingness, which begins the system, can nonetheless "retrieve the '*gediegne* abundance' of existence" (62).[4] The disrespectability of modern political developments consists in its inability to retrieve anything from its negative point of departure: it begins "not the system but existence, with nothing" (64).

Neither Hegelianism nor modern political movements are, however, able to grasp, and therefore bring to a halt, the "newer" negativity in which everything loses its points of reference, its horizon, its stand and stature. What escapes Hegelian conceptualization and the politics of amnesia is on the one hand "life" and on the other "language." The *figure* of the snowy plains of Russia allows Kierkegaard not precisely to *grasp* the negativity of "the whole newer development" but to put it on display and therefore fix it, perhaps even *freeze* it. A language altogether devoted to figuration, rather than to the conceptualization of phenomena or the implementation of plans, might in turn have a chance of similarly freezing this negativity in place; a language of this sort is *literary*. So the relation of life to literature becomes the nexus of Kierkegaard's scattered "papers." This relation can be read in two ways: as the *life of literature* on the one hand and the *literature of life* on the other.

Examining the life of literature and the literature of life constitutes the principal activity of *Papers*. The literature of life is, of course, "biography"—not, to be sure, "factual" biography, for reasons that will soon be apparent, but the fictional presentation of life, the generic forms of which are the ancient epic and the modern novel. To the extent that the novel constitutes the language of life, "biography" in the widest sense of the term, Kierkegaard is justified in making "constant reference" to a recent novel whose development beyond previous examples of this genre consists in presenting a vain, altogether empty character at its center. An analysis of such emptiness is in a favorable position to show in precise terms the character of the nothingness about which Kierkegaard plans to speak. But Kierkegaard does not simply choose Andersen's *Only a Fiddler* out of the blue; the choice emerges out of an exposition of the life of language, which in this case means the Danish literary tradition. The very idea of a life of language seems, however, to belie the primacy and independence of "life" over and beyond conceptual determination. But it would do so only on two conditions: that language be altogether exhausted in conceptuality and that life be reserved only for the registers of the organic and the biological. If literature itself undermines the first condition, the leveling characteristic of "the whole newer development" undermines the second. It is hardly surprising, then, that literature in the age of leveling should be the most pressing concern of Kierkegaard's *Papers* and that the relation of literature to leveling should occupy its attention. For this reason, *Papers* makes "constant reference" to a novel that is incapable of bringing the movement of negativity to a halt.

Poul Møller, Conversation

Papers does not abandon the prospect that "the whole newer development," stamped as it is by negativity, can come to a halt. The prospect of this break manifests itself in the emergence of a perspective from which one can present life in the medium of language. For this reason, the idea of the "life-view" (*Livs-Anskuelse*) becomes the decisive one for the entire review, if not all of Kierkegaard's subsequent papers. With this idea in hand, Kierkegaard can sketch the life of Danish literature in general and evaluate Hans Christian Andersen's novel in particular. Since each life-view relates language to life and life to language, the development of this idea, a development that will soon take Kierkegaard into the realm of "spirit" and into the business of delineating distinct "spheres of existence," holds out the promise of doing something more than mere exposition: it can show the place from which the modern movement of negativity, whether it find its expression in Hegelianism or in the politics of amnesia, can be held back.

The enthusiasm that the young Kierkegaard expressed upon hearing Schelling's declaration that Hegelianism will be swept aside with a "positive philosophy" is similarly motivated: the "positive" ought to be able to put a stop to the thoroughgoing negativity of "the whole newer development." Since, however, Schelling's "positivity" leads without fail to a "philosophy of mythology," not to the idea of a life-view, it fails to carry out the task *Papers* assigns not to philosophy and certainly not to mythology but to literature, as the language of life.[5] Only a properly deployed and appropriated view of life, not the supposition of anything "positive," brings negativity to a halt, and it is hardly an accident that such a life-view can be found in the *anonymous* author of a story called "A Story of Everyday Life."[6]

On the basis of this anonymous author's literary production, Kierkegaard can for the first time present the life of Danish literature as one in which life survives its own negation and does so precisely as a "life-view." Still living after negating every precedent and every continuum, still alive even after having begun with the most meagre and insignificant of material, the author of "A Story of Everyday Life" surpasses even Hegel, for the literary presentation of negativity, its exposition in language, puts a halt to its vertiginous movement. The "little" people who populate the stories of "everyday life" are, to be sure, of no historical significance, especially when compared with the "world-historical individuals" whom Hegel extolled; they are also not "the people" modern political movements have in their amnesia raised to significance, since they do not participate in mass social movements. But for Kierkegaard, the "little" people presented in the stories of "everyday life" are by virtue of the presentation alone able to put a halt to the negativity characteristic of Hegel and "popular" politics: "We shall try to orient ourselves a little in our novel and short-story literature, reminding readers that here, too, a similar attempt to begin from the beginning and from nothing has taken place, has actually been realized, for we do not know how to describe in any other way the cycle of short novels that began with *En Hverdags-Historie* [A Story-History of Everyday Life] (with nothing)" (64).

Although these stories of "everyday life" broke with the literary tradition and therefore began "with nothing," they are nevertheless able to give "testimony to the poetic specific gravity of existence" (65)—testimony, therefore, of the deep foundation in a particular life-view of these stories concerning insignificant characters. Out of this life-view, whose anonymity contributes to its efficacy, language overcomes the negative tendencies of "the whole newer development," and so the one who reviews such stories has only to do "his best *favere lingua*" (65): the favor of the language, its happy life, emerges from a literary presentation of historically insignificant lives whose roots are in a particular life-view. *Critique*, on the other hand, takes over at the precise moment no life-view comes to light; the failure to arrive at a life-view can be *read* not precisely in the "insignificance" of the lives presented in literature but in the failure to make this "insignificance" significant, a failure that can appear as the massive *effort* to make a failure—in the case of Andersen, a failed "fiddler"—seem somehow significant. The choice of *Only a Fiddler* for a critical reading is therefore anything but arbitrary: as a novel of a failed "artist," it tries to make something of this failure, and the very failure of this effort, which amounts to a failure of significance in general, serves as the matter of reading.

The traces of this double failure of significance make up the text under review. For this reason, the reading of this text cannot appear as a "conversation" with the author; rather, the text emerges because its "author" has failed to make his work into an independent work, because, in other words, he has thus failed to attain a "lifeview," because, in short, his literary production has failed to put a halt to the development of negativity. Kierkegaard therefore cannot agree with his recently deceased teacher and friend Poul Møller, who in *his* review of a novella by the author of "A Story of Everyday Life" had conceived of the critical review as a specific mode of "conversation." To the extent that *Papers* eschews conversation in favor of polemics and indeed makes it impossible to converse with the author in the space of a critical review, it amounts to a rebellion against Møller, who in 1837 was no longer alive. Although the tradition in this case may be only as old as the brief relation between teacher and student, Kierkegaard too sets out from the slogan "Forget the tradition!"[7]

The conception of the critical review as a "conversation" constitutes the doctrine that in Kierkegaard's work has been actively forgotten. According to Møller, the critical review should not fall prey to the systematic intentions of German academics or the digressive commentaries of French feuilleton writers. For the critical review to have any validity, it must move in a very specific place: it "moves in the region of conversation [*i Conversationens Region*]."[8] Møller never underestimated the difficulties of carrying out the "conversation" that constitutes the critical review, especially now that "a class of writers who have surrendered themselves to the poetry of despair and nihilism [*Fortvivlelses og Nihilismens Poesie*]"[9] has arisen. Despair and nihilism make "conversation" all the more necessary, yet all the more difficult. For as Møller takes pains to explain, "the period of European poetry" whose name is associated with Goethe has come to a close, and with it, the "poetic harmony" grounded on the "individuality of the author" has expired.[10] Without an individuality, there is no one to converse with. But this pronouncement stops neither Møller nor Kierkegaard from writing reviews; neither wishes to surrender literature to "despair and nihilism," and both undertake their critical projects so that the negativity characteristic of "the whole newer development" will not have the last say.

But the modes of critical reading advanced by Møller and Kierkegaard differ on the decisive question of "conversation": whereas the teacher makes his reading into an intimate dialogue with the author, the student, from the very first lines of the review onward, breaks off all conversation: "A word in advance [*Forord*] breaks up [*bryde*] no dispute, one is used to saying; this preface [*Forord*] at least disrupts [*afbryde*] the continuity of the dispute I have had for a long time with the actual author of this treatise" (55).[11] The breach in the "dispute," as the breakdown of conversation, gives rise to a critical reading, for a *critical* reading has no other text than the breakdown itself. From its inception, *Papers* breaks up the continuum of "conversation" and thus begins with *no spoken word*: it begins, rather, with a caesura, which in its turn becomes the matter of reading. Once "conversation" has broken down, a space opens up in which the "actual author" of *Papers* can touch upon what the deceased Møller, Kierkegaard's most intimate partner in conversation, called the "remarkable emptiness in literature."[12]

That Kierkegaard does not shy away from this "emptiness" and even throws himself into an empty reading of its traces in the text of an insignificant novel sufficiently distinguishes his critical procedure from the one recommended by Møller, and this critical procedure at the same time justifies his title, *From the Papers of One Still Living*. If this title is not understood as a cryptic message about the person of Søren Kierkegaard—and everything in his concept of authorship will be directed against such an interpretation—and if it does not in addition refer back to a non-Danish literary tradition,[13] it can be understood as a *declaration*: both the language and life, both certain "papers" and an uncertain "author," have survived the immersion in the "remarkable emptiness" (Møller) characteristic of "the whole newer development" (Kierkegaard). "Literature" and "life," each in quotation marks, live on, barely, in the critical reading of a "remarkable emptiness."

Life-View

Declaring himself still alive, Kierkegaard refers himself at every point to the moment when life stands still—in a "life-view." But it can hardly be maintained that he has resolved all the problems associated with this newly coined *terminus technicus*. Indeed, the course of Kierkegaard's writing can largely be viewed as an attempt to discover a perspective from which to present various life-views as discrete "stages on the way of life." Insofar as every "life-view" rests on a total negation but nevertheless acknowledges "existence" and presents "life" in language, it cannot help but appear contradictory. Contradictions of this sort could perhaps be resolved through Hegelian formulations whereby "life" negates itself and at the same time preserves itself at a higher level, but it is precisely the point of the term "life-view" to displace the conceptual apparatus through which Hegelians subject "life" and "existence" to the thoroughgoing negativity that characterizes "the whole newer development."

If the contradictoriness of the term "life-view" was simply consigned to the Hegelian phraseology that the character Phrase interjects into Kierkegaard's contemporaneously written play *The Battle Between the Old and the New Soap-Cellars*—"Phrase: Life is going out from itself returning to itself" (115)—then the idea of life-view would amount to nothing but that: a mere phrase, the expressive content of which emerges not from the struggles of a distinct life but from a particular phase of philosophy, Hegelianism. And indeed the battle in which Kierkegaard is as much participant as witness in *Papers* turns on the relation of a life-view to its double yet nonsymmetrical negation: the negation of life in "death" on the one hand and the negation of language in "phraseology" on the other. The very term "life-view" can turn into a concept and become conceptualized on one explicit and one implicit condition: that it *not* be dependent on the death of the organism and that this technical term not be converted into a mere "phrase." These two conditions underlie the battle acted out in *Papers* and determine its ambiguous status between literary critique and critique of life itself: the character of the *novelist* is therefore as important for Kierkegaard's review as the characters of his novel.

Kierkegaard explicitly counters those who would associate a life-view with organic death when he first discusses the meaning of the term: "We readily admit a certain approximation [to the final attainment of the standpoint of a life-view] in the fullest sense of the word but also say stop in time, before we are saddled with the consequence, annulling our whole view, that the life-view proper commences first (*demum*) at the hour of one's death or perhaps even on one of the planets" (77). If the death of the organism is the condition for the possibility of a life-view, then no *life*-view can be attained, or "life" ceases to be a simple organic matter, and "existence" is no longer subject to the ontological predicates attributable to a living substance. But if death is the enabling basis of a life-view in which every life-view, along with life, is systematically disabled, then Kierkegaard's review, which is only on the way to attaining a life-view, is annulled. And *this* annulment is, once again, "death," the negativity in which one sinks whenever a life-view is no longer attainable.

It therefore seems that Kierkegaard must keep his idea of the life-view removed from a "death" that is pointless precisely because it offers no view of life whatsoever; otherwise, his effort to present the life of language and the language of life—both Danish literary history and Hans Christian Andersen's novel—will prove unfit to bring the negativity of "the whole newer development" to a halt. And yet Kierkegaard cannot simply protect the concept of life-view from death, and this inability on his part to keep the term "life-view" free of "death" becomes apparent as he defines the basic characteristic of authorship:

The poet himself must first and foremost win a competent personality, and it is only this dead and transfigured personality [*døde og forklarede Personlighed*] that ought to and is able to produce, not the many-angled, worldly, palpable one. How difficult it is to win oneself such a personality can also be seen from the fact that in many otherwise fine novels there is to be found a residue [*Residuum*], as it were, of the author's finite character, which, like an impudent third person, like a badly brought up child, often joins in the conversation [*ofte snakker med*, often starts to chatter] at unseemly places. (82)

The poet must have died and been transfigured if a "poetic shelter"—against the cold, against certain death—is to emerge out of life. Death inhabits the life-view so completely that any appearance of the poet in the poem undercuts its poetic character: it ceases to be a poem at all. The "death" of the author is therefore the fundamental condition on authorship, and to the extent that the author is "dead," the movement of negativity has come to a halt. Such is the point of a "life-view": it is grounded in the negativity of "death," but for this very reason it is able to bring all the negativity of "the whole newer development" to a standstill. But—and here the asymmetrical relation between "life-view" and death makes itself known and at the same time exposes the "life-view" to a specifically linguistic mode of negativity—the eruption of negativity into the novel takes place whenever the author, "like an impudent third person," breaks into a literary work.

At this point of interruption the conversion of life into literature fails. The conversation that constitutes the literary text breaks up, and this breakup constitutes the locus of Kierkegaard's critical reading of Andersen "as a novelist." Such interruptions know no laws; they arise, to be sure, from the absence of a life-view that is itself enabled by a "death" and "transfiguration" of the author, but the emergence of these absences, these traces of failure, is as incalculable as they are uncontrollable. No poet can accomplish this act of interruption because a poet *as such* cannot interrupt the conversation that constitutes the poem. "No one" interrupts the poem, "no one" disrupts the novel, but this "no one" is, oddly enough, the *actual* poet or *real* novelist: the poet or novelist, in other words, who writes papers but has no "life-view" from which to write. The conversation that makes up a literary text falls prey to a caesura and then continues, altered, devoid of significance, utterly incapable of bringing its own negativity to a halt.

The accomplishment of a life-view excludes the interruption of the literary text, as a "conversation," by a definite empirical author. Nothing is more antithetical to a life-view than these interruptions, for the precise reason that the author who attained a life-view has already "died" and therefore cannot disrupt the conversation of which he is the author, except as a paradoxical ghost, a ghost who is all too *alive*, who has not transfigured his life in accordance with a life-view. And yet if death cannot be excluded from the life-view, it is not so simple to exclude such interruptions, and these interruptions are the very modes of negativity that, like every life-view, resist conceptualization. For "death," no longer a univocal concept, traverses both the life-view and the interruption of its conversion into a literary "conversation." Both are subordinated to a "death" that marks the *end* of this development: the life-view as the telos that puts a halt to the movement of negativity; the interruption of the conversation as the *limit* at which all talk of teleological calculation, including that of "development" and "authorship," is brought to an abrupt stop. This interruption of a conversation, which does not amount to the advent of silence, constitutes the linguistic negativity that interrupts the explicit transfiguration of life designated by the term "life-view," almost as though it were the residue of some alchemical process.

A life-view is not a particular view on life, not even a view on life at large, for the achievement of a life-view leaves neither life nor vision unaltered: life presents itself *in language*, and the language of this presentation resembles a "conversation" that cannot be interrupted by the empirical subject who has lived through finite, determinate, "lived" experiences. Such a conversation, as a resolutely fictional presentation of life, does not consist in an exchange of views among empirical partners; indeed, everything empirical, everything that appears to an identifiable subject, has disappeared and turned into something else, into a "view" that no longer has anything to do with perception but is linguistic through and through. No wonder Kierkegaard presents this transfiguration of life into a life-view as the very experience of the Logos, as transubstantiation:

> A life-view is more than a quintessence or a sum of propositions maintained in its abstract neutrality; it is more than experience [*Erfaring*], which as such is always fragmentary. It is, namely, the transubstantiation of experience [*Erfahringens Transubstantiation*]; it is an unshakable certainty in oneself won from all lived experience [*Empirie*], whether this has oriented itself only in all wordly relations (a purely human standpoint, Stoicism, for example), by means of which it keeps itself from contact with a deeper lived experience [*dybere Empirie*]— or whether in its heavenward direction (the religious) it has found therein the center as much for its heavenly as its earthly existence [*jordiske Existents*].[14]

Transubstantiated experience is free of all empiricity, all "lived" experience; it is thus free of experience if experience is a matter of having "lived through" a complex of occurrences. It is in turn associated with a "death" in which earthly substance translates into the spirit of Logos. But the spirit of the Christian Logos cannot define this transubstantiation if the possibility of a Stoic life-view, a life-view in which fate has been overcome, is conceded. If, however, this concession were not made, no "deeper experience," no experience of the abyssal loss of "lived" experience in the depths of "earthly existence," could even be envisaged. Once transubstantiation is, at least for a moment, free of its theological foundation, it can then present itself as the translation of the Logos from empirical "views" into a sustained linguistic presentation: a "conversation" without empirical subjects, a conversation in which life presents itself but does not make known any particular, definite, empirical lives. Breaking off conversation with empirical subjects conditions the achievement of a life-view; the interruption of this conversation, by contrast, indicates that a life-view has not been achieved. Reading those moments of interruption, which are indices of a radical failure to sustain a conversation without empirical subjects, constitutes in turn the task of the critical review. Critical reading therefore comes down to this: deciding on those places in the text, as a "conversation," in which empirical, "lived" experience leaves its marks. The criterion of this decision and therefore of critique in general has been named: it is the eruption of "chatter" (*snak*), the "impudent" disruption of genuine conversations, even of those one has with oneself. But the eruption of "chatter" has yet to be distinguished from the advent of genuine conversation; the empirical character of the former contrasts with the "transfigured" nature of the latter, but the difference between empirical and transfiguration, "lived" experience and "life-view," demands its own, perhaps always indecisive criterion.

Andersen then serves as a test case: a case to test the possibility of deciding between the empirical and the nonempirical. Since the decision involves this particular distinction, no empirical test is possible. Andersen's novel is, on the contrary, a test of readability, the readability of the eruptions of reference and empiricity in a "conversation" that is supposed to sustain itself without empirical viewpoints. And the name for the marks that such eruptions of empiricity and interruptions of self-sustaining conversations leave behind is "hieroglyph." Reading does not consist, for Kierkegaard, in the decipherment of these "sacred scripts" but in letting them remain without meaning: "If we now look and see how things are with Andersen in this respect, we find the relationship to be just as we expected. On the one hand, single propositions stick out like hieroglyphs [*Hieroglypher*] that at times are the object of pious veneration. On the other, he dwells on the individual phenomena coming from his own experience" (77). Experience of life that has not been "transfigured" or "transubstantiated" interrupts the course of the discourse and leaves a meaningless mark, a "hieroglyph," behind. To make the point even clearer, Kierkegaard appends to the word "hieroglyph" a footnote in which he compares the interruption of a discourse with the tendency to begin every "conversation" with a nonreferential "maxim" (77): a phrase, like the epigraphs with which Andersen begins each of his chapters, that has nothing to do with any "lived" experience. Referring to "lived" experience and speaking without any relation to "life" are equally implicated in "chatter."

Hieroglyphs, as concealed references to the "lived" experience of the author, and maxims, as nonreferential propositions that cover a "maximum" number of applications, are both untranslated, untransubstantiated, insubstantial, and therefore insignificant marks: language no longer in the service of meaning. Because these inscriptional interruptions remain untranslatable, they earn the "rational" sanction of the maxim or the religious sanction of the *hieroglyph*, an object of "pious veneration" (77). And yet, according to a logic unique to the "chatter," both hieroglyphs and maxims are untranslatable and indecipherable precisely because they are all too translatable and all too decipherable: their significance can be found in the "lived" experience of an empirical subject. Without a life-view, Andersen inadvertently interrupts his own literary representation of a life, and this self-interruption indicates his failure to appropriate his own life: he is not himself but an "impudent third person" (8), and he is not himself because he constantly refers to himself. Empiricity, as "lived" experience, leaves peculiar marks: interruptions of transcendental—or "transfigured," "transubstantiated"—conversations, and these interruptions are themselves inscriptions that are unreadable since they are all too readable.

The logic of reading, if one can still speak of "logic," must thus match the peculiarity of these marks; it is the very logic of Kierkegaard's review: each moment and mode of interruption is marked out in a discourse that is itself characterized by a break with the concept of critical reading as "conversation." Such reading cannot be so easily distinguished from the marks it reads, and Kierkegaard justly titles his text not "papers from a recently achieved life-view" but "from papers of one *still* living," so alive in fact that someone could very well interrupt, "like an impudent third person," the text of the review. The impudence does not consist in the negative imperative "forget the actual" (64); rather, the impudence lies in a linguistic mode of negativity, "chatter," that according to its own peculiar logic is all too positive. For this reason, chatter cannot be subsumed under the negativity that characterizes "the whole newer development," and the achievement of a life-view cannot put it, this mode of negativity peculiar to language, to a stop. The aim of critical reading, by contrast, is to do so; therein lies its uneasy justification. But in order to justify itself, critical reading would then have to distinguish itself—by some sure criterion—from interruption, "hieroglyphs," and "chatter."

Spilling Ink

The negativity of interruption, "hieroglyphs," and chatter does not obey the traditional rules of logic; each in its own way is positive to the extent that each imposes itself on a continuum of communication. The hieroglyphs that owe their origin to interruption are unreadable precisely because they are all too readable: they refer back to the empirical, "lived" experience of a particular life. But these hieroglyphs, as residues of reference, are potentially everywhere. For reference to "lived" experience is irreducible. Nothing can be done to prevent reference from accidentally taking place, no matter how many precautions one takes. The decisive position of critical reading derives from this undeniable characteristic of language: nothing, not even the transubstantiation that takes place in the achievement of a life-view, can guarantee the total reduction of "lived" experience or the complete erasure of reference to a particular life. Critique points out such reference and presents it as failure, but it can only do so if it too participates in the failure to reduce empiricity. Hence the "constant reference" to a particular writer; hence the constancy of reference in critical practice that has praise only for those who are able to erase all reference to themselves. Kierkegaard's ability to read Andersen's novel and to critique him in such relentless terms is predicated on his absorption into the linguistic mode of negativity that characterizes this novel, and his search for the marks of interruption, for "hieroglyphs" and "chatter," is itself guided by the ineluctable and uncalculable eruption of secret—and for this reason piously "venerated"—writing: writing, in other words, that does make reference to "lived" experience and that uses these points of reference to reconstruct the significance of the text.

If the text—or the "conversation"—is significant, it makes no such reference. Such is the point of the term "life-view." Only a failed text lets itself be read according to points of reference to a writer's "lived" experience. How ironic that this mode of reading and its corresponding conception of writing should support so much of Kierkegaard scholarship. How ironic that so often "secrets" involving the personal life of Søren Kierkegaard—his father or Regina Olson or anyone else—should be considered the ultimate point of reference for the reading of works he did not even sign. How ironic that Kierkegaard's very accusation against Andersen should be transmuted into venerations of the "secrets" inscribed in his conversations with himself. But aside from these ironies, which should perhaps be expected, and aside from the conception of "mastered irony," which in Kierkegaard's *Concept of Irony* elaborates on the doctrine of life-views with "constant reference" not to a failed novelist but to a unique ironist, namely Socrates, the irony of this mode of reading can under no condition be set aside. For if, as Kierkegaard says, irony finally consists in "absolute subjective negativity"[15] and subjectivity, as privacy, is itself understood to be a privation, it names the negativity that characterizes "the whole newer development": the negativity that is "mastered" in a life-view because every life-view, each in its own way, absorbs the empirical subject and erases all "lived" experience. "Chatter," by contrast, designates the ineradicability of "lived" experience, an ineradicability so extreme that phrases that have nothing to do with life, like epigraphic "maxims," are included within its space.

For this reason, "chatter" not only *precedes* the "mastery" of irony but *exceeds* irony: its mode of negativity cannot be captured in ironic discourse as long as the latter is seen to erase empiricity and to reduce "lived" experience to nil. If, however, irony names something other than "absolute negative subjectivity" and in fact exposes a place in which the "live" subject, without positivity and without absolution, reappears to interrupt the function and purity of discourse, then it belongs squarely to the "logic" of chatter, not the circular logic of Hegel that figures so prominently in the as yet unwritten *Concept of Irony*:

> I am aiming, rather, at the uncertainty, conditioned by the poet Andersen's misrelation to both his person and the fund of knowledge necessary for a novelist—at the conditioned shaking of the hand, which causes his pen not only to make blots but also to make gossip [*betingede Rysten paa Haanden, som g jør, at hans Pen ikke blot slaaer Klatter, men ogsaa slaaer Sladder*], and which characterizes his style to the extent that it thus becomes difficult to copy. And although, as I survey the mass presenting itself to me, I now feel in a singularly ironic manner [*ironisk*] at once so rich and so poor—so poor, I say, because I almost do not know where to begin or where to end—I do, however, catch a glimpse of a way out in the comment made earlier, that the whole has its origin in his misrelation to himself and to the necessary fund of knowledge.   (89)

At the precise moment when the utterly unoriginal Andersen proves inimitable—and therefore proves "in an ironic manner" quite singular—Kierkegaard captures the unique eruption of irony by imitating himself word for word. Such self-citation gives Kierkegaard an equally unique hold on a situation that threatens to collapse into asymmetrical reversal: Andersen ironically turning into the inimitable "genius" whose negative image he wishes to present in *Only a Fiddler*. But this self-citation just as surely demonstrates the hold that the interdiction on reference, the imperative to absorb all "lived" experience into a life-view, exerts on Kierkegaard as reader. For he cannot simply stop with one assertion of Andersen's misrelation; he needs to say it twice. And this doubling corresponds to the double effect of the misrelation itself: blots of ink flow onto paper, and "chatter" spills over into the conversation; ink thus ruins (*slaaer*) the papers, and nonsense strikes down genuine dialogue (*slaaer sladder*). Indecipherable ink stains and insignificant "chatter" substitute for each other..

The hieroglyphs that enter the continuum of Andersen's novel and the chatter that disrupts, if only momentarily, a genuine conversation are both related to the misrelation whose origins is, of course, the failure to translate "life" into a life-view, failure to erase reference to "lived" experience. Hieroglyphs and chatter designate, therefore, the "same" negativity of language against which a life-view distinguishes and defines itself. Unlike conceptual negativity, such negativity does not allow for distinction or definition: unruly ink blotches are hardly able to keep things clear and distinct. Nowhere is Kierkegaard more clear about this blurring of lines than when he envisages the "chatter" that will stain his own papers:

> As an extension of what has been developed, we can now add a special discussion of *Kun en Spillemand*, which will of course essentially keep within the territory demarcated by the foregoing and within the question of the poetically true, limited not by an arbitrary papal demarcation line but by the indeed invisible, yet all the more real one given in the concept. And it is only for the sake of appearances that we would construct a little outwork in order to keep an eye on a detachment of enemies, who are not actually enemies, however, since they agree with us in absolutely nothing [*i slet Intet*], but who must rather be considered as some chatterers who belong nowhere [*intetstedhjemmehavende Snakkere*] and who will probably not refrain from pointing out that what I say may indeed be true but that it by no means follows from this that the Andersenian position is untrue.   (94–95)

The "logic" generated by the corrosive negativity of chatter—of interruption, hieroglyph, ink-blots—operates here in plain view: an "invisible" mark is "more real" than a visible one; an outwork is made integral; enemies are not enemies, *not* because they are friends, still less because they are partners in a reciprocal conversation, but because the "conversation" in which they participate consists in speaking of *nothing at all;* and finally *everything is true,* Kierkegaard's standpoint no less than Andersen's point of view, everything having already turned into a truism. No community, no commonality, no communication takes place in this empty place of the integral outwork. Chatter belongs "nowhere" to the precise degree that it communicates "nothing." And "no one" chatters: not individuals, although "chatter" is everywhere associated with an individual's misrelation to himself; not "groups," since group members would have to be able to converse with one another about *something* if they were to be considered members of a group at all; not even "fictional personalities," inasmuch as the medium of fiction conditions the presentation of a life-view and thus never fails to strike a blow at chatter. "Chatter"—like impudent interruptions, like hieroglyphs, like ink stains—takes place, and when it does so, as in Andersen, its space becomes altogether inimitable: a topic like nothing else, a topic about which no one can speak because speech about definite "lived" experiences, referential discourse, spills ink on, punctuates, and defiles the literary work and as a result, the language of life.

"Sympathetic Ink"

Not even a life-view can protect an author from "chatter," although a life-view has perhaps no other point, from the perspective of literature, than the protection of language from the eruption of this mode of linguistic negativity. For anything can be read as an interruption, as a "hieroglyph," as "spilled ink," as "chatter." Language—and above all the language of life—cannot dissociate itself from its referential function, its relation to "lived" experience. Since the very positivity of reference makes up the negativity of "chatter," slogans of positivity do not lead out of "chatter" but into its heart. So corrosive is "chatter" that the opposite of referential language can just as easily present itself under its banner: "maxims" of conduct, which preface but do not determine action, are just as chatty as anecdotes referring to "lived" experience. To the extent that the negativity of "chatter" cannot be opposed by a firm position and even undoes every opposition it encounters, it proves far more unmethodical and far more destructive than any of the various negativities through which "the whole newer development," beginning with Descartes,[16] receives its impetus.

In the end Kierkegaard concedes as much. The conclusion of *Papers* makes reference to Kierkegaard's own "lived" experience and to this extent capitulates to the "chatter" that he has taken such pains to mark out in this reading of Andersen's *Only a Fiddler.*

Critical reading is supposed to supplement the achievement of a life-view by distinguishing those authors who had "transfigured" experience from those who, having failed to do so, make reference to their empirically determined lives. A string of reference points, as marks of failure, is the outcome of this critique. However, since language cannot renounce reference to "lived" experience, critique cannot help but fail. And the mark of this failure brings Kierkegaard's critique to a conclusion—in *praise* of Andersen as one whose text lets the reader refer not to Andersen himself (this is its failure) but to *the reader himself,* or Kierkegaard.

To make this situation more tenable, Kierkegaard makes a distinction between "critique" and "reading." Whereas the aim of the latter is to show the "lived" experience of the author, the process of the former is to relive *in language* one's "lived" experiences. Self-reference turns out to be reading itself, and it can hardly be denied that reading, so understood, makes every word into an interruption, into hieroglyphs, into spilled ink, into what Kierkegaard now calls "sympathetic ink." With these words of sympathy, Kierkegaard concludes his first literary text:

> With regard to what I have to say in conclusion—prompted by the misrelation, certainly on the whole conceded to be factual, between a reading and a criticizing world's judgment of Andersen, insofar as this misrelation has also repeated itself in my consciousness—I could wish that I might succeed in speaking about this just as personally as I have tried to keep the foregoing free of any oblique relation to my personality. That is, as I reproduce the first stage, the recollection of a variety of poetical moods [*poetiske Stemninger*] is brought to life, moods with which every poetic life [*digterisk Liv*], even the most obscure (and this, in a certain sense, perhaps most of all), must be interwoven. And as I once again seek to retain every single one, the one displaces the other so rapidly that the totality of them assembles as if for departure in one single concentration, assembles in itself the necessity of becoming a past and thereby evokes from me a certain nostalgic smile as I consider them, a feeling of thankfulness as I recollect the man to whom I owe it all, a feeling that I would prefer to whisper in Andersen's ear rather than confide to paper [*betro til Papiret*]. . . . I wish to say this to

Andersen rather than write it because such an utterance is on the whole very exposed to misunderstanding, something, however, I hope that I shall be able to put up with if only Andersen, in order to avoid it, will hold what I have written with sympathetic ink [*sympathetisk Blæk*] up to the light which alone makes the writing readable and the meaning clear.   (101–2)

Whereas Andersen's misrelation to himself underlies his misrelation to the world, the misrelation of *the world* to *language* makes its way into Kierkegaard's "self" and in turn brings about his own misrelation to himself. Since this misrelation amounts to a failure of reference—language, in other words, does not reach the world—Kierkegaard's misrelation to himself consists in an inability to speak of himself without speaking of another, even if that other is a novelist who fails to the extent that he constantly refers to himself. No one, however, can exercise any control over the misrelation of language to the world, and unless the self plays a part in this failure, no god can claim to restore it. A certain "sympathy" then accrues to Kierkegaard's reading as it renounces critique. Nothing Kierkegaard has *written*, not a word of his *critique*, is his own, but this self-estrangement, which has of course characterized every literary production undertaken on the basis of a life-view, does not owe its origin to a "transubstantiation" of "lived" experience; it consists in fragmentation without origin, which again and again refers to scenes of the intensely lived, "original" time of youth. For the essential, and essentially apotropaic, difference between being "personally" engaged in writing and engaging one's "personality" in reading does not rest on a transfiguration of empiricity accomplished in complete isolation from the world but on the misrelation of language to the world. Naive efforts to repair this misrelation are, as it turns out, "chatter." But so too are sophisticated ones. For each "reading" that defines itself against "critique" and each "speaking" that defines itself against "writing" repeats the misrelation and makes this repetition into a mark of its own inability to attain the status of "author": every moment of reading becomes one in which self-reference interrupts the text and leaves in its train

glyphlike stains whose character is sympathetically called "sympathetic ink."

"Reading," as it is called in the end, spills "sympathetic ink":
sympathetic at the very least because Kierkegaard sympathizes with
the plight of Andersen. For neither writer nor reader can erase
"lived" experience. And what is "sympathy" other than this inability? Reference to empirical life cannot be eliminated without at
the same time eliminating language. So any language that still lives
has no choice but to interrupt itself and thereby produce hieroglyphs, ink stains, or "chatter." After reading Kierkegaard's concluding concession, it is even impossible to maintain that the term
"life-view" is itself the mark of Kierkegaard's own "lived" experience, a mark from one who is "still" alive—or stillborn. "Invisible
ink" is sympathetic to the extent that it lets like-minded individuals communicate to the exclusion of all others. Yet it is just as
surely unsympathetic to the extent that these individuals make up a
clergy who by virtue of a technical device rule over an otherwise
illegible and doubtless illegitimate writing. On the basis of this
potentially vicious device, hieroglyphs are instituted, and ink is
spilled. And every word in Kierkegaard's *Papers* is made as invisible
as the supposedly necessary dividing line by which he attempted to
separate himself from those enemies who are not in fact his enemies and before whom he can marshal no line of defense: those
who "chatter" (95).

Chatter so little opposes itself to the authentic communication
of the hieratic few that the lines of demarcation between these
apparent opposites erase themselves every time they are drawn.
The selection of the "few" is thus an utterly arbitrary affair, not one
predicated on "genius," least of all the kind of genius to which
Andersen pays homage.[17] Kierkegaard "himself" interrupts his
"own" discourse, disrupting the continuity of his own work to the
degree that his "moods" break up the continuum of the text to
which he devotes his reading. Nothing is left, therefore, but the
invisible borderline on which "chatter" flourishes, and "chatter"
emerges as the always inappropriate name for the eruption of that
which undoes the overall continuity and totality of life enshrined

in the idea of the "life-view." But chatter is just as much the condition for its possibility, for only in the medium of chatter can one work oneself out of an original misrelation and in making reference to oneself communicate with oneself. "Chatter" can thus designate the continually disappearing difference in whose shifting movement the very possibility of relating the self to itself is disclosed. For this reason, the one who chatters can be neither a real enemy nor a real friend.

Kierkegaard's self-interruption takes place under the ever-vanishing sign of invisible ink; it overflows his papers, like the "gossip" that flows onto Andersen's novel (89). And in this superfluity—the reader can skip over all the pages, for nothing is said in them—*Papers* loses and finds its home. Kierkegaard's nostalgia is not for a lost totality, not for a lost life or a lost life-view, not for a lost past whose leveling and oblivion have been progressively accomplished in "the whole newer development," but is for those "lived" experiences, those lost "moods," indeed those lost and multiple "lives" that by allowing him to make reference to himself make it possible to have a relation to himself. Nowhere could he be brought into closer relation with the "chatterers who, belonging nowhere, having no home [*intetstedhjemmehavende Snakkere*]" (95). For at the precise moment of speaking in response to reading, which is distinguished from the estranged moment of delivering a critique in writing, he is no longer "himself," no longer a self at home with itself, but "lives" only in self-reference. The referential function of language in self-reference makes the self possible in the first place and at the same time exposes every word, and therefore the language of life no less than the life of language, to "chatter."

To consign to "irony" Kierkegaard's nostalgic insistence on fragmented "lived" experience in a text so singularly concerned with the virtues of particular life-views in which all "lived" experience is "transubstantiated" would doubtless link this early effort with the more famous master's thesis on "mastered irony," but it would at the same time miss a mode of negativity more corrosive than the standpoint of irony before "absolute subjective negativity"—the mode, namely, in which all points of view, all reference points, do not vanish into a nonconceptual, "existential" nothingness but *fail* to disappear. Out of this failure, against which there is neither shelter nor protection in language, there arise illegible and yet all too legible, blotted and yet all too clear, invisible and yet all too visible, unreadable and yet all too readable "lines of demarcation."

Style

The vanishing point of every distinction Kierkegaard wishes to draw, including the distinction between a life-view and fragmented experiences of life, looks like the obliterated and leveled landscape toward which the "whole newer development" is drawn and against which Kierkegaard, armed with the idea of a life-view, sets out to do battle. But such is not quite the case. For oblivion and leveling are real enemies. The vanishing point is not: it indicates the impossibility of drawing battle lines and declaring real enemies; the withdrawal of all points of reference leaves in its retreat the disruptive marks that, as ineradicable references to "lived" experience, constitute "chatter." But Kierkegaard leaves room for *another* mode of combat, a mode that doubtless belongs to "the whole newer development" but nevertheless refuses to take part in the effort of Hegelians or political propagandists to "begin with nothing." Like the activity of the author of the "Story of Everyday Life," this other mode of combat is waged on the level of language, but it does not depend on a momentous transubstantiation of "lived" experience into a life-view. Since it belongs to "the whole newer development," moreover, it cannot count as an *enemy* of modern negativity but acts instead as a corrosive integral agent, a nonenemy that is not for this reason an ally.

Carefully woven into the extraordinarily complex and highly idiosyncratic vocabulary and syntax of *Papers* is therefore another mode of negativity that is at once linguistic and counteractive. Here, if anywhere, one should find protection against "chatter"; here, if anywhere, Kierkegaard should be able to shelter himself from a "sympathetic" relation to Andersen. For this mode of specifically linguistic negativity goes against the modern age and fights against its leveling tendencies; it is, moreover, a mode of linguistic negativity that expresses itself not in the language of fictional, "transfigured" life but in that of *critique*. Nowhere else could Kierkegaard so effectively inscribe himself into the text of *Papers* and therefore have the opportunity to refer to himself without referring to any particular "lived" experience.

This shelter and protection against "chatter" resides in *style*. Kierkegaard discloses no names when he undertakes a characterization of style under the aegis of "the whole newer development," but the anonymity of the stylist only emphasizes the resemblance that the stylist bears to Kierkegaard himself—or "Kierkegaard himself," Kierkegaard as a pseudonym, a Kierkegaard to whom no "lived" experiences could be attributed:

> If we see the same phenomenon [as seen in Hegel] evoked by a genuinely original character's natural opposition to the whole modern phraseology [*moderne Phraseologie*], if we see such a one, raised high above the crowd by the deep artesian force belonging to genius, stand like an imposing statue, completely enveloped in the rich draperies of his homemade terminological cloak [*hjemmegjorte terminologiske Kappes*]—but yet so egoistically enclosed in himself that there is not the least rag the "gaping mob" can clutch—then we must indeed thank God that such a Simeon Stylites reminds us of what self-reliance [*Selvstændighed*] is but also regret that the misdirection of the age required such sacrifice.[18]

No longer can the opposition to modern phraseology call for a return to so-called natural language. Not only is "natural" language itself part of modern phraseology, but this return vindicates modern phraseology in general. For it guarantees that natural language, having returned, will constitute a new phraseology. The only opposition to phraseology is not silence but *petrified speech*: speech frozen into stone and therefore speech that no longer speaks, no longer enters into conversation but stands there alone, like a statue. And yet this statue does not simply stand there, nor does it stand for anything other than itself; it stands *out* there as an inadvertent monument to "the whole newer development" and in so standing out interrupts the constancy of this development. Since, however, the age is "misdirected" because its every tendency points toward oblivion and leveling, the self-erection of this Stylites, this pillar dweller, is *not* like the modern developments with which Kierkegaard opens his discussion; it has nothing to do with Hegelianism or recent political movements founded on the slogan "Forget the actual." So opposed is the emergence of stylistic uniqueness to this oblivion that it makes an impression on an otherwise leveled landscape; it marks a point of reference toward which a "younger person who is striving after something higher" (72) could look. But—and this is decisive—*only the eye* could rest there. *For the statue cannot speak*; it cannot enter into conversation, into genuine dialogue, into communication at all: it is a pure point of reference, out of communication and yet entirely linguistic; it does not, to be sure, refer to "lived" experience but, as the reference point itself, constitutes the interruption of all so-called "conversation." Its stony speech communicates nothing, for as the point of reference for any "view" of life that wants to lift itself above the leveled landscape, it is the very "thing," or the "nothing," communicated.

Stylistic uniqueness is taken to the point where there is no style in language but only a stylus that punctures conversation. The monumental infantilism of such a stylus does not amount to silence, nor does its stance of opposition bring it down to the same level as those against whom it has been defined, namely, "the many," "the crowd," "the levelers." For the stylus shares neither criteria nor measures with the crowd, least of all one defined in common language. The incommensurability of this phenomenon, then, consists in its inability to oppose *anything*: it is not an enemy; it is not a friend or an ally; it is not subject to common or even general criteria; it is not *anything definable* without, however, thereby becoming "ineffable." Petrified speech, frozen into its own "homemade" shelter, is the other side of "homeless" chatter: its "opposition" stands in precisely the position that disallows all oppositional terms. Nonenemy meets nonenemy, and on this empty but not at all "leveled" battleground Kierkegaard plays out his polemic against someone he would whisper friendly words to if only he could refrain from writing. On this ground, statuesque incommunicability as "style" (Kierkegaard) and flaccid communicability as "prattle" (Andersen) prove themselves intimately related, indeed almost identical. For this reason, chatter disrupts every discussion of unity and identity, above all those undertaken under the direction of a "life-view" and in turn of "existence."

Communicatio Idiomatum

The intimate relation between a monumental denial of communication in speech ("style") and an ignoble overflow of communication ("prattle") does not escape Kierkegaard. They come together when the points of reference for communication are no longer simply "lived" experiences but the experience of one's "life." Reference to oneself cannot help but produce "style" and "prattle" in turns. Such reference is dramatized in the remarkable preface to Kierkegaard's *Papers*. For in the preface "style" and "prattle" struggle against each other, the "author" of the text wishing them kept hidden, the "mediator," as editor, trying to force them into the open. The anonymous editor undertakes the task of retrieving the "papers" from his intimate friend and, "against his will," publishing them. So intimate is the relation between "mediator" and "author" that only in tandem is the authorship of the text possible. And yet their intimacy is never such that they could constitute an authentically unified existence: "Although I love him [the author] 'with tongue and mouth and from the bottom of my heart' and truly regard him as my sincere friend, my *alter ego*, I am still far from being able to describe our relationship by substituting another expression that might perhaps seem identical: *alter idem*. . . . We are, therefore, so far from being able to rejoice as friends in the unity for which poets and orators in their repeated immortalizations have only a single expression—that it was as if one soul resided in two bodies—that with respect to us it must rather seem as if two souls resided in one body" (55). The genesis of *Papers*'s publication thus devolves onto the structure of intracorporeal communication: communication with "oneself" on whose basis the "self" can announce itself to a public and thus "publish" itself in the first place.

Only under one condition can the "author" communicate with the medium, or "editor," and therefore with himself. His otherwise pervasive forgetfulness, which makes him into a manifestation of "the whole newer development," must be interrupted by a secure point of reference, indeed *the* secure reference point on which every other reference to "lived" experience depends: "our well-known, but also frequently forgotten, true home" (56). Upon the eruption of a relation to "*our . . .* true home," as the home of both author and editor, the former can finally be "himself": "He closes himself up, silent and secretive in his *aduton,* so that he seems to avoid me, in whom he otherwise usually completely confides, from whom he otherwise has no secrets, and it is only in a vanishing reflection [*forsvindende Afglands*], as it were, of what is moving in his soul that I, in a strangely sympathetic way [*sympathetisk Maade*] (explicable only by an incomprehensible *communicatio idiomatum*), feel what is stirring inside him" (56).[19]

Once again, sympathetic ink has been spilled. The "vanishing reflection" lets the secrets stored up in the *aduton,* including those of *Papers,* be read for a moment. But this reading cannot do without the secret, which as Kierkegaard's theological vocabulary already suggests, is "incomprehensible," even mysterious: no communication without a secret, but the secret cannot be communicated. The "medium" does not disclose the secret but at most communicates its secrecy, and he can do this only because communication itself has become, for him, *communicatio idiomatum:* idiomatic, idiotic, even infantile communication; communication with oneself when there is no one, and certainly no unified "one," with whom to communicate; communication of one "substantial nature" with another, when neither one nor the other, neither author nor editor, is "substantial." The insubstantiality of every communication then comes out of this *communicatio idiomatum.*

From the Papers of One Still Living could not have been open to a public without a *communicatio idiomatum* in which this public, and therefore its every reader, cannot participate. A "medium" of communication is needed, but this "medium" is just as incapable of reading as anyone else. For this reason, he has to appeal to a "sympathy" through which the secrecy of the secret is communicated and, as "sympathetic ink," spills out. In reading the "idiomatic" communication of the author, which makes the author into a stylist, the role of the "medium" is confirmed; he makes self-reference into reference points for communication, and these points of reference make up, and break up, the "lived" experience of the author: "This little treatise was also finished, and I, as the medium through which he telegraphs with the world, had already taken charge of it" (57).

Once medium and author are distinguished in this way, the author can preserve his "standpoint" from all contact with "lived" experience; he will have no choice but to publish everything "mediately"—indirectly, that is, through the mediation of various telegraphic pseudonyms. And this telegraphic communication, "idiomatum," can then define the whole of Kierkegaard's subsequent "authorship."[20] Doubtless the medium, who is not Kierkegaard, enrolls the now fictional author of *Papers* into the program of authorship that the treatise itself aims to vindicate and that, when driven to its limit, gives rise to a host of pseudonyms. But the medium, who is Kierkegaard's first anonym, does not turn into someone altogether distinguished from the "real" author, the one who signs himself *Kjerkegaard*; in the vanishing point, on the contrary, the distinction itself vanishes, and the text arrives at an idiomatic-idiotic communication in which, as the medium concedes but the author cannot, *nothing is communicated.* Perhaps this "nothing" is itself an absolute idiom, but no one, strictly speaking, can decide on this matter. The very undecidability of this matter implies an imperative, to wit, that of contentless, insignificant "tautological" writing:

> Furthermore, I know very well what blinds you. Author's vanity, my dear "Poor thing, can't you give up the vain hope of being an author of four sheets?" . . . Pure nonsense [*Slidder Sladder*]. All you have said means nothing and is nowhere at home [*har Intet at betyde og intetsteds*

hjemme], and since, as you know, the chatter that is nowhere at home [*den Snak . . . som intetsteds har hjemme*] is always more than enough, I will not hear another word. The treatise is now in my hands, I have the power to command. Therefore: straight ahead, march. The word is: what I write, this I write [*Parolen er: hvad jeg skrev, det skrev jeg*]. (57– 58, translation modified)

The author's defense of his denial of publication may amount to "pure nonsense" (*slidder sladder*), but this denial of access to the *aduton* of "lived" experience alone lets him become an author. Authorship itself is based on a defensive pronouncement that because it refers to nothing but never stops referring, is sheer "chatter." *Everything spoken* in ever-deeper conversations with one-self and in ever more inclusive conversations with others descends into "chatter" because it is based on a speech that "means nothing and is nowhere at home." Referring to a "nothing" that is "himself," the author—who stands for every genuine speaker, every authentic engagement in language—breaks into the sacred place in order to shelter its sacredness. Such is the logic of "chatter": it is a counterlogic, but not a counterlogic, like that of Hegel, who sublates the principle of contradiction to achieve a more inclusive "science of logic," nor is it a counterlogic that glorifies irrational, "lived" experience; rather, it is a counterlogic to the extent that it rewrites every word in terms of *tautology*: "Write—but write only what is written!" The self-referentiality of tautology never leaves language; it never refers to a "self" who has lived through a manifold of experiences; it refers only to a selfless language that however cannot do without an "I" and can never in turn suffi-ciently distance itself from "lived" experience: "What I write, that I write."

These words, which repeat Pontius Pilate's words concerning a sign that designates the site of a dead god,[21] do not fill up a space of emptiness or fulfill a prophecy or even a promise; rather, the tautology depletes language of any place of fulfillment and names this depletion "writing." The topic of this writing could henceforth hardly be anything but "nothing": insubstantial, contentless, insignificant if not, strictly speaking, "meaningless" language. Every reference point for this writing belongs to this topic, so it is no wonder that the text sets out to counter negativity in the vast variety of its modern manifestations through an idea of "transubstantiation" that is supposed to leave no "lived" experience, no empirical points of reference, behind. Nothing can then be communicated but the altogether idiomatic, yet the very *communicatio idiomatum* that lets the text be written in the first place breaks off— with the martial imperative to "march." Not only is communication with others dependent on an interruption of the *communicatio idiomatum,* but the latter, as a designation for the communication between the two modes of substance that make up God's essence, takes place only in a moment of interruption, as the very "order" of interruption, "March!" Without authority, this word no longer means anything. *Papers* in turn interrupts the order of meaning; its force, and not its meaning, lies in breaking up (as if it were a police whistle) every communication, every speech, every conversation. Such is in fact the upshot of its opening words: "A word in advance [*Forord*] breaks up [*bryde*] no dispute, one is used to saying; this preface [*Forord*] at least disrupts [*afbryde*] the continuity of the dispute I have had for a long time with the actual author of this treatise" (55).

The interruption opens the space for a medium through which communication takes place, and this medium undoes the immediacy of "lived" experience. But a medium never has authority; only an author does. The author in turn communicates nothing and is nothing, not even an author, without a medium. The one *chance* for the communication of "nothing" and not simply a negative, "critical" communication resides in a defenseless, unapologetic exposure to the threat that the medium so clumsily represents: the threat, namely, of empty speech, tautology, giving orders without the authority to do so—"chatter." Such exposure, which rules out silence from the start, gives an oddly affirmative character to the linguistic mode of negativity with which, and not *against*, Kierkegaard is engaged. Not a "life-view," not even "existence," but "chatter" alone has a chance, and it is only a chance, to thwart "the whole modern development."

For this reason, Kierkegaard has no choice but to register his ultimate sympathies with Andersen. *From the Papers of One Still Living* is not a lamentation for the passing of continuity, the oblivion of tradition, the leveling of everything superior and trustworthy, or the forgetting (for instance, but only as an instance) of what it means to be a Christian. No recollection can escape the interruptions of continuity that make up "chatter," since these interruptions let the self communicate with itself in the first place. The strange ability of "chatter" to dismay—to disable, to alarm, to scare, to set off anxiety—stamps the elusive character of Kierkegaard's subsequent papers.

§ 2 Algebra, a Rejoinder:
The Concept of Anxiety

> The preponderant and prevailing interest in the ex-
> plication of and occupation with concepts in our
> age is something that indicates that our age is de-
> moralized or demonized.
>> —Kierkegaard, a note to himself

Orientation in Science

Unlike *From the Papers of One Still Living* and in marked contrast
with its near namesake, *The Concept of Irony*, the treatise that bears
the title *The Concept of Anxiety* and is written under the guise of
Vigilius Haufniensis does not seem particularly interested in "the
whole newer development" and even appears quite content to
eschew all talk of contemporary history. Whereas the very structure
of *The Concept of Irony* is historical to the extent that it presents the
ironic life-view of Socrates as an equally ironic turning point in
"world history," the necessary outcome of which is the emergence
of modernity,[1] *The Concept of Anxiety* evinces a single-minded
devotion to the exposition and explication of a single "concept."
From the first sentence onward, it presents itself as a contribution
to "science" (*videnskab*), and its scientificity lets it ignore the
motley occurrences of the day. The preface emphasizes the author's
extraordinary indifference to "the whole newer development" and
above all to the new methods of deciding who holds the authority
in nonscientific domains: "When it comes to human authority, I
am a fetish worshiper and will worship anyone with equal piety,
but with one proviso, that it be made sufficiently clear by a beating
of drums that he is the one I must worship and that it is he who is
the authority and *Imprimatur* for the current year."[2] Such clarity is

reflected in the goal of the treatise itself: the concept under investigation is to be as clearly distinguished from other concepts as one drumbeat from another. These drumbeats indicate that any *reading* of the treatise is mediated by this illegitimate temporal authority and is therefore implicated in the issue of the age.

The authority of science, by contrast, is supposed to evade the perennial revolutions to which the author humbly submits his publication. Thinking the concepts of science, unlike reading the treatise, should therefore begin with an absolution from historical reference. No other conclusion could be drawn from the interleaf instruction to the reader, which, to be sure, refers to "our day" but does so only to dismiss its claims in favor of the demand for scientific light: "The age of making distinctions is past. It has been vanquished by the system. In our day whoever loves to make distinctions is regarded as an eccentric whose soul clings to something that has no long since vanished" (3). Whereas the ability to distinguish among ever-changing historical authorities has so thoroughly vanished that the author can commit himself to a perennial revolution, the ability to make distinctions in the service of science, to expose and explicate a determinate concept, can still be recalled, and this recollection establishes the terms in which the author can carry out his project; it would be, in Platonic terms, the recollection of the absolutely ahistorical, the recollection of Ideas.

Concepts, like Platonic Ideas, do without history, and the recollection of Ideas has nothing to do with reading; it implies, on the contrary, an immediate intuition of something in its eternal essence. If *The Concept of Anxiety* conceived of concepts as Ideas, it too would have nothing to do with history, and the recollection of these concepts would immediately put a halt to the effort of "the whole newer development"—to "begin with nothing" and therefore to "forget the actual." However, if concepts were conceived as other than Ideas, concepts would have an historical dimension, and this dimension would open itself to reading, not recollection. Now the impossibility of making concepts into Ideas makes itself known in a specific concept, namely, anxiety. So the exposure and explication of this concept, as the unique concept that undoes any conception of concepts as eternal Ideas, makes the very status of conceptuality, and therefore science and scientific rationality, into a problem, and into a "scientific" one at that.[3] *The Concept of Anxiety* cannot therefore help but return to the inception of history to conceive of anxiety in the first place, and it must likewise return to "the whole newer development" as the very phenomenon of ever-vanishing "distinctions," of leveling, amnesia, and beginning "with nothing." This "nothing" is, as everyone already knows, the "object" of anxiety, so *The Concept of Anxiety*, by making this "nothing" into its *scientific* topic, repeats the task of *From the Papers of One Still Living* in conceptual, as opposed to critical, terms.

The scientific authority of the concept cannot entirely remove itself from the perennial revolutions of political authority; the authorities who allow the treatise to be published are not erased in the recollection of its ideational content. "Ideology" is perhaps a name for an attempt on any front to shelter *some* authority—be it an Idea, be it a "fetish" (8)—from this exposure of all generalities to the loss of "distinctions." But the outcome of this exposure is the thoroughgoing undermining of all claims of authority. The author's declaration that he worships fetishes is not an arbitrary whim on his part but an integral part of "the whole newer development" in which he, like every other author, participates: all authority is seen to rest on fetish worship; all alterations of authority are arbitrary; everything finite dissolves and leaves "nothing"—nothing substantial, nothing significant, nothing of rank—in its place. Out of this "nothing," which anxiety will discover, there arises not only the treatise but also the very "development" of the thoroughgoing negativity that *Papers*, with its intermittent "ideology" of conservation, was still trying to withstand:

> Socrates says that it is terrible to be deceived by oneself, because one always has the deceiver present; similarly, one may say that it is fortunate to have present such a deceiver who piously deceives and always weans the child before finitude begins to bungle him. Even if in our time [*i vor Tid*] an individuality is not educated by possibility in this manner, our age nevertheless has an excellent characteristic for

each one in whom there is a deeper nature and who desires to learn the good. The more peaceful and quiet an age is and the more accurately everything follows its regular course [*sin regelmæssige Gang*], so that the good has its reward, the easier it is for an individuality to deceive himself about whether in all his striving he has a beautiful but nevertheless finite goal. In these times, one does not need to be more than sixteen years old in order to recognize that whoever performs on the stage of the theater of life is like the man who traveled from Jericho and fell among robbers. Whoever does not wish to sink in the wretchedness of the finite is constrained in the more profound sense to struggle with the infinite. Such a preliminary orientation is analogous to the education by possibility, and such an orientation cannot take place except through possibility.   (160)

"Our age" allows for a preliminary orientation, which like all orientations does not take place on the basis of an inference, least of all on an inference whereby the "infinite" results from the determinate negation of the finite. The "education by possibility" precludes such inferences as it likewise excludes all points of reference for the cognition of actuality. Nothing would be more mistaken than to conceive of this age as one in which the acknowledgment of "the infinite" emerges out of a recognition that everything finite is henceforth null and void. On the contrary, the single distinction through which "our age" proves itself exceptional lies in its discrediting of all "regular" calculations, including those of determinate negation. The "possibility" that carries out the "education" is not the negation of the actual as it reveals itself in cognition; it is, rather, *fictionality*. "Education by possibility" names a suspended mode of cognition, one that can never escape from a certain "deceptiveness." And this inadvertent deceptiveness, which undermines rules no less than trust, belongs to "our age."

This age thus *orients through its very disorientation*: East and West are as difficult to distinguish as anything else. Once the concepts with which science works no longer reveal themselves as Ideas and are, in "our age," unable even to present themselves as *rules*, science ceases to function. Or the medium of science becomes *fictionality*, and its method becomes reading. Reading the fictions of orientation toward a fixed point—such would then be the unique scientific undertaking of "our age." Without any point of support, this undertaking cannot but happen upon anxiety as an orienting concept. Its lack of support does not, however, imply that anxiety erases all points of *reference*, even if East and West are no longer distinguishable. For the language of this treatise, as the language of anxiety itself, again and again speaks of "nothing." This *impossible* point of reference, which undermines any finite and definite "fiction," constitutes the problem against which *The Concept of Anxiety* stumbles.

Kant, Conversation

The Concept of Anxiety presents itself as a stalwart defender of rules, above all, the rules to which scientific disciplines are bound. The opening words of the introduction declare that "every scientific problem within the larger compass of science has its definite place, its measure and its limit" (9).[4] To break with the contemporary breakdown of rules, to recall the now forgotten distinctions, to draw science out of the oblivion into which it has recently fallen, thus defines the preliminary goal of the treatise as a whole: it assigns this task to its introduction. And the treatise insists on rules and the distinctions that go along with them for the precise reason that nothing scientific, nothing conceptual, no *treatise*, could begin without them. "Begin" means here: inaugurate movement. Movement based on negativity then becomes the most pressing concern of this introduction, and its pressure resolves itself on a single point: that the word "negativity," as it has been used by Hegel in the *Science of Logic* and his "scientific" followers, leads to misconceptions on all fronts: "The negative lends a hand, and what the negative cannot accomplish, play on words and modes of speaking [*Ordspil og Talemaader*] can, just as when the negative itself becomes a play on words" (12).

The word—not by chance "the negative"—comes into play because it ceases to be effective; it no longer works. Words out of work, which are *only* words and no longer concepts, lead to misconceptions, the principal misconception being the deception of conceptuality: *everything* seems conceivable, including the inconceivable, and the *name* of the inconceivable, of that which cannot be brought into any conceptual calculation but nevertheless earns a name, is "sin." Without a concept of sin, "negativity" can only present itself as a word out of work, a word that has no role to play in the scientific analyses undertaken in *The Concept of Anxiety*. Since, however, sin is a matter of freedom, it is as little capable of being captured in a concept as freedom itself. This Kantian argument, which denies the "ideality" of freedom and ensures that freedom remain altogether "practical," sets the stage for a "proof" of existence on which Kant's entire critical enterprise is founded: "Freedom is never possible; as soon as it is, it is actual, in the same sense as it was said in an older philosophy that if God's existence is possible, it is necessary" (22).

Just as Kant's *Critiques* replace the God of classical metaphysics with the practical reality of freedom as the foundation of every future metaphysical program, *The Concept of Anxiety* eschews all "proofs" of God's existence in favor of freedom's self-exposition, and this self-exposition, like Kant's presentation of the "fact of freedom,"[5] needs no deduction. No wonder, then, that Kierkegaard always refuses to accede to the competing claims of Fichte, Schelling, and Hegel to have "actually grasped Kant's skepticism" and to have overcome the limits of Kantian critique by means of certain methodological "slogans" (11), and nowhere is the grasp of "Kant's skepticism" stronger than in *The Concept of Anxiety*. For this skepticism, like all skepticism, denies the ability of concepts to grasp everything; the limits of the grasp of the concept is as much a problem for Kant as it is for Kierkegaard. Not to grasp the limit as a problem is to strike idle "slogans" for the simple reason that the limit of a concept—as the worldly objects to which it refers, on the one hand, and as the inconceivable, on the other—constitutes the force of resistance against which words alone do work.

If the decision whether a philosophical treatise belongs to the tradition of Kantian critique depends on how it presents the function and concept of freedom, and there is no better criterion for this decision, then *The Concept of Anxiety* should surely be considered a distinctly Kantian text: freedom has no other place than "practice," and only freedom determines good and evil.[6] *The Concept of Anxiety* could then be understood as a forerunner of the movement "back to Kant" and indeed as a more significant forerunner in this regression than Schopenhauer's contemporaneous attempt to rescue Kant from the speculative systems of Hegel and Schelling. For it does not, as Schopenhauer recommends,[7] do away with the pillar of Kantian critique: the "practical reality" of transcendental freedom, the "fact" of reason as the facticity of ethical worldhood.

But the Kantian character of *The Concept of Anxiety* does not prevent it from striking into new territory, that of the "psychological." Whereas Kant dismisses all "psychological" orientations and more broadly all "anthropological" digressions as detrimental to the establishment of a metaphysics of morals,[8] Kierkegaard concedes to "psychology" a preeminent place in the account of freedom: the place from which one cannot *not* speak of freedom but a place that likewise cannot make freedom into a theoretical thesis. The "psychology" of *The Concept of Anxiety* therefore has nothing to do with the *psychologia rationalis* with which Kant was familiar and whose foundations he destroyed in the "Paralogisms of Pure Reason," nor do the anthropological determinations of the treatise have anything in common with Kant's anthropology from a "pragmatic" point of view.[9] The "psychology" of anxiety, on the contrary, exposes a critical reef whose danger Kant had recognized when he made an attempt to ground a metaphysics of morals but from which he merely retreated.

The advancement of Kant's concept of freedom, which amounts to radicalizations of its roots in the incomprehensibility of freedom and the "radicalness" of human evil,[10] no longer sets out to justify such a metaphysics; a "psychologically oriented" radicalization sets out from the key "psychological" concept, the reef on which the Kantian enterprise founders, namely interest: *inter-esse*, the "between" of being, being-in-between. With incomparable sureness, *The Concept of Anxiety* designates the point at which the meta-

physics of morals hits ground: " 'Repetition is the interest of metaphysics, and also the interest upon which metaphysics founders;
repetition is the watchword in every ethical view. . . .' This first
statement has reference to the thesis that metaphysics as such is
disinterested, something that Kant had said about aesthetics. As
soon as interest steps forth, metaphysics steps aside" (18, translation
modified). As the third section of *The Foundations of the Meta-*
physics of Morals makes clear, interest in freedom as the timeless
origin of morality and the new foundation of metaphysics is the
point on which the whole project threatens to collapse.[11] Vigilius
Haufniensis, "the watchman of Copenhagen," gives the "watchword" in which this foundering on "interest" is spoken: the word
is, of course, "anxiety."

The concept of interest, derived from Poul Møller and applied to
projects of metaphysical foundation, doubtless includes an affective dimension, but the deployment of this dimension in the
critique of metaphysical foundations does not amount to a relapse
into pre-Kantian appeals to "immediacy," appeals for which Jacobi
can be credited and from which Kierkegaard, like Møller, takes his
distance.[12] Indeed, the particular "feeling" of which the treatise
wishes to conceive—anxiety—is anything but "immediate." One
must become aware of it; it must be clarified, and to this extent *The*
Concept of Anxiety is enrolled in an "enlightenment" project: the
dispelling of magic wherever it may appear, including in the exalted realm of science. And since a certain magic of words has
recently raised itself into a "science of logic," the treatise takes
aim at this supposed science: the body of *The Concept of Anxiety*
tries to undo the magical spell exercised by the various "things"
over which one seems to be anxious, whereas the introduction
claims the more modest task of exorcising the spell of certain
magical words, more exactly the word-association through which
Hegelianism has tried to erect a "science"—"negativity" as "mediation" and "reconciliation":

> What is quite proper in logic, namely, that immediacy is *eo ipso*
> canceled, becomes in dogmatics idle talk [*Passiar*]. Could it ever occur

to anyone to stop with the immediate (with no further qualification), since the immediate is annulled [*ophævet*] at the very moment it is named, just as a somnambulist wakes up at the very moment his name is named [*hans Navn nævnes*]? . . . One rejects synthesis and says "mediation." Very well. Brilliance, however demands more—one says "reconciliation," and what is the result? The propaedeutic investigations are not served by it, for naturally they gain as little in clarity as does the truth, as little as a man's soul gains by having a title conferred on him.   (11–12, translation modified)

Immediately upon speaking "immediacy," immediacy is broken. But a broken immediacy does not amount to its determinate negation, to "mediation," still less to the reconciliation that is promised with the appearance of every mediator. Broken immediacy is, rather, "idle talk." At this point the word *interrupts itself*: it is not a word in which a concept is expressed but is only a "word," without the ability to incorporate itself into conceptual thought. A word no longer subservient to its concept is, however, a word *at a standstill*, a word on idle, not a real or effective word. The introduction collects such words and puts them to work in the treatise: "negativity," "mediation," "reconciliation" will not be submitted to conceptuality, still less to the Hegelian *Begriff*, but to the concept *of* anxiety: a concept *in name only*, a "word" in which conceptual expression is suspended. Only against the limits of *another* science, which would be a science of the other, do any of Hegel's words do work, but this science of the other—or philosophy of freedom, or dogmatic of sin—is no longer a science, no longer even a philosophy; its language is in turn no longer conceptual but *conversational*.

Here is where the difficulty begins, however. If Kierkegaard's *Papers* founders on the irreducibility of reference, then *The Concept of Anxiety* stumbles onto the irrevocability of conceptuality: words still mean *something*, even in the "feeling" of anxiety, and this surviving "something," which ought to have been reduced to naught in the experience of anxiety, makes language into "idle talk." And this experience cannot do without language; it cannot be immediate and "pure." Anxiety has the power to counter the spell of "negativity," to bring it back into conceptual rules and demarcations, but the countering agent is itself the disease. The introduction could not be more clear on this point: to counter this spell exercised by words, the treatise, reiterating Poul Møller's advice for those who wish to engage in literary criticism,[13] recommends what it cannot deliver—"conversation." In "conversation" language goes back to work. For—and here is where *The Concept of Anxiety* tries to resolve the difficulty from which it begins—conversation can, unlike scientific writing, uphold limits and at the same time reduce conceptuality to naught. The topic of conversation is, as a result, impossible to address; not only is it inconceivable, but its putative name, "sin," merely indicates its uniqueness and its impractical practicality:

> Sin does not properly belong in any science, but it is the subject of the sermon, in which the single individual speaks as the single individual to the single individual. In our day, scientific self-importance has tricked pastors into becoming something like professional clerks who also serve science and find it beneath their dignity to preach. Is it any wonder that preaching has come to be regarded as a very lowly art? But to preach is really the most difficult of all arts and is essentially the art that Socrates praised, the art of being able to converse [*at kunne samtale*]. It goes without saying that the need is not for someone in the congregation to provide an answer, or that it would be of help continually to introduce a respondent. What Socrates criticizes in the Sophists, when he made the distinction that they indeed knew how to make speeches but not how to converse, was that they could talk at length about every subject but lacked the moment of appropriation [*Tilegnelsens Moment*]. Appropriation is precisely the secret of conversation. (16)

Scientific exposition of a concept cannot suffice. But at the precise point where it seems that its opposite, "conversation," will emerge to save words from dissolving into the indifferent defining system of the infinite Hegelian *Begriff*, it shows itself to be as atopical as the topic of conversation itself. For "conversation" no longer has anything in common with what is commonly called conversation: it does not consist of two partners exchanging views; it is not composed of questions and answers; it does not consist of dialogue and has nothing to do with dialectics; it is not even a matter of bringing something—a thought, an idea, a consistent subject matter—to light in speech. Every conception of conversation based on the idea of *apophansis*—bringing something, as a substance, to light—and its translation into the scholastic as well as idealistic concept of the proposition is annulled. In its place one finds the an-apophantic par excellence: a *secret*. "The secret of conversation" cannot be spoken because its exposition in language would implicate conversation in *conceptuality*. The inconceivable—freedom, "sin"—thus slips out of the conversation, and the conversation ceases to be a conversation at all; it becomes idle talk. "Appropriation," by contrast, names the mode of "grasping" that does without concepts.

However, since appropriation alone lets one speak properly, science at its limit—and what science does not test its limits?—supports itself on this basis, even as it by definition fails to meet the test; a scientific exposition of a topic is never its appropriation. Science speaks properly, to be sure, but this very propriety in speech contributes to the loss of what is proper to conversation as such, appropriation. To the extent that science distinguishes itself from conversation, it fails to appropriate the topic under discussion and thus fails to finds its place in the topic it treats. The site of this failure is the concept. For the concept of something secures the meaning of words; it makes the words into proper ones, terms appropriate for the determination of a context. Conversation, by contrast, speaks "improperly," without concepts. Conceiving of a word and fixing it into a concept make conversation impossible, but since a proper conversation distinguishes itself from improper conversations, including the "lengthy speeches" of the Sophists, it cannot do without its *own* concept. Conceptuality cannot be altogether reduced in "conversation," and the residuum of the concept is found in the concept of anxiety: a concept of "nothing," but not, for that reason, a nonconcept. The possibility of conversation, and therefore of language properly speaking, rests on the "work" of *this* concept, not the Hegelian *Begriff*, because it should reduce the all-inclusive claim of conceptuality and thereby make room for the inconceivable, incomprehensible, incommunicable "secret of conversation."

Nowhere, therefore, does Kierkegaard oppose anxiety. Unlike *From the Papers of One Still Living*, this treatise calls for the thoroughgoing negativity that "in our time" has made "education by possibility" a necessity. Its very commitment demands that it recount and account for the process of deconceptualization in which language is made free for conversation. The residuum of this process is composed of dispersed words, like "anxiety," whose propriety and univocity are shattered from the start. These words are marks of a double failure: to grasp in a concept and to appropriate into "existence." Reading these words becomes the task of the treatise proper.

Historicity, Topicality

Whereas according to a famous saying of Spinoza, the concept of a dog does not bite, the concept of anxiety does. It does not have its home in a different ontological register than the phenomena it singles out. For like *The Concept of Anxiety*, the "object" of anxiety is "nothing": "If we ask more particularly what the object of anxiety is, then the answer, here as elsewhere, must be that it is nothing. Anxiety and nothing always correspond [*svare*] to each other" (96). Anxiety and "nothing" answer each other *without question*. Such is the consistent "problem" of the treatise: the collapse of the distinction between concept and phenomenon makes the reduction of conceptuality into a concomitant reduction of empiricity, but these reductions annihilate neither conceptuality nor empiricity; rather, they leave "nothing" behind, and this "nothing," as an ineradicable residuum, calls on anxiety once again, thereby repeating the process ad infinitum. This "problem" first presents itself in "psychological" terms as the so-called mind-body problem: anxiety is a "symptom" of the misrelation of the mind, or the "soul," to the body, which like all symptoms, indicates something else. But the psychological "problem" is itself a discovery of anxiety. So the "something else" turns out, again and again, to be "nothing," and anxiety ceases to be a symptom in any simple sense *of* anything, including a mind-body misrelation, but is instead "itself": it is, in other words, again and again *insignificant*. For this reason, "chatter" and "idle talk" never cease to intrude upon the exposition of the concept, and the experience of anxiety is of the "self" as it comes across its "own" insignificance.

The ontological register of anxiety is not "psychology," since the body is as responsible for the misrelation as the soul; the register is rather *language as such*, language as it distinguishes itself, always unsuccessfully, from "mental" concepts on the one hand and the "bodily" field of primary referents on the other. This unsuccessful effort at distinction, which constitutes an effect of anxiety as such, leaves language unable to rid itself of concepts and their referential dimensions: the *concept* of anxiety cannot therefore eradicate the *historical* character of the phenomenon, and *The Concept of Anxiety* has no choice but to become an exposition of what makes history, as the primary dimension in which reference occurs, possible in the first place. The condition of possibility for history is the uneasy condition in which anxiety, as "education by possibility," makes itself known. Such a condition is, according to an always inappropriate "dogmatic" representation, before the fall into "sin." Knowledge of anxiety, which is never immediate, is not knowledge by way of concepts, or empirically ascertained, but is the exposure of, and by, its inner possibility.

Historicity without history—historicity without reference to actual occurrences but only exposure of its field—is a topic of scientific treatment in *The Concept of Anxiety* because history itself is always *new*; necessity, which is governed by rules and conceived in already secured concepts, has nothing to do with novelty as such. For all its indifference to empirical history, *The Concept of Anxiety* is nevertheless, and indeed for precisely this reason, at every point *topical*. The "new" is its element. Regular historical occurrences are not discussed and do not fit into its scientific mode of treatment, but this very elision makes the text all the more topical, all the more a matter of a topical town crier, a *vigilius haufniensis* who like all town criers does not have time to reflect on, much less devise reasons for, actual and "necessitated" occurrences. Written by a town crier, the topicality of *The Concept of Anxiety* exceeds even that of a local book review. As every periodical attests, topicality is never a matter of causal explanation; there is no time and no distance to conceive of explanations: the danger—be it fantastical, alluring, "present," or promised—is already at hand. "Topical" means a *unique place* is decried. And the topicality of *The Concept of Anxiety* consists in decrying the danger to which the city, indeed "civilization" itself, is exposed. The threat is at the city gate, and the pathos of this threat, which is "discovered" (15) in anxiety, is precisely the mood in which its "psychological deliberation" takes place. What is "discovered" in anxiety is not therefore simply "nothing" but a *topical* "nothing": the atopos in which the "new" springs forward, interrupting the rule of conceptuality and likewise making history possible.

"The Speaker Is Language"

Anxiety discloses the possibility of history, for it is the condition in which every historical event takes place: every event, that is, in which something *new* happens. The inception of history in the fall into the atopical field of "sin" names the "problem" to which *The Concept of Anxiety* turns. Regular historical "development," by contrast, does not presuppose anxiety and is not, properly speaking, historical. "The whole newer development," inasmuch as it is the unfolding of a continuum, is of no concern to *The Concept of Anxiety*; its concern is the condition prior to history and indeed the a priori condition on novel events. Nothing like Hegel's distinction between "objective spirit" and "subjective spirit" can operate as a mediating term between "psychological" phenomena and "historical" institutions because this distinction loses sight of the one to which *The Concept of Anxiety* devotes its analytic labor: the distinction between possibility and actuality. Only the possibility of history, of the "new," deserves scientific treatment; its actuality demands something equally and yet incomparably new. If, for instance, the new is sin, only another sin, or "repetition," is equally and incomparably new enough to meet the demands of actuality. The constituent moments of historicity are therefore presented in relation to what has no constitution and therefore cannot be explained: actual history insofar as its foundation involves freedom. The method of presentation is not a demonstration of the a priori conditions whose ultimate basis and justification is a highest principle or axiom; rather, the presentation constructs various concepts through which one can make sense of a "prior" condition.

"Prior" to history, whether of the human race or a singular being, is the condition of innocence, and this condition consists in ignorance, which in turn is likened to the state of "dreaming" (41). History itself is therefore at bottom a matter of knowledge, awareness, awakening. The task of a town crier is to awaken to knowledge, so the *historical* task of the particular town crier who writes *The Concept of Anxiety* is to awaken the town to the knowledge of what is discovered in knowledge itself. Because of this double inflection, Vigilius Haufniensis can anxiously cry to others of threatened borders, boundaries, and distinctions as he nevertheless proceeds to cut off all conversation with his fellow townsfolk; he can, as he everywhere insists, "deliberate" with no one but himself and yet issue a decree that the danger is near.

The decree and the decry are both contained in anxiety. It traverses the distinction between articulate announcement and inarticulate cry. For this reason, it can serve to elucidate the condition on hereditary sin both "progressively" and "regressively," in terms of both an articulate statement of the danger encountered and an inarticulate intimation that danger threatens. But the ambiguity of anxiety does not exhaust itself in this simple opposition between articulate and inarticulate, mature and immature; the very ambiguity of articulateness is constitutive of anxiety. Everything discerned in anxiety and every threat it discloses not only decries a threat but describes this threat—as a promise: at the very least, a promise of awakening, of knowledge, of "science" based on concepts through which everything, including unfamiliar threats, can be submitted to normative regulation. The single defining feature of anxiety whereby definition itself loses its univocal character—the feature, namely, of ambiguity, "double meaning" or *Tvetydighed* (43)—does not consist simply in psychological ambivalence. To be sure, the treatise underlines the description of "anxiety [as] *a sympathetic antipathy* and *an antipathetic sympathy*" (42), but this ambiguity proceeds to unravel all interpretative constructions of a univocal discourse: every threatening word promises; every promising word threatens.

So ambiguous is anxiety that it, like a paradox, becomes altogether inconceivable. But unlike a paradox, it does not point beyond itself—to its resolution at the very least—but points nowhere, and this "nowhere" to which it directs attention and indeed *responds* is precisely itself: it points to "itself" before the self, as the mind-body relation, is posited; it speaks of "itself" when the self of which it would speak is absent. Not only is anxiety therefore self-referential, but its self-referentiality denies language the very substance that as the subject matter of a sentence it would need to strike ambiguity down, including the substantiality and permanence of an "I" who could refer all its sentences to itself. Without a substance disclosed in the subject matter of a sentence, without a subject who can refer all substances to itself, language loses its power to define things, to make distinctions, to express concepts, and thereby to determine a specific field of reference. In referring to itself, which is not a "thing" and gives no point of reference, anxiety opens up the linguistic space of the self, as the relation of mind to body, but the space thereby disclosed is *only* linguistic. In this space the self takes place. *The Concept of Anxiety's* representation of the fall into "sin" presents the arrival of the self in the place of utterly self-referential language as an event in which concepts and their fields of reference, not the self itself, flourish. The reducibility of concepts is in turn the measure of every "new" arrival, hence every historical event.

The treatise rejects those "clever" theories of the fall into sin that suppose that the prohibition itself instigates the transgression, for the simple reason that this prohibition would have to suppose a prior cleverness; it would have to presuppose that someone *understood* the prohibition and above all understood itself as the subject of prohibition. The deictic "thou" so emphatically deployed in the original threat—"Thou shalt surely die" (Gen. 2:17)—would have to have referred to a substantial subject to which the self-referentiality of anxiety bars reference. Every prohibition is already inhibited by the prohibition on reference to every substantial and self-subsistent subject, and this prohibition constitutes the threat— of "death" as an inconceivable word—to which anxiety responds. Incapable of concepts and incapable of reference, the language of anxiety nevertheless speaks of "itself." This speech of language "itself," not the speech of an already constituted subject nor the announcement of a prohibition to an a priori posited individual, is the presupposition of "hereditary sin," the fundamental condition on history in which the possibility of history is disclosed and the character of history as knowledge of ever-altering prohibitions is stamped:

> Innocence still is, but only a word [*et Ord*] is required and then ignorance is concentrated. Innocence naturally cannot understand this word, but at that moment anxiety has, as it were, caught its first prey. Instead of nothing, it has an enigmatic word [*gaadefuldt Ord*]. When it is stated in Genesis that God said to Adam, "Only from the tree of knowledge of good and evil you must not eat," it follows as a matter of course that Adam really has not understood this word. . . . After the word of prohibition follows the word of judgment: "You shall certainly die." Naturally, Adam does not know what it means to die. On the other hand, there is nothing to prevent him from having acquired a notion of the terrifying, for even animals can understand the mimic expression and movement of the voice of a speaker without understanding the world. . . . Because Adam has not understood what was spoken, there is nothing but the ambiguity of anxiety. (44–45)

Just as the ambiguity prohibits reference to the one who stands under judgment—and therefore this "one" is as lacking in unity as "the [many] animals that understand the voice of a speaker without understanding the words" (45)—neither the prohibition nor the judgment need refer to a divine source of these communications. The treatise even denies access to a divine voice that would have been understood according to the "mimic expression" characteristic of animals. Without this source, the dominant resource to which *science* appeals to let language speak turns out to be a *concept* personified, the figure of "innocence": "Innocence can indeed speak, inasmuch as in language it possesses the expression for everything spiritual. Accordingly, one need merely assume that Adam talked to himself. The imperfection in the story, namely, that another spoke to Adam about what he did not understand, is thus eliminated. From the fact that Adam was able to talk, it does not follow in a deeper sense that he was able to understand what was said" (45).

By making Adam self-sufficient, the story is perfected for the purposes of clarifying the concept of anxiety—title of both the treatise and the section. "Adam," who is only the *figure* of innocence, can attain such self-sufficiency to the extent that he already stands for a concept. As the figure of anxious innocence, he corresponds to, or "converses" with, "nothing," and this "nothing" constitutes the point of reference for all figures. As a figure, Adam participates in conceptuality without, however, being conceivable according to any given rule. Such is his "freedom." But the very figurality of Adam denies him the ability to be the unambiguous speaker in any conversation. "No one" speaks to "nothing": language "itself" speaks. Concept and reference are both reduced in an "original" language, a language no longer conceivable in the *narrative* representation of the fall: "The imperfection in the narrative—how it could have occurred to anyone to say to Adam what he essentially could not understand—is eliminated if we bear in mind that *the speaker is language,* and *also* it is Adam himself who speaks" (47, italics added).

Adam, as a figure, and language "itself" speak in turns—or at the same time, in a colloquy that is anything but a dialogue. Unlike innocence, language is not unambiguously a personified concept; it is not itself a figure, and it has no figural function unless it, "language," means precisely "innocence," in which case it would be a concept. "The speaker is language" means, however, that conceptuality does not belong to language. Language speaks without concepts, without significance to anything but "itself." But insofar as the speech of language is a *prohibition*, it cannot do without concepts that specify a field of reference—let it be "knowledge of good and evil"—to which the prohibition applies. Language can just as little do without concepts as it can do without figures of speaking. For this reason, language is never the unambiguous speaker. The figure—of innocence, alias Adam—*also* speaks. If language were able to speak on its own, without figures who speak and therefore without figures of speech, the radical ambiguity of anxiety, which reaches into the "root" of knowledge, would be canceled, and language would turn out to be a substance after all, albeit a negative one. The ambiguity of anxiety thus reaches its most radical point when the speech of language "itself" loses the simplicity of its origin and a figure speaks as well. Since *The Concept of Anxiety* cannot count on the simplicity of an origin, it cannot account for the "origin of language":

> If one were to say further that it then becomes a question of how the first man learned to speak, I would answer that this is very true, but also that the question lies beyond the scope of the present investigation. However, this must not be understood in the manner of modern philosophy as though my reply were evasive, suggesting that I *could* answer the question in another place. But this much is certain, that it will not do to represent man himself as the inventor of language. (47)

Human subjectivity, figured as innocence, could not on its own originate language so long as language *also* speaks. The colloquy of figure and language gives rise to the dominance of concepts, the primary purpose of which is to put this confusing colloquy in order. Since the published text of *The Concept of Anxiety* is supposed to stick to "psychological" observations, it will go no further; it will not answer the question How did the first man learn to speak? But one of Kierkegaard's drafts almost ventures into "dogmatics," and the serpentine figure of confusion emerges out of a remarkable self-colloquy: "If anyone wishing to instruct me should say, 'Consistent with the preceding you, of course, could say, "It [the serpent] is language,"' I would reply, 'I did not say that'" (185).[14] The "I" who speaks here not only did not say such a thing but *could* not; the monstrosity of the serpentine "it," which could mean *anything,* excludes the possibility that any "I" can lay claim to speech. In speaking, both the figure and language, both Adam and "it," speak. This doublespeak corresponds at every point to the "double meaning" of anxiety, and it likewise so thoroughly confounds any univocal, unambiguous understanding that no conception of Adam as a mere figure or language "itself" as merely self-referential can stand.

In the earliest speech, as the colloquy of figure and language, a *communicatio idiomatum* takes place. Language "itself" speaks (along) with a figure of the self. Nothing, of course, is communicated in the *communicatio idiomatum.* Out of this "nothing" every concept and every one of its fields of reference springs. Whereas it has often been thought that talking with oneself, however pointless, not only ensures communication but is indeed the very securing of communication,[15] "original" communication is presented here as *communicatio idiomatum* at cross-purposes, so cross indeed that the "self" and every purpose for which it enlists its speech, including the purpose of prohibiting itself, is nullified. At bottom, all talk of anxiety is talk of "nothing": it has no point of reference, and its concept is nil. But this nontalk is not the end of language, and concepts and points of reference are not reduced to nothing. Quite the contrary, nontalk is the inception of language, and this inception stamps its subsequent character as thoroughly as "original sin" stamps the character of the speaking species. The speech of language "itself" (along) with the figure of the self cannot constitute a genuine conversation; it interrupts everything that would call itself a "conversation," but the speech nevertheless goes on. Self-colloquy, *communicatio idiomatum,* continues to speak without a continuum to which this speech could be assigned; it continues to speak *nothingly.* It is not by chance that "nothingly" is not a genuine word: its function disperses into the idleness of "idle talk," the "emptiness" of "empty words," the "smallness" of "small talk," and the nullity implied in all talk of "chatter."

Science, no doubt, assigns its language the task of putting a limit to loose talk and thereby bringing "chatter" to a halt. The language of science, however, is that of knowledge, and this language never ceases to bear the stamp of its origin in a more original colloquy, a *communicatio idiomatum* to which every concept and every field of reference bears witness: the colloquy of language "itself" (along) with a figure of the self. Science therefore cannot bring "chatter" to a halt; its limits, which are always concepts, and its points of reference, which are always conceptually demarcated, condemn language all the more effectively to speaking "nothingly." Knowledge does not restore ignorance, but the language of knowledge is indebted to that of "innocence." Ambivalence with regard to science thus marks the entire enterprise undertaken in *The Concept of Anxiety.*

Such ambivalence finds its characteristic expression in the founding of a *new* science, that of "psychology," which is no longer supposed to grasp the character of things but the "nothing" discovered in anxiety. The irreducibility of concepts in the exposition of this new science goes to show that the language of science, even this new one, cannot escape its debt to "chatter." The "problem" of "original sin" comes down to this: "chatter," which is original language, outgrows its origin and corrodes the very language that is determined to bring it to a halt. The problem that "a man of science" poses therefore finds expression in a question that he, who is supposed to know, cannot unambiguously answer: "That the man of science ought not to forget himself is entirely true. . . . His philosophical enthusiasm will make him so absent-minded that he needs a good-natured, level-headed wife whom he can ask, as Soldin asked Rebecca when in enthusiastic absent-mindedness he also lost himself in the objectivity of chatter: 'Rebecca, is it I who is speaking?' " (51). Any speech that responds to this question with the self-assuring statement "I speak"—or what amounts to the same, "I think"—cannot hope to bring "chatter" to a stop, for it too participates in the original colloquy at cross-purposes.

Spirit, Sexuality

But it would be quite a surprise if *The Concept of Anxiety*, having given the first word to anxiety, also gave it the last word and this word was "nothing." *Science* is doubtless unable to bring anxiety into line, but something else should be able to do so. Such is spirit, *Aand.* Nowhere does the introduction to the treatise hide science's inability. Vigilius Haufniensis vigilantly respects the limits of science so that he may keep his "psychological" discovery of "nothing" from being nonsense, and he, as the very figure of a scientific spirit, is driven by his exposition of historicity to undo the very distinction between the language of knowledge and that of ignorance. But he is as little inclined to let anxiety have the last word as the author of *Papers* will let the negativity that characterizes the "whole newer development" deliver the final verdict on life and language. And just as *Papers* drafted the concept of life-view into the service of critique so that it could hold back the progressive unfolding of oblivion and leveling on all fronts, *The Concept of Anxiety* enlists a term to mark off the limit of the new science of psychology. "Psychology" means discourse on the soul; the limit it must respect is therefore that of the soul, namely, spirit. The function of spirit, as limit concept and limitation on the conceptuality of "psychology," thus parallels the function of the term "life-view" in the critical determination of Andersen's failed novel. *The Concept of Anxiety*, moreover, introduces "spirit" in precisely the same place that *Papers* calls upon the idea of a "life-view"—when the thoroughgoing negativity that has stamped the character of history is exposed to a specifically linguistic "nothing."

Unlike the acquisition of a life-view in *Papers*, the positing of spirit in *The Concept of Anxiety* does not simply hold back the ongoing development of oblivion and leveling. And the whole of history, not just "the whole newer development," is characterized by a certain negativity, for the first spiritual position is one in which the self disposes of itself and deposits itself into "sin." To the extent that sin is "negative," nothing could be more negatively qualified than the original position of spirit. But the treatise will not outright declare, to use the title of the last chapter in *The Sickness unto Death*, that "sin is not a negation but a position,"[16] since the word "negation" has, as the introduction insists, corrupted science. The original positing of spirit disposes of innocence, and yet it is only in the positing of spirit that the motility and momentum of falling has a chance of being held back. For only spirit posits something— *oneself*, "existence"—about which one can finally speak. In the unconditional positing of spirit, which does without empirical as well as conceptual conditions, some*thing* arises that takes the place of empty self-referential language—the self itself. The self takes the place of language "itself." Such is the thesis of spirit:

> That anxiety makes its appearance is the pivot upon which everything turns. Man is a synthesis of the psychical and the physical; however, a synthesis is unthinkable if the two are not united in a third. This third is spirit. In innocence, man is not merely animal, for if he were at any moment of his life merely animal, he would never become man. So spirit is present, but as immediate, as dreaming. Inasmuch as it is now present, it is in a sense a hostile power, for it constantly disturbs the relation between body and soul, a relation that indeed has persistence but does not have endurance, inasmuch as it first receives the latter by the spirit. On the other hand, spirit is a friendly power, since it is precisely that which constitutes this relation. What, then, is man's relation to this ambiguous power? How does spirit relate itself to itself and to its conditionality? It relates itself as anxiety. . . . Innocence still is, but only a word is required and then ignorance is concentrated. (44)

Spirit takes the place of the radically ambiguous "word" in which ignorance is concentrated, and "sin" in turn takes the root. The ambiguity of "spirit" therefore matches that of this word; its "double meaning" doubles that of anxiety. Spirit posits itself in the very space opened up by the self-referential colloquy of this original "word." For this reason, the "object" of anxiety is not only "nothing" but also that which takes its unique place, namely, spirit. Over spirit, and so over *oneself*, one is anxious, so much so that "self" and "nothing" constantly exchange places until the moment when spirit posits itself unconditionally, without reference to either of the relata that make up the relation of the self to itself. Only in the unconditional positing of spirit, which takes away every historical condition, is there the prospect of striking down the "ambiguity" that spirit inherits from anxiety.

Spirit consists in the relation of body to soul; in spirit, body and soul relate to each other, so any misrelation of one to the other is a "spiritual" misrelation. The original positing of spirit, which constitutes "original sin," leaves as its residuum a misrelation in which each of the relata stands outside the relation. The expression of this outstanding characteristic of spirit is precisely *generation*. For spirit stamps the *slægt* (race, generation) with psychosomatic difference: with, in other words, *gender*. Over this difference spirit hovers, and to it anxiety never fails to refer. If the a priori condition on history is the "nothing" of anxiety, its actualization takes place through the constant replacement of this "nothing" with the stroke of the *slægt*, with generation and gender. Out of these outstanding marks of spirit history takes place. However, since the replacement of "nothing" by the strokes of generation and gender can have no preordained aim, the history generated in this constant replacement can have no fixed telos. Instead of a telos outside itself, history is assigned a *task* for which one solution after another is proposed:

> And no explanation that explains Adam but not hereditary sin, or explains hereditary sin but not Adam, is of any help. The most profound reason for this is what is essential to human existence: that man is *individuum* and as such simultaneously himself and the whole race, and in such a way that the whole race participates in the individual and the individual in the whole race. . . . At every moment, the individual is both himself and the race. This is man's perfection viewed as a state. It is also a contradiction, but a contradiction is always the expression of a task, and a task is movement, but a movement that as a task is the same as that to which the task is directed is an historical movement. Hence the individual has a history. But if the individual has a history, then the race also has a history. (28–29)

No individuality can arise without spirit. But spirit itself "cannot be conceived as sexually qualified" (79). *The Concept of Anxiety* touches upon precisely this inconceivability, for individuality—and therefore "existence"—cannot dis-qualify itself, not even when spirit has posited itself unconditionally and transparently (80). Therefore, when one insists that "the whole race participates in the individual and the individual in the whole race," no reified concepts of "the race" are in play; no "realism," in the scholastic sense, undoes the primacy of "existence." For the whole race is nothing other than its individuals, uniquely outstanding, and therefore stamped into a *slægt* (race, generation). Each individual, as outstanding, participates in this stamping, and this stamping partakes of the individual because the race "exists" solely as the stamp on the individual: as sexuality, that is, *driven* to the task of stamping out precisely what under no condition can be so qualified, namely, spirit. On the basis of this lack of qualification, spirit alone has the ability to make the "qualitative" leap into the hands of its maker. Sexual qualification and the qualitative leap into the altogether unqualified, the "absolute," are therefore mutually exclusive, absolutely unequal. And it is in the sexual drive that sensuousness turns into sinfulness, hereditary sin imparts a sensuousness now qualified as sexual-sinful, and history undertakes to complete a task that like tasks in mathematics, has no telos other than its own solution.

Sexuality, driven to the task of stamping out spirit, makes every new anxiety into a repetition of the old one, with a single difference: "generic difference" (69). Since this difference is from the perspective of spirit "nothing," it comes out of and turns into the "object" of anxiety: "The sexual is the expression for the uncanny contradiction (*Widerspruch*) that the immortal spirit is determined as *genus*. This contradiction expresses itself in the profound *Scham* that conceals this contradiction and does not dare to understand it" (69). The concealed contradiction then reveals itself as "the beautiful" (69), but the beautiful, as the luminous appearance of shame, does not exhaust the ways "the uncanny contradiction" can be revealed without, however, being resolved. Each attempt to understand this contradiction according to determinate concepts does so. To resolve the contradiction is, by contrast, to *speak against it*. Speaking against "the uncanny contradiction" means countering the "diction" of sexuality, of generation and gender. But the "object" of each of these uncanny "dictions" is a mode of *difference* that from the perspective of "unqualified" spirit is precisely nothing. "Qualified," and therefore *historical*, language takes as its point of reference this "nothing," always refers in one way or another to this "it," and shamelessly develops *concepts* in order to reduce "it," the point of reference, to naught. Such is the point of the concept of anxiety as it is developed in the science of "psychology." Only an "unqualified" language, which would not be that of science, could, it seems, counter the "uncanny contradiction" and bring the progressive march of negativity to a stop. Such a language would have to do without concepts and could refer only to *itself*, to spirit posited unconditionally and without qualification. The unconditional positing of language, which is known as "naming," therefore cannot be far removed from any discussion of the concept of spirit.

"Algebraic Naming"

The exposition of the various ways "the uncanny contradiction" can reveal itself, without resolution, occupies much of the analytic labor of *The Concept of Anxiety*. The content no less than the motor of history is at bottom this drive, this *Drift*: not simply as the "sexual drive"—a name that says very little here and above all would have little to say to the Copenhagen over which Vigilius watched[17]—but as the driving out of spirit and its concomitant replacement, again and again, with *difference*. Such difference is not simply generic, not simply confined to the "two sexes" whose physical and psychic opposition Vigilius takes for granted. The variety of differences that replace spirit under the compulsion of the so-called sexual drive, the compulsion to forget the origin and to call this forgetting "knowledge," makes itself manifest in the very effort by *The Concept of Anxiety* to reduce differences in accordance with certain "algebraic" (113, 128, 137) designations, hence to conceive of individualities according to mathematico-conceptual notations: not, in sum, to replace "existence" by imaginative *imitations*, as Vigilius states when he mounts his most lucid defense of his "experiments" (54–55) but instead to displace the field of the imitative, the mimetic, the theatrical, and the reenacted with an altogether different field, a field of difference whose very name, "algebra," refers to a system of notation incapable of referring beyond its self-defined operations and indeed insists on its own strange "beyondness," its undeniable *foreignness*. For algebra, the operation no less than the word, does not owe its origin to the West, to Christendom, or even to the greater Roman orbit whose borders Vigilius surveys.

　　Orientation in science, as the turn eastward, begins with the word "algebra." For nothing could be more intimately related to that which resolves "the uncanny contradiction" and to this extent speaks against those modes of difference that from the point of view of "unqualified" spirit are precisely nothing. Spirit consists in the relation of the mind to the body when it posits itself as a relation; it unifies, or reunifies, the relata of this relation. In Greek, such unification goes by the name *synthesis*; in Arabic, the word is *ja'bara*. "Algebra," as the rejoining of dismembered members,[18] posits dissevered relata in a reunited and now "healthy" relation. Algebra therefore heals misrelations. To the extent that the equations that arise from such rejoinings of displaced relations claim to be expressions of *truth*, they show an even greater affinity with the syntheses of body and soul that are supposed to take place in the positings of spirit. Indeed, "algebra" even describes the act of positing this synthesis since it includes the "re" of reuniting and thus refers to the *repetitive* character of every "spiritual" positing. But all the same, *algebraic* rejoining of displaced relata never refers to a lost wholeness and does not arrive at organic health. Not "sickness" and "death" but "task" and "solution" are the terms in which its equations occur. However closely it parallels the synthesis of spirit, the syntheses of algebra do not animate and as a result cannot spiritualize the relevant relata. Algebra emerges in this way as the doppelgänger of spirit, a "spiritual" double that haunts spirit insofar as it again and again rejoins displaced relata but never gives them "new" life. No language of spirit can hope to escape its double, a language of "algebraic naming" (128) in which arbitrarily posited designations and therefore *names alone*—not things, not "individuals"—are "new."

So arbitrarily posited are the "names" that populate algebraic equations that they cease to refer to anything outside the system of its equations. These "names"—let them be *A, B, C, x, y, z*—are not simply *pronouns*; they do not simply replace nouns or names but are the systematic replacement of anything that claims meaning on its own, the thoroughgoing undermining of all independently meaningful expressions. Anything algebraically named, including every letter, is meaningful only as one relata in the relation, so the positing of the relation *itself* makes these "names," which as letters are dismembered words, into names in the first place. Nothing else happens in the positing of spirit *itself*: the relata of this relation— soul, body—are significant only in the positing of spirit, and only in the "unqualified" positing of spirit as spirit are these relata related to one another as a transparent, genuine, and therefore "true" identity. From systematically posited relations the "names" of algebra acquire meaning; from unqualified positings of spirit the relata of "psychology" gain significance. So closely related are "algebraic naming" and spiritual positing that the language of spirit could easily be taken to be an "algebraic" one, especially when *The Concept of Anxiety* continually calls upon certain "algebraic" names to present and explicate various "qualified" and therefore "imper- fect" positings of spirit—the positings of spirit in which spirit is not posited unconditionally.

"Original" language, as the language of anxious innocence, is itself algebraic: "Adam was created; he had given names to the animals (here there is language, though in an imperfect way similar to that of children who learn by identifying animals on an A B C board)" (46). Spirit has not yet been posited, yet language never- theless presents itself in its most perfect algebraic form: every "name" is arbitrarily posited, and only in an equally arbitrary system of naming, "an A B C board," do they have any significance. On their own, these "names" are nothing; their point of reference is, as usual, the "nothing" of anxiety. However, if "original" lan- guage, which is "imperfect" because spirit has yet to be posited, shows itself to be as "algebraic" as the language of spirit, the unique criterion by virtue of which languages could be decisively distinguished no longer holds, and the language of spirit can no longer counter "the uncanny contradiction" that difference qualifies spirit. The "perfection" of language may lie in the "spiritualization" of its original letters, but this spiritualization can consist in the positing of them only in their relation to one another, and this positing is, once again, the "original" act of naming, a linguistic act in which the colloquy of language "itself" and the figure of the self take part together. To the extent that Adam's "imperfect" language has no guides, no tutors, no rules, it is the very language of anxiety, but to the extent that the very same language is *freely posited*—without convention, without association—it is the "perfect" language, the language of spirit.

Spirit, as the relation of the self to itself, is supposed to posit itself in the place opened up by language speaking of "itself" to "itself." Spirit thereby releases the self, as a relation, from its imprisonment in quotation marks; the self of spirit becomes something other than the so-called self-reflective pronoun and posits *itself* in its place.[19] Each topic discussed in *The Concept of Anxiety* after its exposition of the fall into "sin" orients itself toward the "perfection" of this replacement; the more "imperfect" the replacement, the more "qualified" spirit's position; the more perfect the replacement, the more unqualified the positing of spirit. "Guilt" closes the arc of possible replacements because it, unlike "shame" or "fate," is inconceivable without spirit. Over guilt, then, spirit at its most unqualified is anxious; guilt constitutes the final determination and to this extent the ultimate significance of the "nothing" to which anxiety always answers and to which its language never ceases to refer. The guilt over which one is anxious is "nothing," and this guilt constitutes the content of "psychological" observations. The "object" of guilt, however, is not "nothing": it is the very positing of spirit as "sin." In the position of spirit, guilt is "nothing" and positivity in turns. No concept of guilt can fail to take these turns— of negativity and positivity, "nothing" and "existence"—into account; this concept, unlike all other concepts, delimits no field of reference but marks out the unique place in which the positing of spirit replaces language "itself." This positing alone should be the point of reference for the concept of guilt, so the language of guilt, which is usually called confession, should annihilate the last traces of conceptuality and have nothing but an absolutely referential function: the function of pointing out guilt; more exactly, of pointing at oneself as guilt and thereby positing *oneself* instead of finding oneself deposited in language.

Nowhere, however, does algebra prove more indispensable than in the exposition of what occupies the content of guilt and thus constitutes its concept: "Because of the form of the investigation, I can indicate the particular state only very briefly, almost algebraically" (113). Soon this "almost" has to be dropped. The more profound the guilt, the more indispensable the "algebraic naming" (128). For the deepening of spirit corresponds to the widening of algebra until in the end "language itself becomes algebraic" (137). In guilt, therefore, at the very point where "unqualified" spirit and "sexual difference" are most intimately joined, algebraic rejoinders multiply, so much so that the "qualification" of spirit no longer presents itself as "sexual" at all. "Sexuality" names, rather, difference endlessly referring to itself without any "self" having been posited to which reference could be made. It is, as it has been all along, "algebraic," joining but never reuniting, propagating difference ad infinitum. It is a *rejoinder* to the positing of spirit, a rejoinder that interrupts the replacement of language "itself" by the positing of spirit.

This interruption is doubtless confounded with the failure of spirit to posit itself without condition and without qualification; it doubtless presents itself as though it were the qualification—and therefore sexualization, "sinfulization"—of spirit. But the algebraic rejoinder to spirit confounds the topic of replacement to the point where the positing of spirit cannot eradicate its every trace of referential indeterminacy. *Concepts* of spirit—and everything involved in its positing—are ineradicable, irreducible, and even indispensable for its presentation. Each algebraic name bears witness to the irreducibility of conceptuality in the very place and on the very topic where concepts are unqualified to speak. The rejoinder to the supposed replacement of language "itself" by the positing of the self itself—namely, the positing of spirit—is "algebraic naming." This rejoinder, which is eminently clear and remarkably straightforward, confounds the very possibility of unambiguous language, language delivered over entirely to spirit that would for this reason perfectly replace the "original" colloquy of language "itself." Algebraic substitution takes the place of spiritual replacement; algebraic conjunction of sameness interrupts and undoes the spiritual positing of the relation of the self to itself. Algebra, as an arbitrary but exacting rejoinder to the claims of spirit, does not replace but *replays* "original" language in historical—sexual, sinful—terms.[20]

Spirit Minus Spirit

The concept of anxiety is a "dialectical" one to the extent that anxiety and conceptuality exclude each other, and so too does every concept concerned with anxiety. Spirit, however, is not concerned with anxiety; its "unqualified" positing, which is never a *self-positing* but nonsexual and nongenerational reception of its unique position, is supposed to replace the "nothing" of anxiety so completely that nothing of conceptuality remains: an outstanding singularity, "existence," is instead pointed out. However, if this "unqualified" positing cannot altogether replace anxiety, if this replacement is impossible to carry out for the precise reason that the "topic" upon which the replacement is supposed to take place has been already confounded, then the concept of spirit is not "dialectical" but *colloquial*: it is not simply a "contradiction in terms" but a "confusion of tongues," and this confusion countermands every claim to distinction in a more radical and more thorough manner than anxiety itself ever could. For this colloquial concept does not demarcate a field of reference but points out again and again the colloquy of language "itself." Conceptual oppositions, which give rise to "dialectics," collapse when the positing of spirit cannot oppose the "nothing" of anxiety. None of the distinctions to which *The Concept of Anxiety* clings—between anxiety and spirit, between "psychology" and "dogmatics," between origins—are therefore valid. The irreducibility of conceptuality does not imply the primacy of "thinking" over "being" but the impossibility of making even this opposition into a dialectical one. So irreducible is conceptuality that the residuum of this reduction, language "itself," revokes the only unconditional distinction and the most pointed opposition that makes its way into the "algebraic" formulations of *The Concept of Anxiety*: the distinction between spirit and spiritlessness.

Spiritlessness, which knows no anxiety, is the ironic—or as Vigilius prefers, "comic" (94)—conclusion to history: "comic" because history concludes not in presence or precisely in absence but in a ghostly nonpresence, and because spiritlessness, in any case, is incapable of coming to a conclusion. The driving out of spirit in spiritlessness is so effective that sexuality itself, as the qualification of, and opposition to, spirit, is likewise driven out; nothing but "limp clamminess" and sudden "fetishism" (95) remain. Spiritlessness leaves history adrift, without drive, without direction, and even without distinctions between past, present, and future. The "fetishism" of spiritlessness corresponds to the regular erection of a "fetish" (8) which marks "our age." What was called "the whole newer development" in *Papers* now goes by the far more incisive name "spiritlessness," more incisive to the extent that its "negativity" no longer presents itself as a *development* but as a retroactive suspension of the very ability to develop or decide. The disjunctive judgment in which decision is lodged—"guilty or not guilty?"—is likewise suspended:

> The life of Christian paganism is neither guilty nor not guilty. It really knows no distinction between the present, the past, the future, and the eternal. Its life and its history go on like the writing in ancient days went over paper [*over Papiret*], when one uses no marks of distinction, no punctuation marks [*Adskillelsetegn*]; rather, one word, one sentence rubs up against another. From an esthetic point of view, this is very comical, for while it is beautiful to listen to a brook running murmuring through life, it is nevertheless comical that a sum of rational

creatures is transformed into a perpetual muttering without meaning [*Murmelen uden Mening*]. (94)

Spiritlessness annuls meaningful language, the very language of opposition in which it, as nonspirit, is written. Spiritlessness recognizes neither temporal nor linguistic oppositions; the points of time, like those of language, are rendered inoperative. Since pointlessness cannot posit itself, since it can never make itself present, the very pointlessness of spiritlessness can be recognized only *in writing*, not in speech; only in writing do temporal and linguistic points show up. In order to make spiritlessness "present," then, everything therein spoken must be made archaic, distant, and utterly *foreign*; spiritlessness shows up only in strange scripts. In spoken discourse, by contrast, every word goes on without a recognizable loss, without the "less" of spiritlessness showing up. Spoken discourse consists in those "murmurings" that are unpunctuated precisely because *nothing*—no speaker, no self—takes up a position in place of language "itself." But this "nothing," as nonpositing, does not oppose the positing of spirit; "it," which can never be subject of a sentence and can never show up as a substance, therefore cannot be the "nothing" to which anxiety always corresponds. This "nothing," which endlessly displaces the replacement of language "itself" by the finite positing of spirit, interrupts even the empty correspondence of anxiety. Opposition to spiritlessness is therefore all the more impossible. If punctuating the "murmuring" of spiritlessness reinscribes a present tense into a discourse that eschews all temporal qualifications, it does so only at the cost of its own presence: it makes all spoken discourse into archaic writing. The language of spiritlessness and that of its supposed opposite share a common, but never substantial, trait, namely, "repetition":

> Spiritlessness can say exactly the same thing that the richest spirit has said, but it does not say it by virtue of spirit. Man qualified as spiritless has become a talking machine [*Talemaskine*], and there is nothing to prevent him from repeating by rote a philosophical rigmarole [*en philosophisk Ramse*], a confession of faith, or a political recitation. Is it

not remarkable that the only ironist and the greatest humorist joined forces in saying what seems the simplest of all, namely, that a person must distinguish between what he understands and what he does not understand? And what can prevent the most spiritless man from repeating the same thing verbatim?   (95)

No one can *answer* these questions, although they are the ones from which *The Concept of Anxiety*, again citing Socrates and reinvoking the claims of science, begins. For no one, no "spiritual" position and therefore no selfsame being, is left over; no one is left to engage in dialogue, as the now utterly foreign text proceeds to acknowledge: "There is only one proof of spirit, and that is the spirit's proof within oneself" (95). Talking machines depunctuate so thoroughly that the place in language "itself" from which spirit is supposed to take its position has been confounded: not lost, not erased but sullied to the point where language "itself" and the self posited in spirit become indissociable and indistinguishable. Both the depunctuation of spiritlessness ("chatter") and the repunctuation of spirit ("writing") share in repetition: the insignificant repetition of "meaning" on the one hand, the repetition of discourse with punctuated marks on the other. Repeating language without points, repeating language with points: they are the same; only the points differ. And the difference of points, the punctual difference, is difference "itself." Difference "itself"—not specific differences and not individual differences but the difference to which every species and every individual owes its existence, even as its existence rests on an identity attained through the eliding of difference itself—cannot show up; it cannot be staged. Or if it comes on stage, if it does show up, it does not appear as the stroke of sexual difference but presents itself as *pure language*—language without meaning, without a qualified speaker, without a point other than its own pointlessness: "When spiritlessness is to be represented, pure nonsense [*ret Passiar*] is simply put into the mouth of the actor, because no one has the courage to put into the mouth of spiritlessness the same words one uses oneself. This is insecurity" (94–95, modified).

The theatrical replacement of speech with "pure nonsense" constitutes "insecurity," but it does not amount to anxiety. Spiritlessness, rather, replaces anxiety, the "object" of which is "nothing," with *stage fright*: not the fear of losing one's voice on stage but the fear of *language itself*, the fear lest one's speaking disclose self-absence, the fear lest the "less" of spiritlessness show up "in the very same words one uses oneself." Verbal "nonsense," as the passing comments that compose *passiar*, would be an enormous relief in comparison to this fright, for it keeps language in its place; it remains subordinate to "oneself," even as it shows, in any stage re-presentation, that language "itself" has already replaced the supposed "self" of the speaker. Hiding oneself in "nonsense" does not, however, conceal chatter but discloses the subordination of this supposed "self" to language, a subordination that the positing of spirit is supposed to oppose. But opposition to "nonsense" cannot consist in making sense; the opposite to "nonsense" is not "significance," and cannot to this extent appear an opposite at all. Rather, the "opposite" is sheer repetition: punctuating the speech, making it into archaic writing, presenting on stage "the very same words one uses oneself." Punctuation, writing, recitation—these interrupt the language of spiritlessness by presenting this language again and again. But since it is impossible to make a decision on the purity of "nonsense," it is impossible to represent the language that interrupts spiritlessness as the positing of spirit.

Spiritlessness cannot do without spirit, but the spirit of spiritlessness does not posit itself; it is, rather, "spirit." Spiritlessness is itself an "algebraic name": spirit "less" spirit. The equation into which this name figures has no equal in the idealistic register of "$I = I$." This equation is spiritlessness = spirit "less" spirit; spirit minus spirit = "spirit." Spirit minus spirit does not equal zero; it amounts to the nullification of spirit as a *position* and the replacement of this positive power with unruly, arbitrary, undecidable concepts—with, that is, "spirits," specters, and haunting apparitions; the "spirits," in other words, that Kierkegaard will later discuss in terms of a certain "spirit of leveling" that has overtaken and underwritten "the present age."[21] In this life of language a concept—that of zero, a null-point in an open and indeterminate set of denotations—proves its irreducibility. Without presence, the life of language survives as "talking machine," as ghosts, galimatias, and drifting phrases: "Spirit may therefore possess the whole content of spirit, but mark well [*vel at mærke*], not as spirit but as the haunting of ghosts, as galimatias, as a phrase, etc. [*som Spøgerie, Galimathias, Phrase, o. s. v.*]" (94).[22]

Into such "spirits" spiritlessness retreats, leaving no trace of body or soul behind; instead, the trace of this retreat is "murmuring without meaning," language without difference, but all the same, language as "pure nonsense," as pure difference to which nothing positive, nothing meaningful or significant, corresponds. To the "spirits" of this spiritless language, which is language "itself," there corresponds a mark, the countermanding command to "mark well." This command has no discernible authority; it does not come from the position of spirit. It arrives from the confounded place in which the positing of spirit is supposed to replace the colloquy of language "itself." The burden of the entire exposition of anxiety comes down to this impossible command: "Mark well." It is a historical command to withstand the forgetting and the obliteration of all distinguishing marks, a linguistic command to punctuate otherwise pointless speech, and a "psychological" command to stay on the alert. But none of these commands can do without a criterion of "wellness," the unique criterion on which *The Concept of Anxiety* stands or falls.

Communicerende

Spirit does not oppose spiritlessness. The "less" in "spiritlessness" is not simply a negation and does not simply indicate a loss. So negative is this "less" that it cannot be opposed to a positive and cannot be converted into a position by any spiritual power. It is so negative, and negative in such a way, that the "less" of "spiritlessness" constitutes and concomitantly institutes a peculiar mode of affirmation. The legacy of Hegel's "negation of a negation" is doubtless in play, as is Kierkegaard's consistently negative evaluation of Hegel's affirmation of modernity,[23] but the oddly affirmative character of spiritlessness expresses itself in the "murmurings without meaning" of disguised "spirits." And if the positing of spirit cannot oppose spiritlessness, nothing can: spirit has been so thoroughly driven out—of itself and thus turned into its other, into "spirits"—that no position, including opposition, remains in force. *The Concept of Anxiety* in turn drives spirit out; it ceases to speak of spirit, as though spirit, having encountered the topic of spiritlessness, had turned into its own specter: a "spirit" that through quotation marks marks itself off from itself, a "spirit" that must write itself off. Spirit then makes use of a substitute so that the criterion of "wellness" can be discovered; that substitute will be called "freedom," for the distinctive trait of freedom is its ability to distinguish good from evil and therefore, one would hope, "marking well" from "marking poorly."

The driving out of spirit takes place in the treatise as the replacement of spirit by the word "freedom." The topic toward which this replacement orients itself is then this: whether the replacement of language "itself" by the positing of spirit, which is freedom, is possible; whether, in other words, spirit can be free of the "murmuring" in which spiritlessness speaks. Freedom's absolution from all relations other than those it posits makes its every term into a self-referential one and makes opposition to its speech a matter not of unfreedom, certainly not of necessity, but of guilt: "The opposite of freedom is guilt, and it is the greatness of freedom that it always has to do only with itself, that in its possibility it projects guilt and accordingly posits it by itself" (108). However clearly this assertion declares the terms of opposition to freedom, complications cannot be kept at bay. For the opposite of guilt should be freedom, but the text leaves no doubt that it is in fact *innocence*; to wit, an innocence that is not opposed to guilt but disclosed along with it:

> The fact that [the religious genius who has turned to himself] discovers guilt so profoundly indicates that this concept is present to him *sensu eminentiori*, just as its opposite, innocence, is also. So it was in the case

of the relation of the immediate genius to fate, for every man has a little relation to fate, but there it ends in empty talk [*Passiaren*] that does not notice what Talleyrand (and Young before him expressed) discovered, although not as fully as empty talk [*Passiaren*] does, that the purpose of language is to conceal thought—namely, to conceal that one has none [*at man ingen har*]. (107–8)

No terms of opposition can withstand the *passiar* into which this passage has ventured. Not only does "empty talk" elude the opposition between noticing and discovering, but the very principle of opposition collapses when the purpose of language, which is so often said to be disclosure, turns out to be concealment, and this concealment, in turn, reveals itself to be the concealment *of nothing*, the concealment that there is nothing to disclose. "Empty talk" does not notice what it nevertheless has already revealed—that no notes and no marks are available by which something could be noticed. *Passiar* cannot notice this discovery because its relation to *fatum*, to "that which has been spoken," obeys the "logic" of chatter: "empty talk" says too much, yet it speaks of nothing at all. The revelation of this emptiness would be fatal to language; it would dislodge its revelatory, apophantic function and condemn every one of its announcements to self-announcements of its lack of selfhood. Opposition to such linguistic nullity demands that language posit its "own" opposite and therefore that language, not spirit, take the place of *libertas*.

The Concept of Anxiety tries to close with the saving word: "Language, the word, is precisely what saves" (124). Salvation, however, is one of many designations of an "object" freedom discovers: "The good, of course, signifies the restoration of freedom, redemption, salvation, or whatever one wishes to call it" (119). In order to save "what saves" of the indeterminacy expressed in "whatever one wishes to call it," in order therefore to make this "wish" to name into the freedom that saves—and first of all saves "what saves" from indeterminacy—the word "salvation" must get to work. The term must be determined against something if it is to be saved from the indeterminacy of anxiety and its various historical replacements: shame, fate, guilt. The determination of the term "what saves" therefore demands an exposition of the opposition to what it signifies, "the good." Opposition to the good, taken to its limit, drives out spirit so thoroughly that nothing but a ghost of spirit remains, and the name for this remnant, a name that is only "rarely" spoken in "our day" (118), is "the demonic." Daimons are "spirits" without the positing of spirit, "spirits" in the plural who, as "the demonic," have a polemical, "unfree relation to the good" (119). Against these daimons—and one might add, against the Socratic daimon to whom he owes his "infinite negative subjectivity"[24]—"language, the word, is precisely what saves." The last place where the words for this salvation should fall into indeterminacy is in the face of the demonic.

Demonic phenomena, as particularly acute misrelations of the soul to the body, are worthy objects of any "psychologically oriented" observation. If Vigilius is on the watch for anything in particular, it is for unnoticed and unmarked demonic "spirits," those "spirits" that an *incarnated* and yet completely "unqualified" Spirit should be able to drive out. In opposition to the absolute positing of Spirit, which no human being can carry out alone, there stands the demonic: it is the limit that "comes to [the good's] boundary from the outside" (119). The word "demonic" therefore serves as the oppositional term par excellence, the term by which the "psychological" observation comes to an end and a "pneumatology" would begin. The words of "psychology" work as long as they oppose the spirit of demonism, and the crowning of this work is the abdication of each of its concepts to something other than mere conceptuality. However, when Vigilius comes to "observe" the demonic and when in turn he wishes to show its relation to "unqualified" Spirit, he gives up observation and falls into a peculiar indeterminacy of citation.

> The demonic therefore manifests itself clearly only when it is in contact with the good, which comes to its boundary from the outside. For this reason, it is noteworthy that the demonic in the New Testament first appears when it is approached by Christ. Whether the demon is

legion (cf. Matthew 8:28–34; Mark 5:1–20; Luke 8:26–39) or is dumb (cf. Luke 11:14), the phenomenon is the same, namely, anxiety about the good, for anxiety can just as well express itself by muteness as by a scream. The good, of course, signifies the restoration of freedom, redemption, salvation, or whatever one would call it.   (119)

The demonic does not exhaust itself in the alternative—scream or muteness. For the multiplication of logos in the very word "legion," and the multiplicity of textual references to this "word," attests to its articulateness, indeed to its overarticulateness, its excessiveness in speech, perhaps even its own parodic *communicatio idiomatum*. The language of "legion," of the logos as it multiplies and divides itself, as it refuses to enter into an equation with itself, escapes the opposition between language and silence, articulateness and inarticulateness, humanity and brutality. Without, however, leading to a higher term, a supreme spirit. That "legion" speaks to the logos means at the very least that "unqualified" Spirit shares in the same words as the demonic displacement of spirit into "spirits," and this sharing of words at the very least suspends the terms of their opposition.[25]

The "observation" of the demonic can have no object other than the exposition of the terms in which demons do "in reality"—as opposed to "in textuality" or even "in Scripture"—oppose freedom. Observation of possibilities, which would appear to be a contradiction, serves to expose us to the concept of freedom by virtue of its very interlacing of actuality and possibility. For as the introduction had claimed, freedom projects possibilities but is itself actual "as soon as it is" (21). The observations of possible opposites to freedom should therefore bring the treatise to a stunning conclusion—a conclusion, in any case, in "inclosed reserve" (*Indesluttede*). And this term of closure serves as a replacement; it takes the place, remarkably enough, of the term against which the entire introduction was oriented, "negativity." When this term, like a *revenant*, returns to haunt the treatise, it is no longer merely idle: it says something, or does something. It says that opposition to freedom, a position against freedom, does take place in a closed-off space.

Vigilius thus retreats in part from his firm stance of opposition to the recent talk of "negation":

> If I were not to call attention to the terminologies of the most recent philosophy, I might say that the demonic is the negative and is nothing, like the elf maid who is hollow when seen from the back. However, I do not prefer to do this, because the terminology in and by its social intercourse has become so amiable and pliant that it may signify anything whatsoever. The negative, if I were to use this word, signifies the form of nothing, just as the contentless corresponds to inclosed reserve [*Indholdsløse svarer til det Indesluttede*]. But the negative has the defect [*Feil*] that it is more externally determined; it defines the relation to something else, which is negated, while inclosed reserve defines the state itself.
>
> When the negative is understood in this manner, I have no objection to its use as a designation for the demonic, provided that the negative can otherwise rid itself of all the bees that the most recent philosophy has put in its bonnet.   (134)

The term "negativity" can be saved for "science" as long as the "bees" of Hegelian philosophy are prevented from using it for the purposes of cross-pollination. "Negativity" invites these "buzzing" bees because it has no fixed determination, and this indeterminacy presents itself as endless substitution of one thing for another: "The negative has gradually become a vaudeville figure [*Vaudeville-Figur*]" (134). So varied is the figure of "the negative" that on stage it can appear as anything but what it is—namely, "nothing." The figurality of the term "the negative" does not, however, simply befall negativity; it is not as though negativity could "gradually" become a figure of endless substitution without this event having its source in negativity itself. The negative, *pace* Hegel, does not work, and does no work for the Concept, because every time the term appears, it turns a determinate concept into a figure of its own indeterminacy, and this figure, which might be called the "vaudeville figure" or the figure par excellence, has no role to play, no function to fulfill, no act to perform.

The Concept of Anxiety therefore devises a figure of this "vaudeville figure": that of enclosure, of being self-enclosed, shut inside. *Det Indesluttede*, "inclosed reserve," takes the place of "negativity" to let the demonic, which would otherwise be absorbed into the figure of endless and contentless figuration, present itself as opposed to *something*. With this opposition the term "demonic," no longer ghostly or magical, can finally go to work. And what enclosure works against is, of course, *disclosure*, which in turn serves as a figure for "communication": "The demonic does not close itself up with something, but closes itself up within itself, and in this lies what is profound about existence, precisely that unfreedom makes itself a prisoner. Freedom is always *communicerende* (it does no harm even to take into consideration the religious significance of the word); unfreedom becomes more and more inclosed [*indesluttet*] and does not want communication" (124).

The opposition of communication to self-enclosure doubtless raises the expectation that something like "dialogue" will arise to oppose the demonic and by opposing it, resolve it once and for all. But the term "dialogue," as opposed to the "monologue" (128) of the demonic, has no place in the exposition, and all expectations of a resolution in conversation, conceived under the dominance of the question, come to naught. Instead of representing "dialogue" or "conversation," disclosure serves as a figure for *communicerende*, a foreign word that because of its very foreignness is raised to the status of a *terminus technicus*. Nowhere is the Latin provenance of Vigilius Haufniensis more decisive. For *communicerende* has no place in the local, colloquial language; it is technical, idiomatic, and foreign, a word of algebra, the word at which the "vaudeville figure" of negativity should come to a stop if this word were not itself subject to the indeterminacy of the term "negativity."

But few terms could be more indeterminate than *communicerende*. For it does not simply mean the transference of a message from sender to receiver. Like the words "communication," *koinoneō*, *Mitteilung*, *meddelelse*, it divides and multiplies meanings, one of which would presumably be "the religious significance of the word." But even this meaning is not unique; the significance of *communicerende* for "the religious" is itself divided and multiplied.

The "religious significance" of *communicerende* does not exhaust itself in the idea of a shared communion wherein the community of those who believe in its founding first becomes a community in its own right, nor does the term in its "religious significance" simply mean the sharing of communion in commemoration of the one who by virtue of an incomprehensible *communicatio idiomatum* brings divine and human substance back into a unified community, thereby binding together (*re-ligio*) man and god. *Communicerende* also means "making common"—the making common on the one hand whereby community and re-ligion take place and thus make a sacred space for communion, and the making common on the other hand of that which is supposed to be kept altogether uncommon, to be held therefore at a distance, to be always unspoiled by commoners.

Communicerende "in its religious significance" also means "defiling the sacred." The term designates the unbinding of re-ligion as much as its binding. The language of *communicerende* cannot escape the threat of profanity to which every making common, every cat-egory, every vulgar-ization, every public-ation is exposed. Nowhere is this threat more clearly stated than in the very Scripture from which Latin technical terms owe their origin and which promises to emancipate its readers from the demon of the law. *Communicerende*, as the Vulgate translation of the Koinic Greek term *koinoneō*, designates "spiritual" pollution: " 'Nothing that goes into a man from outside can defile him. But the things that come out of a man are the things that defile [*ta koinounta*; *communicant*] him.' . . . He told them, 'It is what comes out of man that defiles man [*koinoi anthrōpon*; *communicant hominem*].' "[26] " 'What goes into the mouth does not make one common; it is what comes out of the mouth that makes one common.' "[27]

What comes out of the human mouth is, of course, speech. Communication therefore doubly defiles: as *communicerende*, it designates the defilement of that which should be held apart, and the agent of this defilement is precisely "the mouth," a figure of communication. Designation and figuration are as closely bound together in *communicerende* as communion and defilement. The being of freedom—"freedom is *communicerende*"—presents itself now in terms of the sacred and now in those of the profane, without at the same time offering a criterion with which one could decide which is which. So sullied, so devoid of the disjunctive either-or, so utterly *confusing* is this term that it too is made common and defiled. Re-ligion, as the binding together of substances first in a *communicatio idiomatum* and then in its sacred community, cannot escape categories, vulgarizations, publications, and in the end—which might be called "spiritlessness"—the defilement of the very terms in which the "religious significance" of words is supposed to find expression. Religion binds and unbinds itself in *communicerende*, which is freedom.

Speaking cannot but pollute the speaker. For the place at which the positing of spirit is supposed to replace language "itself" is not simply confounded by an original colloquy but is thoroughly sullied. The division and multiplication of the meanings that inhabit *communicerende* is an index of the muddle. And the demonic, as a name for a negativity so corrosive that it exceeds determinate negation, shows itself to be the outstanding communicable disease, more distressing than anxiety, indeed the unease of *communicerende* itself. The demonic insists on this: communication no longer serves a sacred communion but serves to sully the speaking self—a self, however, that "is" only in making itself common, making itself other, defiling itself even as it upholds the law. Such sullying cannot be captured by the disjunctions through which *The Concept of Anxiety* tries to maintain terms of opposition: enclosure or disclosure, unfreedom or freedom, silence or speech. The sullying of *communicerende* releases the demonic from its enclosure in the figure of enclosure, *ex*-communicating language from any determinate "spiritual" position and likewise excommunicating spirit from the confounded position of language. *Communicerende*, as communion in the sacred, does not oppose excommunication but on the contrary rejoins excommunicants in an already interrupted, never successfully accomplished *communicatio idiomatum*. If communication and excommunication do not oppose each other, nothing can oppose anything.

Crossing Communication Out

The most idiomatic of all communications must be that of freedom. For any freedom that does not imply the ability to speak on one's own, idiomatically, cannot be considered freedom in the eminent sense. To distinguish the idiomatic "monologue" of the demonic from the *communicerende* of freedom becomes an impossible task, especially when language, not the positing of spirit, emerges as the force that undoes the enclosure and to this extent brings the constant buzz of "the negative" to a halt: "Here disclosure is the good, for disclosure is the first expression [*Udtryk*] of salvation. One therefore says the old word [*siger man for et gammelt Ord*] that if one dares to name the word [*nævne Ordet*], the sorcery's enchantment disappears, and therefore the somnambulist wakes up when his name is named" (127, translation modified). *The word wakes "itself" up.* The enclosure of the word in itself, where the word "itself" is disclosure, makes its disclosure of "itself" to "itself" into an immediate and therefore magical event: immediacy is annulled (10); dreaming spirit awakens (41); freedom is restored (119).

All these determinations of falling and restitution draw their resources from the word as it wakes itself up. And what it wakes up to is "itself," not the positing of spirit that takes place in the replacement of a linguistic "self" by the self of spirit. The word awakens to the confounded, unclean, "defiled" place of this replacement. In *The Concept of Anxiety* this place of defilement goes by the necessarily inadequate name "the concept." The outstanding figure of this place is therefore antonomasia, the replacement of name by concept, concept by name, noun by pronoun, pronoun by noun.[28] The place of replacement does not, however, receive this rhetorical name; instead, it finds an "algebraic" one, indeed the name of names that is not, however, a divine name or a divine symbol but an absolutely open name that replaces absolutely determined concepts; an utterly literal name, *the* algebraic letter: the letter-name of dispelling, the sign of multiplication, the index of crossing-out, and crossing-over—*x.*

X marks the spot: on this spot the positing of spirit is supposed to replace language "itself." The algebraic name *x* stands for anything. As the letter in which philosophy concedes a "skepticism" and marks out its inability know anything in itself—"the transcendental object = x"[29]—the *x* stands for the thing itself; it stands for the mere position of being. Standing for everything, however, means that it stands against nothing, and this is precisely the case: *x* opposes nothing and yet, being able to replace everything, it leaves nothing the same; it draws everything into "the concept," or more adequately stated, into language "itself," language without the position of a speaking self. The *x* is a name of names; it "is" the constantly discussed "nothing" of anxiety to which no categorical determination of nothingness applies: not an *ens rationis*, not a *nil privativum*, not an *ens imaginarium*, not even a *nihil negativum*, the *x* stands out and thus ex-ists, as it crosses "itself," and thus its own emptiness, out. Not, however, in order to fill itself up again. For the *x* can never escape its always active emptying out. Colloquialisms, idiomatic turns of speech, are never more appropriate than when the topic of discourse is *x*:

> In everyday talk there an expression that is very significant. It is said of a person: "He will not come out with it [*han vil ikke ud med sproget*]." Enclosure is precisely muteness [*Stumme*]; language, the word, is precisely what saves, what saves the individual from the empty abstraction of enclosure. Let *x* stand for the demonic, the relation of freedom to it something outside *x*; the law for the disclosure of the demonic is that against its will it comes out with it [*rykker ud med Sproget*]. In language lies communication [*Communicationen*]. (124, translation modified)

Colloquialisms conspire with algebraic formulations to deliver the dictum through which the existence of the demonic, and therefore the contradictory existence of negativity itself, comes into speech. The demonic, which consists of utterly empty abstraction, can be designated by *x* since *x* is precisely that: utterly empty abstraction. But *x* is not simply the demonic; "it"—and the quotation marks are necessary here to the extent that *x* multiplies itself and sets itself apart—stands *for* the demonic, stands in the confounded, "defiled" place of negativity, and is therefore even further removed from its "own" emptiness. "It" is the *making empty* of demonic emptiness, the place toward which the demonic is attracted precisely because "it," this spot marked x, is the site of abstraction pure and simple, the site of "the concept," not of "existence." To the degree that the demonic is attracted only there, to the degree that the demonic lets itself be designated by x, the x is an even greater emptiness, an even greater point of disorientation, an ever more untoward negativity than the demonic could ever imagine: it can only imagine this—its own negativity—as conceptuality.

The language in which the demonic gives itself up turns out to be the most abstract and the most colloquial at the same time, the most contra-dictory without being therefore paradoxical: the language of "algebraic naming," a language of the name, or of the letter, that names the replacement of all concrete names; a language in which nothing, not even thoughtlessness, is concealed; a language without essence or depth; a logos, if this word can still be used to designate language, of *ex*'s: an "ex"-isting language that is nevertheless more "abstract" than any scientific, conceptual one. The tilted cross lets other crosses enter into language—only to "come out with language" (*ud med Sproget*), to lose language to abstraction, to empty its contents into the outward and untoward pointers of the x. Not only is the demonic drawn towards the topic of the x, but its drive (*rykke*) draws everything else, indeed every-*thing*, in its path: "Let the enclosure be x and its content x, denoting the most terrible, the most insignificant, the horrible. . . . What then is the significance of the good as x? It signifies disclosure" (125–26). No longer is there even the pretense that something—the good, which "of course, signifies the restoration or freedom, redemption, salvation, or whatever one could call it" (119)—stands outside the x. Nothing can stand outside so long as x stands for everything, and the x is, once again, this sheer coming outside itself: disclosure not of something, not of nothingness, but disclosure "itself," communication interrupted by a topical rejoinder to which nothing communicated corresponds, communication no longer capable of communicating anything, communication as ex-communication.

Only one force holds the drive of the *x* back: "the age as a whole" (139). The spiritless public that inhabits the "present generation" and separates itself into opposing camps of heretics and orthodoxy still resists the *drift* of this *x*. If orthodoxy represents the communion of communicants and heretics the communion of excommunicants, then the opposition of these two communities comes down to the opposition of communication to excommunication, perhaps the most ferocious opposition of all. "The age as a whole" will not let the *x* stand for everything, anything, and finally for the "nothing" of demonic negativity that cannot be captured in a figure or opposed by a determinate concept. Unable to abandon itself to the pull of this *x*, the age clings more and more to definitions, to determinations of meaning, to destinies and destinations, to precisely those "distinctions" that *The Concept of Anxiety* sets out to uphold against the uncertainties of "our age."

No one is more prone to hold on to discussions—and above all, the distinction between right and wrong—than the ortho-dox. Of the orthodox man and the camp of communicants he represents, the treatise states: "He knows everything, like the man who can prove a mathematical proposition when the letters are A B C, but not when the letters are D E F" (139–40). The knowledge of the one who "knows everything" is, of course, limited to specific letters, which are taken to mean something in themselves; for this reason, this all-knower does not know algebra and has no familiarity with algebraic naming. Replacing each of these letters with another letter and in the end each with *x* would not, however, procure knowledge; "science" would not begin at this point but would constitute a rejoinder to every claim to the knowledge of distinctions, even of the terms in which opposition is supposed to take place.

At this point, one could doubtless say that an Adamic language, which consists of names like "A B C" (46), has returned; ignorance is restored. But not innocence. For the abstraction of which *x* is, after all, only an outstanding name never fails to dislodge ignorance and replace it with—concepts. Unable to come to a stop even in the restoration of Adamic language, the pull of the x, out of language and out with language, interrupts all talk with disjointed "algebraic" rejoinders. The drift of the x empties every communication, including the communication of emptiness, and lets something be said only to the extent that every topic communicated is confounded, defiled in the rigorous sense, ex-communicated in this manner: "Let the topic of discussion be x." Such is the countermanding command, the outstanding rejoinder, toward which *The Concept of Anxiety*, otherwise dedicated to a "nothing" discovered in a particular psychological state, is drawn. And so too is all talk in "our age" (160) and of "our age," an age in which communication again and again crosses itself out.

§ 3 Autopsies of Faith:
Philosophical Fragments

> There is a rambling of loquacity that in its inter-
> minability has the same relation to the result as the
> incalculable lists of Egyptian kings have to the his-
> torical outcome.
>
> —Kierkegaard, "Diapsalmata" (*ad se ipsum*)

The Difficulty of Thought

"I can put my own life on the line, I can in all seriousness jest with my own life—not with another's."[1] Thus Johannes Climacus closes the preface to *Philosophical Fragments* and cuts off all communication with his fellow human beings: jesting and seriousness become the modes of being through which he, in his isolation, relates to his life, and this self-relation is determined in language as the interrogative mood, the unique mood in which conversation with oneself, if not *communicatio idiomatum*, can take place. He has put his life into question. On the title page, just below his name, as an addendum to and perhaps as a clarification of its strange formality, Climacus poses a set of questions, the final instance of which— "Can an eternal happiness be built on historical knowledge?" (1)—demands an answer that will not fall prey to jest and therefore no longer needs a mark of seriousness. He cannot even hope to deliver an answer to this question so long as language is determined by the play of jest and occasional marks of seriousness. Until Climacus can learn a language that does without jest and does not therefore need to mark the onset of seriousness, of "really" meaning whatever is said, his relation to his own life will remain in question. To jest in all seriousness is to question the jest (*at spørge spogen*). To question the conception of language as jest (*sprog som spøg*), and indeed the conception that the essence of language, always directed elsewhere, is jest. To question whether wordplay—*spørge, spøg, sprog*—and thus the word that falls prey to such play, constitutes the essence of language, to question whether the interrogative mood determines the mode of language through which one can relate to oneself as a self-same being, is jest. To jest in all seriousness is to question whether language itself, and not that questionable language whose seriousness can never be assured, has indeed come into being. It is to question how one relates to oneself in this other language, and finally to question whether language without jest (*sprog uden spøg*), if it has come into being, has not already been slain in jest and, by virtue of the wordplay that haunts this discourse, whether it henceforth turns into a specter (*sprog som spøgelse*).

Climacus's proposal to jest in all seriousness demands an index of seriousness that does not fall prey to jest, and he closes the preface by locating just such an index in the thought, not a conception and not a picture, of death. What Kierkegaard wrote in his dissertation on irony holds true for his encounter with philosophical discourse in general—that "the ironic nothingness is that deathly stillness in which irony returns to haunt and jest [*spøger*] (this last word taken wholly ambiguously)."[2] Once the thought of death is lost, the jest, the *serious* jest, whose rules are unfathomable precisely because irony undercuts every attempt to bring them to light, turns into either a hopeless mockery or an unendurable burden: "I have only my life, and I promptly put it into play whenever a difficulty appears. Then it is easy to dance, for the thought of death is a good dancing partner, my dancing partner" (8). This dance is a conversation, a turning-about; alone, Climacus will con-verse with the thought of his own nullity. In this sense alone is his life in question, and on this question alone—"Am I alive?"—does the conversation with himself, who is perhaps not there, turn. So little is Climacus in control of this turning, this dance with the thought of his own nullity, that it depends upon an "occasion," which like all occasions escapes from the schemata of causality in which control itself is grounded.

A summary of the occasion that gives rise to this dance: a moment of difficulty emerges, life comes into question, and the jest begins in earnest. But how does such a difficulty (*vanskelighed*) arise? Did not Socrates ground philosophical discourse on the position that all difficulties are self-imposed, hence only illusory difficulties, problemata and hypotheses projected by someone who does not yet know himself? Each problem of this sort is destined to be overcome. Under the Socratic interpretation, a difficulty is simply illusory; the one in trouble confounds its source when he refuses to see that since he brings the difficulty forward, it is *his* difficulty and to this extent not an impediment to his ongoing project. The one who con-verses with Socrates can never trip, however often aporias appear in the way. But the difficulty that makes the game serious cannot be merely an illusory difficulty, and the only difficulty that occasions a game played in earnest would be a difficulty completely removed from the provenance of prob-lemata and hypotheses projected by human beings. It would not be possible for a self-imposed difficulty to reach beyond the position of the self, and with this proposition, Climacus maintains, Socra-tes—and the entire philosophical project he set into motion—rests satisfied.

The ironic satisfaction of Socrates resides in the propounding of such a position: "A man cannot possibly seek what he knows, and, just as impossibly, he cannot seek what he does not know, for what he knows he cannot seek, since he knows it, and what he does not know he cannot seek, because, after all, he does not even know what he is supposed to seek. Socrates thinks through the difficulty in the doctrine that all learning and seeking are but recollection" (9). By thinking the difficulty *through*, Socrates abandons the thought of death—"it becomes a demonstration for the immor-tality of the soul" (9–10)—and he begins to dance and therefore to con-verse with his fellow human beings, "for even if a divine point of departure is ever given, between man and man this remains the true relationship" (10). If one recognizes that it is one's own project that occasions the difficulty, the project becomes the cause of the difficulty, and insofar as the cause of the difficulty is oneself as

ground, the game never has a chance to become serious. Or, in
what amounts to the same, seriousness is never sustained within
the game. When Socrates thinks death, he *thinks it through* and
thereby misses it.

   In order to pose a difficulty that thought cannot penetrate and
thereby to challenge philosophical discourse at its source, Climacus
must pose what he himself cannot pose; in other words, he must
not pose the difficulty. It—and every question in which it presents
itself—must come from elsewhere. And yet the attempt to locate
this "elsewhere" is as contradictory an exercise as the proposal that
one pose a difficulty that no one, by definition, can pose. For to
locate it is *eo ipso* to locate it within one's grasp and therefore in the
end to locate it within one's self-conception. The difficulty, therefore, cannot be located, yet the project of locating it, of addressing
its questions, defines philosophy, the very discourse to which Climacus is committed, if only in part. Certain constitutive categories
of philosophical discourse, including those of *anamnesis, Erinnerung,* and conceptual analysis, are unthinkable outside the project of securing a location from which the difficulty of philosophy
itself issues. Addressing the questions in which this unrecognizable
difficulty makes itself known demands that one be able to give an
address for the difficulty. Doubtless the aporias into which Socrates
was led are *difficult,* but they are themselves only questions, modes
in which the difficulty presents itself. And the address of this
difficulty is itself already known: it is addressed to human beings,
each of whom can respond to questions.

   Given this address, Socrates can engage in a conversation that no
longer concerns the difficulty but its modes of presentation, that is,
the various questions posed to him by those who, as human, are
within his grasp. No such conversation is possible as long as the
difficulty is *not* the question, and the two—difficulty and question—are no longer recognizable as one. To the extent that he
retains the identification of one with the other, Climacus remains
philosophical; to the extent that he has put this identification into
question, which is precisely the difficulty questions cannot address,
every philosopheme he articulates undergoes a certain fragmentation. If, however, he simply relented in his search for the location of

the difficulty and as a result abandoned the interrogative resources of philosophical discourse, the difficulty would no longer present itself as *one* difficulty, the dance would turn into an interminable series of con-versations, and the thought of his own death would turn out to be legion, each a result of the various autopsies, or self-reviews, he is about to perform.

Proposing to Abandon the Question

The source of the difficulty is as yet unclear, and as long as this source remains obscure, there can be no proposition about the source, no proposition that makes sense of the source and thus no resolute response to the question it proposes. Only the ability of this difficulty to interrupt philosophical discourse is a guide for the inquiry. Insofar as every proposition is brought forward by a human being, no proposition can escape the position prescribed by Socrates: propositions result from pro-positioning; hence no problems that are *in principle* unsolvable can arise. The proposition, according to the tradition inaugurated by the Greeks and formalized in Aristotle, has been the privileged locus of truth. The *Organon*, as the repository of the tools Socrates employed, begins with the contrasts between mere signification (*semantikē*), rhetorical discourse, and the proposition itself (*apophansis*)—that discourse "in which the true and the false reign."[3] If the Socratic position is unavoidable, the proposition must be considered that mode of language which, by asserting something about an object and concomitantly making sense of that object, secures access to truth.

So, when Climacus sets *Fragments* into motion with his own "Propositio," he at once begins to speak about something, to make sense of something, and to seek entrance into the realm of truth. Or at least he signals that his discourse remains within the provenance of the distinction between truth and falsehood:

> *Propositio*:
>
> The question is posed by the unknowing one, who does not even know what has given him occasion [*Anledning*] to ask it thus [*at han spørge saaledes*]. (9)

Yet no proposition, strictly speaking, has come forward: only a question has been asked, whose specific terms remain hidden; the circumstances that surround the enunciation are alone described. No one knows whence the question came.

Such a difficulty is simply unthinkable from Socrates' perspective. The question that initiates *his* inquiry—"To what extent can the truth be learned? With this question we shall begin. It was a Socratic question" (9)—must proceed from the mouth of a human being. Significant questions emerge only from a self that maintains itself, and since "the condition and the question contain the conditioned and the answer" (14), the message transmitted by the true proposition that corresponds to the question addressed to oneself always remains within one's power to grasp. The circumstances of the question *mean nothing*. Such a proposition summarizes the Socratic position. The meaninglessness of the circumstances make every difficulty turn into, at worst, an aporia: "Thus the truth is not introduced into the individual from without but was within him" (9). The circumstances in which the question arises recede into insignificance once the true proposition is ascertained. The interrogator is therefore a midwife, one who does not enter into a familiar relationship with the bearer of truth, and a difficult occasion (*anledning*) in which a question presents itself is completely insignificant in comparison to the response. The eternal validity of the response testifies in turn to the oblivion to which the thought of death has fallen: "If I were to imagine myself meeting Socrates, Prodicus or the servant-girl in another life, then here again neither of them could be more to me than an occasion [*Anledning*], as Socrates fearlessly expressed by saying that even in the underworld he proposed merely to ask questions; for the ultimate thought of all questioning is that the man asked must himself possess the truth and acquire it by himself" (12–13).

The first alteration of the Socratic position, and the alteration into which everything else in *Fragments* is drawn, consists in abandoning "the thought of all questioning," which turns out to be self-continuity. Any attempt to locate the source runs the risk of succumbing to an illusion, which is precisely the illusion of questioning, of inquiry and interrogation. The possibility of such illusion constitutes the most extreme danger that Climacus faces as he tries to bypass the resources of the Socratic question. However often Socrates only gives the impression of asking questions when in fact he knows the answer, this illusion amounts only to "irony," and the real character Socrates has merely climbed the ladder of questions and answer *beforehand*. Johannes Climacus, by contrast, has climbed no such ladder. If the source of the question to which he addresses himself could be recognized, it would prove to be himself, hence the resources of the Socratic question—the continuity of the selfsame self, who has posed the question to himself beforehand—would once again prove sufficient. But if the source of the question was in principle unknowable, if it arose from an ignorance that is not merely the negative mode of knowledge but constitutes a negativity in which questions, answers, and knowledge are all exposed to an unlocated difficulty, then the Socratic position would not prove ineluctable.

The Socratic question turns inward upon itself and turns into an inquiry into the source of its own performance. By asking "To what extent can the truth be learned?" Socrates presupposes a pedagogical process and thus a distinction between the teacher and the student, a distinction that further reflection, conducted from Socrates' position, cancels upon the realization that there can be no essential difference between the teacher and the student. For the *question* leads teacher and student to themselves, as it likewise constitutes their community. Without essential difference—without, to speak with Aristotle, difference in essence—the teacher and the student occupy the same relationship toward the truth as it presents itself in the proposition. The Socratic question thus transforms itself into a statement about the source of the one who speaks and thus about the essence of the interrogator. The capacity to differentiate the essence of the speaker from accidents that accompany his speech becomes the decisive problem, and as long as one neglects the possibility that there may be difference in essence, absolute difference, the problem is solved and resolved in every truthful response.

A proposition thus presupposes a primordial positing of its source, that is, a declaration that the speaker is human and that there are no essential differences among human beings. The two moments in the Socratic question: (1) the truth is eternal, so any particular enunciation of it is "so incorporated with it that I cannot, so to speak, find it, even if I sought it" (13); (2) the source of the enunciation is always determined to be human, and since there are no essential differences among human beings, each one ends in exactly the same relationship to the truth. The eternity of truth, which overshadows any enunciation of it, and the essential sameness of all speakers, which negates all consideration of the speaker's accidental characteristics, are the two turns in the explication of the Socratic question. Its decisive character consists in a mode of "significance" whose relation to the meaningfulness of propositional discourse ceases to be unproblematic the moment truth is no longer a matter of apophansis.

Climacus's "Project of Thought" will then cast the resources of Socrates' inquiry aside. This project throws away both of its constitutive moments: first, truth is not eternal but is *the* eternal, so its enunciation is an event that carries "decisive significance [*afgjørende Betydning*]" (13); second, the source of the enunciation is as yet undetermined, so the possibility of difference in essence cannot be so wholly neglected. However, because truth and falsehood are no longer assigned to propositions but, by contrast, to the speakers themselves, it now seems as if language, along with the Socratic question, had been cast aside. And if Socrates' position can indeed secure the absorption of language into propositional discourse, including that of the question prepared beforehand, Climacus's project would have nothing to do with language and would soon have to do without language altogether.

But the exhaustion of language in the proposition is perhaps the first illusion Climacus must confront. Propositional discourse, which is founded on proposing a question, has always had an ambiguous nature. Since a proposition is both linguistic and non-linguistic, both assertion and meaning, the transition between the two, the convention by which one is tied to the other, indeed the transubstantiation of one into the other, has always been an exemplary difficulty of philosophical discourse. It is precisely the problem encountered in an *idealization* whose temporal conditions do not pass into the idealized object, that is, into a "meaning." Climacus's project of positing an event of decisive significance is, by contrast, the thesis that language arrives *in time* and that this language, from which propositional discourse ultimately derives and toward which it always tends, is irreducibly temporal. Climacus, in other words, takes temporality seriously. And this is the irony of *his* "own" project. Far from being a step outside language, it is prompted by the possibility that language, and not an already constituted medium of meanings, comes into being.[4] The "Project of Thought" thus turns in upon itself and asks how it could have come into being, how Climacus could have learned the language now at his disposal, and the Socratic solution—the doctrine of recollection—precludes the possibility that language is ever in fact or "seriously" learned. Socrates must in turn be cast aside. The one who learns language cannot recall anything precisely because he cannot call upon anything at all.

At this point, however, another philosophical proposal seems to fill in the gaps left by the Socratic account. In continuity with his early career as one who made a serious effort to doubt everything, Johannes Climacus could have directed his efforts toward the one proposition that, according to Descartes, "is necessarily true every time it is uttered by me."[5] Climacus could, in other words, have asked for the conditions of possibility of uttering this momentous proposition, *ego sum*, and thereupon pointed out how we can come to assert it. But in *Philosophical Fragments*, Climacus, who has learned from negativity of "the whole newer development" and has as a result taken it to its climactic limit, turns toward its *negation* and therefore asks how one could learn to say *ego non sum*, "I do not exist." Whoever has not learned to speak in this way has not learned language in all seriousness.

To learn to articulate the proposition *non sum*, the teacher must not only prompt the student to recognize that such is the case, or has always been the case, but must first offer him the condition under which this proposition can be asserted. To teach is thus to grant the condition of assertive self-negation: "In *the movement*, a man becomes aware that he was born, for his previous state [*Foregaaende*], to which he is not to appeal, was indeed one of 'not to be' " (20). But could one not respond to Climacus's proposal by affirming that "I do not exist"—and thus language (*sprog*)—is now used only in the service of jest (*spøg*)? This particular juxtaposition of words appears to *mean nothing*, and the meaninglessness of this sentence—or its lack of seriousness, its not being meant—returns to support the Socratic procedure. And at this point of extreme negation—when meaning and significance no longer mean the same thing, and the same "thing" can no longer be seriously disclosed in speech—an unnamed voice interrupts Climacus's self-questioning and in this interruption enacts the very disruption of continuity to which *non sum* attests. The voice, which belongs to no one in particular, says that Climacus's "own" project does not belong to him, and *this* anonymity underlies the seriousness of *non sum*. For it is not "I" who says it, so it could be spoken in all seriousness: "This, as you see, is my project! But perhaps someone will say: 'this is the most ridiculous of all projects. . . . You are like the man who in the afternoon exhibited for a fee that in the forenoon anyone could see free of charge' " (21).

Climacus's proposal, it seems, is merely an echo of certain sounds everyone recalls having heard, "words" that seem to make sense, but since the particular circumstances within which they were learned recedes upon reflection, these "words" can be counted only as jest, disconnected phrases that have never in fact informed the serious interactions that define communal life. Climacus does not contest the unnamed voice but insists upon its acuteness: everyone has heard this jest, his "own" project, but no one can recall having invented these "phrases" or indeed ever having learned them: "Is it not curious that something like this exists, about which everyone who knows it also knows that he has not invented it, and this 'Go to the next house' does not halt and cannot be halted, even though one were to go to everybody? Yet this oddity enthralls me exceedingly, for it tests the correctness of the hypothesis and demonstrates it" (22). The echo enthralls Climacus because he cannot recall having learned to say *ego non sum*, and he cannot even image how anyone could have taught it to him or made it up: "It would indeed be unreasonable to require that a person discover at daybreak [*opdage*] all by himself that he does not exist. But this transition is precisely the transition of rebirth from not existing to existing. Whether he understands it later certainly makes no difference" (22, translation modified).

Daybreak discovers nonexistence, but this discovery cannot of course consist in the appearance of a phenomenon to a subject. Nor, however, is "nothing" discovered, as in anxiety, since the discovery is of one's *own* nonexistence. For such a discovery to take place, another, and not simply oneself faced with a phenomenon about which one can form propositions, must already be in place, but the place of this other is as little susceptible to elucidation as the nonexistence discovered at daybreak. The other to which this discovery owes its origin "exists" only in language, not in phenomena and not in apophansis. *Understanding* "makes no difference" to this language so long as understanding takes its stand from the coming-to-appearance and determination of a subject matter in speech. A language in which one learns to say *non sum* cannot, by contrast, escape the spectral moment of daybreak in which all hermeneutic questions, all questions of understanding and all questions addressed to understanding, make "no difference." Difference is not made in understanding; rather, the difference of the self to itself, as it is articulated in *ego non sum*, disrupts the operation of understanding to such an extent that it "itself" cannot be understood.

The discovery of nonexistence could be saved from the accusation of nonsense if a distinction could be drawn between saying and meaning. Whereas the former inhabits a linguistic register, the latter belongs to the domain of the mental, the psychic, or the spiritual. The independence of language from meaning can be seen to enact itself in the assertion *non sum* and by so appearing, saves the order of phenomena. For one can doubtless say *non sum* and yet not mean it, and since language has no indubitable mark of seriousness, a mark that is not at once exposed to jest, the call to serious-

ness demands a flight from language toward extralinguistic intentions, ascertained motivations, typical behavior, and the like.
Seriousness, by all accounts, does not reside in language but is
posited or deposited by the speaker therein. Climacus does not
offer a detailed treatment of the concept of seriousness, but in the
introduction to *The Concept of Anxiety*, which may also serve as the
introduction to *Philosophical Fragments*, seriousness receives a thorough treatment. Seriousness is said to be a *response*, indeed the
singular *voicing* that conditions every response; it is the mood
(*stemning*) that answers (*svarer*) to "sin."[6] Language that arrives in
time is not at first apophantic discourse but pathetic voicing. The
word "sin" perhaps prejudices the issue, however, especially when it
is understood as "negativity" and therefore, according to the account of *The Concept of Anxiety*, contributes to the erasure of
disciplinary domains from which each issue stems. *Philosophical
Fragments* does not use this word, nor does it conceive of sin as
"negativity" and thereafter determine its logical or dialectical character. Not "negativity" but "difference" is the term on which
Philosophical Fragments turns, and the difference to which seriousness responds is not the difference established in identity but a
difference more original than the self-identity of the "I" who
speaks.

The difference to which seriousness responds "is" *absolute difference*, a counterpart to "sin" but not a negativity by virtue of which
the immediate is annulled and mediation carried to its conclusion.
But if "sin" is replaced by "absolute difference," the term "seriousness" cannot remain unaltered: it turns into *sorg*, "care" or "sorrow." Sorrow responds to absolute difference, and the voice of such
sorrow escapes apophantic discourse because absolute difference
can never occupy the position of the subject and can never appear
as substance. The response of sorrow to absolute difference breaks
down every propositional context, leaving only one word in this
breakdown: "I'm sorry," or more succinctly, "Sorry!" This confession is the word of so-called serious speech. Whether it belongs
to *human* language, however, is in question: "And just as that royal
sorrow [*Sorg*] is found only in a royal soul and most human

languages [*Menneskers Sprog*] do not name it at all, likewise all human language is so self-loving that it does not intimate such sorrow" (28).[7]

Sorg—seriousness responding to absolute difference—cannot maintain a secure mark in the language of apophansis, so it seems to withdraw completely from any language in which the proposition is thought to define its essence. But this withdrawal is the illusion in which the aporias of Socratic discourse disappear. For *sorg* is not sorrow over a determinate object defined in relation to question and answer; it does not depend upon prior acts of denomination and predication, and in particular, it never presupposes a primordial positing of the speaker whose essence is determined to be human. Seriousness, as *sprog* that has come into being, is rather sorrow over absolute difference, and the source of this language differs in essence from the human being.

A Language of Names, Absolute Difference

The source, therefore, is not human. At this point, the Aristotelian *Organon*, as the instrument of propositional discourse, provides the grid through which the source receives a preliminary definition. The expression *to ouk anthrōpos* (the not human) serves in fact as Aristotle's example of an *onoma aoriston* (indefinite nominal phrase).[8] Since the phrase specifies only what is not, it will always fail to refer to something in particular. But for Climacus, this nondetermination indicates that the Socratic inquiry and its formal organization in the Aristotelian *Organon* have been suspended. In the "Propositio" the question emerges from the "unknown one" whose voice remains undetermined; the source of the question is without delimitation. It could come from anywhere except human beings. Yet this exception provides a first indication of the direction toward which the "poem" (*digt*) of language's coming into being might orient itself. Although the attempt to locate the source must be carried out without the resources of the *Organon* and thus without the aid of propositional discourse, it is only because Climacus dares another proposition that he can even set out on his attempt to dictate such a *digt*: "But in order to get started, let us state a daring proposition [*dristig Proposition*]: let us assume that we know what a human being is. In this we do indeed have the criterion [*Criterium*] of truth, which all Greek philosophy *sought*, or *doubted*, or *postulated*, or *brought to fruition*" (38).

This proposition is particularly risky because it assumes a kind of self-knowledge that was unavailable to Socrates. The paradox of his thought, according to Climacus, is that he, who knew more about the being of *anthrōpos* than any other human being, still asked himself whether he himself was a man or a monster (*Phaedrus*, 229 E). The "daring proposition" does not, however, amount to an *answer* to the question What is man? This question is not put to rest; rather, *questioning* itself, including the question of the genus to which one belongs, has come to an abrupt, uncalled-for, irresponsible end. With the end of questioning comes the "daring" of the "proposition" as pro-positioning: taking a forward position, a position prior to the question, its aporias, its answers, and its hermeneutical projects. The "not" of the nominal phrase "not human" does not determine a subject. It is not determinate negation, and its negation of determinate negation suspends the proposition; it does not turn the proposition into a dialectical one. And yet, the language of this "not" is still *human*. Such is the daring of Climacus's proposition. The disturbance of human self-knowledge nevertheless makes room for a language. The kind of language disclosed in this disturbance has already been named: it is a language of indefinite nominal phrases, a language of *names* in which every name issues from a nondetermining—and to this extent, "infinite"—"not." The language of names thus takes over Climacus's "project" and replaces every term determined in propositional discourse by one that determines nothing. In place of apophansis there arises an "algebraic naming" in which each name issues from an unknown, in-finite variable, namely, x: "But what is this unknown against which the understanding [*Forstanden*] in its paradoxical passion collides and which even disturbs man and his self-knowledge? It is the unknown [*det Ubekjendte*]. But it is not a human being, insofar as he knows man or whatever else he knows. So let us call this unknown something: *the god.* It is nothing more than a name we give to it" (39).

Every decisive word in the "Project of Thought" emerges from the same act of algebraic nomination: "Let us call this something *x*," and the something has no other being than that of a mere name. No recollection functions in this algebraic act, for there is nothing to recall, indeed no words upon which to call, until the command "Let us call this something *x*" has been carried out. And then each name has no function other than to recall the moment of algebraic nomination—the moment, in other words, of learning the language of names. From this recollection, which has nothing to do with psychology and even less with interiorization, there arises a temporalizing language, a language in which time and timing are of the essence. For each name has no other meaning than the moment of its nomination. The "Project of Thought" thus gives itself names with which to think: "Let us call it *sin*" (15). "Let us call him a *savior*" (17). "Let us call him a *deliverer*" (17). "Let us call it: *the fullness of time*" (18). The naming of the moment brings into this language of names its own moment of naming. And yet this moment is not one in which the language of names recalls itself to itself. For each name issues from *lader os* (let us), and these peculiar words assume the indeterminacy to which the names themselves, as replacements for *x*, are immune. "Let us" is at once a demand and a request, a demand-request addressed to no one in particular and undertaken in the name of an impossible "us": impossible because Climacus is alone as he projects his "Project of Thought."

The confounded source of the names, an indeterminate "us" who demands and requests an equally indeterminate as well as unspoken authority, cannot leave the names themselves untouched. And the confusion overtakes the very word that Climacus insists is "only a name" (39), namely, "the god." For the "the" indicates that "the god" is not *simply* a name, and soon Climacus recalls that "the god" is a "concept" (41). The irreducibility of the concept makes itself known in this alteration, and it's an irreducibility that stamps the character of Climacus's thought. For the conceptualization of the name, antonomasia in reverse, thus turns out to be the very project of *thought*. The proper name turns into the "general" name, which because of its generality is improper but which by virtue of its generality generates determinate and therefore proper thought.

At this point the "nonhuman" can receive no predicate and has no extension; its "infinitude" is, on the one hand, conceived according to the predicate "divinity," but since the character of such infinitude is linguistic—and beyond that, is linguistic in denying the powers of predicative language, *in-finite*—the predicate cannot be the basis for the conception of the subject, of *the* god, not of God, a god or even divinity. Conceiving of the infinite phrase doubtless gives reason for calling the unknown *x*, but under no condition does this reason justify the concept expressed in "the god." It is, rather, the conflict between conceptuality and linguisticity, between the conception of the infinite and the indefinite language of names, that gives rise to "the god" and at the same time robs this thing, or rather this phrase, of even nominal meaning: it is at once phrase and thing and yet again neither one. Each name in the language of names becomes in the train of "the god" a *pseudo-*name, not precisely a false name but a name that denies its nominal status and a concept that denies its conceivability.

When both the discourse of the proposition and the language of names are thus disturbed, when the criteria of both languages are undecidable because each disrupts the other, when in sum *nothing is said*, the infinite phrase, as pseudo-name, stands as the indistinguishable mark of the limit to sense (*forstand*). No position stands before this limit, so at this abyssal point, the understanding (*forstanden*) encounters its opposite:

> What, then, is the unknown? It is the limit that is continually arrived at, and therefore when the category of motion is replaced by the category of rest it is the different, the absolutely different [*det absolut Forskjellige*]. But it is an absolutely different in which there is no distinguishing mark [*Kjendetegn*]. Defined or determined [*Bestemmet*] as the absolutely different, it seems to be at the point of being disclosed, but not so, because the understanding [*Forstanden*] cannot even think the absolutely different; it cannot negate itself but uses

itself for that purpose and consequently thinks the difference in itself, which it thinks by itself. It cannot absolutely transcend itself and therefore thinks itself as above itself only the sublimity that it thinks by itself. (44–45)

If the understanding thinks through the absolute difference, its care and sorrow turn into a negligent assurance of proper differentiation whose self-affirmation comes out in the attribution of sublimity and the experience of the sublime. Such negligence shrinks away from the grave question. The only way the limit to the understanding can be respected is through a vigilant sheltering of the absolute difference. But it is not an easy matter to shelter the absolute difference, for it—if indeed reference should be made with a singular pronoun—cannot be distinguished. Once again we run across the difficulty: to stand before (*forstand, propositio*) the absolute difference precludes the possibility that one could recognize one's forward position; to think the absolutely other of the understanding and not to *think it through* demands the abandonment of definition and determinate articulation. Mere appellation, indefinite designation that affords no predication, is in truth all that the thought of the absolute difference, the thought of strict nonsense, and hence the thought of death can together propose.

But when the difficulty emerges, *neither* the Socratic solution— "Socrates thinks the difficulty through" (18)—*nor* Climacus's anonymous project, which amounts to a projection of pseudo-names, proves sufficient. For even to call upon *the* absolute difference presupposes the capacity to differentiate absolute difference from itself: this name must be distinguished from that name, this thought from that thought, and these distinctions relativize absolute difference, indeed relativize "it" in relation to "us," the *ones* who speak in the name, or pseudonym, of Climacus: "Let us. . . ." *The* thought of *the* absolute difference cannot be a thought among others; it cannot be a thought that one merely entertains or a thought one decides to think. Still less can "the god" be a name that an indeterminate something, beyond the god, or the demonic demiurge of this god, lets "us" speak. However weak a demonstrative "the" may be, it still serves to demonstrate, and in the act of demonstration it speaks *of* the absolutely other and thereby makes sense of the absolutely other of sense.

Dispersion, Collection, Departure

"The Project of Thought" not only cannot be Climacus's project; it cannot even be a project *of* thought, that is, thought's project. The definite article—*det bestemte kendeord*—includes the two moments the thought of the absolute difference can never accommodate: the moment of definition and the moment of determinate articulation. *The* absolute difference goes unmarked, without a *kendeord*, yet it still seems to let something, *the*, stand before it. Strictly speaking, *the* thought of *the* absolute difference is completely insignificant. The *the* will never make a whit of sense.[9] If, moreover, Climacus himself is not to fall into complete nonsense— and such a possibility is never to be discounted but encountered— he must break with the entire philosophical tradition and declare that thought is thoroughly removed from the understanding; it includes no synthetic function; propositions are not expressive of thought; and thought is not a synthetic activity that somehow gives rise to propositions but is rather the care for, and sorrow over, the absolute difference.

Thought thus enters into the most intimate possible relation with pathetic "nonsense," language given over neither to concept nor to name but given in their mutual confusion. The Aristotelian *Organon* has withdrawn to make room for the thought of the absolute difference, indefinite demonstration and indeterminate disarticulation. And yet the displacement of the *Organon* opens the thought of the absolute difference to a multitude of confusions. The understanding, in combination with the power of imagination, breaks up the utterly indeterminate name of the unknown and scatters it with rhetorical flourish, just as the Jews were scattered after the destruction of the Temple: "Unless the unknown (the god) is not merely the limit, then the one thought about the difference [*den ene Tanke om det Forskjellige*] is confused with the many ideas about the differences. The unknown is then in *diaspora*, and the understanding has an attractive selection from what is available and what imagination can think up (the monstrous, the ridiculous, etc.)" (45).

The diaspora erupts from the dispersion of the *single* thought of *the* absolute difference, or in what amounts to the same, from the abandonment of conceptual thought to the name and the conceptualization of this name as a pseudo-name.[10] So controverted is the word "diaspora" that against its own rhetorical intention it designates the content of the "pagan imagination" (45). Only insofar as the rhetorical intention of the word, as the designation of an exile *into* a Greco-Roman orbit, has been suspended in favor of its interpretation as the polytheistic content of a pagan imagination can opposition to the diaspora maintain the opposition of Socratic inquiry to the "Project of Thought." The "diaspora" names a dispersion that results from a reluctance to accept the compulsive burden of thinking matters to the point of aporia; it thereby dulls the difference between the interrogative mode, which reaches aporia after aporia, and the difficulty, which is not a question but still less an answer. Dulling this difference lets the understanding cede its right to think the limit to the imagination and thus recedes from the scene altogether. The "pagan imagination" against which Socratic inquiry works takes its point of departure from those various unities—or gods, "idols"—which are imagined to inhabit the limit of understanding.

But the diaspora can also present itself as a temporal one, a destruction and exile of time as a unity in which the imagination, or the empirical imagination, the one that makes lively images, plays no role: "Or," Climacus writes as he sketches the "dialectic of the moment" and explains the scandal that the Jews attribute to the announcement that the moment *has already come*, "the moment is supposed to be constantly about to come; one *looks for it*, and the moment is supposed to be *worth looking for*, but since the paradox has made the understanding absurd, what the understanding considers worth looking for is no distinguishing mark [*Kjendetegn*]" (52). Vigilence with regard to, and with highest respect for, the future does not dull the difference between the interrogative mood and the one that without question answers to absolute difference; instead, it puts this difference off. Everything in Climacus's project comes down to a renunciation of this strategy of deferring "the moment" of difference: absolute difference stands in opposition to absolute deferral and *must* do so as long as it works against to the Socratic question. For the compulsion of Climacus's project rests on the a priority that Socrates had already recognized and bequeathed to philosophical discourse in the doctrines of "remembrance" of its a priori content. The very *necessity* of Climacus's search to locate the source of the difficulty, its compulsive character, lies in the priority he assigns to the past, and this priority demands that he take his point of departure from the earliest Greek doctrine of the a priori and distinguish the pastness that gives rise to his compulsive project from the pastness that because of causal necessitation, develops into the present.

Climacus therefore breaks up his text to show that the past does not necessarily give rise to the present. In an "Interlude," Climacus so radicalizes Aristotle's argument in *De Interpretatione* that it no longer makes sense to say that the past and present in contrast to the future are somehow necessary, and since knowing a necessary connection remains an indispensable mark of knowledge (*erkendjen*) in general, it no longer makes sense to assert that one can recognize a temporal moment and thus gain historical knowledge. Such a moment discloses only the constant annihilation of possibility in actuality, an annihilation whose recognition requires an organ that both responds to the momentary and organizes it within the general dispersion that makes up time: "It is clear, then, that the organ [*Organet*] for the historical must be formed in likeness to this, must have within itself the corresponding something by which in its certitude it continually annuls the uncertitude that corresponds [*svarer*] to the uncertainty of coming into existence—a double uncertainty: the nothingness of non-being and the annihilated possibility, which is also the annihilation of every other possibility" (81). Belief or faith is this organ: "Now *Tro* [belief, faith] has precisely the required constitution" (81). *Tro*, like all organs, indicates both the condition of needing an organ (and hence the absence of an intellectual intuition) and the activity of organizing. Both condition and realization, both passive and active, faith functions as that apparatus by virtue of which the diversity of sources sounds one note—the "synthetic" moment that does without conceptual thought. Faith then gives access to uniqueness; it is the *conditio sine qua non* for organizing a dispersion of time into a unique order; it is the difficulty—without question.

But to consider faith an organ, to think of it as organizing a multiplicity into a unity, is surely to miss the point of Climacus's project. Although he often speaks of faith on analogy with cognitive organs—"the eyes of Faith," "the ears of Faith" (69–70)—and even describes it is as an organ whose structure rests on an analogous relationship to its "object" (40), he insists that faith and belief are not "forms of knowledge" (62); the analogy that imposes a connection between it and its erstwhile "object" is simply a-logical. And even as he writes that faith has an "object" and thereby indicates that as an organ it provides a criterion of coherence by means of which disparate perspectives turn into a single objective sense, he undermines the very notion of objectivity when he assigns the "object" contradictory predicates. In accordance with his fierce retention of the pillar of the *Organon*, the Aristotelian principle of noncontradiction, against its recent Hegelian assault (108), Climacus rejects the object *as* an object of knowledge since it is the unification of contradictories: "that happy passion we call faith, whose object is the paradox, but the paradox unites the contradictories and is the historical made eternal" (61). If, however, it is not an object of knowledge, no one has the right to consider *an* object in the first place.[11]

So faith is a form of knowledge but does not assume the form of knowledge; it both provides a criterion for unification and refuses the principal criterion of all thought. It, like the paradox—the unknown, the god, or whatever else one might call difficult— cannot be thought through; it cannot be made into a matter of knowledge; so every attempt to predicate it leads to the limit of thought and the parameters of the *Organon*. Thus, Climacus affirms, faith is as unknowable as the unknown and "as paradoxical as the paradox" (65). As an organ, it can only turn in wonder upon itself and "*in pausa*" (80) contemplate from its singular position the miracle that it can contemplate anything at all, that singular "something" to which there is no other access. It organizes no other sense than the sense of its own organization, so in contrast to every mode of knowledge, this organ can perceive only one thing, and it can perceive it only once.

The moment, the singularization of the absolute difference, is the very instant, the only instant, of its operation: the blink (*Øieblikket, Augenblick*) within which the organ perceives itself and perceives the extirpation of its perception. The paradox of faith is therefore entirely different from the paradoxes encountered in understanding: whereas the understanding is paradoxical only in its attempt to stand before itself, that is, only *in* the attempt that recognizes the absolute difference, faith is paradoxically itself. There is neither a stipulation nor even a promise that *at some moment in the future* it will encounter its own undoing. For faith is *about* only itself, and it makes sense only *of* itself. Its self-reflexivity then comes to propositional discourse as the self-referential proposition, the self-acknowledged stumbling block to the Greek *Organon*, the suspension of propositional discourse in propositional discourse: "I do not exist." To speak thus in all seriousness is to speak of oneself and yet to have no one to speak of. Faith, in speaking of itself, must be its own definitive object, but in order to be so, it must abandon itself as a determinate object.

When Climacus begins to explore the analogy with the sense organs, he therefore moves from the rather banal analogy—a human being "receives the condition from the god, and so beholds his glory with the eyes of faith" (70)—to the paradoxical formulation "He is contemporary as a believer, in the *autopsy* of faith (*i Troens* **Autopsi**). But in this autopsy every non-contemporary (in the immediate sense) becomes a contemporary" (70). Faith sees with its own eyes, sees itself, *and* sees itself with its own eyes at the point of its own death. It must see itself yet cannot see itself, for the moment of sight is the moment of death: its knowledge turns into the knowledge of death, its thought into the thought of death.[12]

It is therefore no surprise that faith has no desire to see: whoever undergoes the autopsy of faith wishes that the sole object "worth looking for" (52) take its leave; it does not want to be seen, so it exchanges sight for story: "But this immediate contemporaneity is merely an occasion [*Anledning*], and this cannot be more strongly expressed than the disciple, if he understands himself, must therefore wish that it be terminated by the departure of the god from the earth" (105). In this departure, which is not quite a *diaspora*, although it cannot be entirely distinguished from one, faith remains absolutely unique. In order to maintain its paradoxical vision, the autopsy must always deliver in the moment of decisive significance the same verdict, yet no one, by definition, can attest to the coherence of the verdict or the sense of its message. The autopsy, where no one is there to see, constitutes a heteropsy in which every eye closes and this closure of the eye, anopsy, is shared: in a "poem," in speech.

"Thus"

The community of faith does not share in a message. It shares an organ, but the organ it shares is already linguistic. The character of this "organic" language has yet to be determined; it cannot be the language of the proposition, or even that of given names. Whereas a proposition refers to something, is about a definite object, and makes sense of that thing, faith never ceases to refer but does not determine the "thing" to which it refers; its affinity with naming is found in this characteristic. But unlike names, faith does not altogether do without sense. Neither making sense of something in conceptual comprehension nor naming something in which all sense is extinguished, faith includes sense without making sense of anything: "Faith is sense for coming into existence [*Tro er Sands for Tilblivelse*]" (84). "Sense for" suspends the distinction between conceptual language and the language of names. The "organic" language of faith does not make sense of anything or stand for anything but sets itself in relation to something. However, since the one who says "I do not exist" cannot speak of a self as though it were a determinate object and furthermore, since coming into existence

(*Tilblivelse*) is not itself an established object but an event that
precludes and undercuts all calculation according to the canons of
necessity, neither the "organic" language of faith nor its "object" can
become subjects of sentences and thereby appear as substances.

"Sense for" becomes more than a mere juxtaposition when the
for no longer designates an atemporal relation (*forhold*). When
"sense for" occurs on its own, singularly, when its occurrence is a
coming forth (*forekome*) out of its own unique circumstance, it
arises from syntactical "death" and begins to say something: faith
holds to a moment *before*. The historical character of faith is thus
found in its "be-foreness." Climacus not only draws toward the
purely positional, senseless, and singular relationship but also *projects* the sense of faith backward, as the event comes forth. This
back and forth, which suspends the back and forth of remembrance,[13] marks the time of faith, the moment of "decisive significance" in which a decisive event—a cut, a caesura—comes to the
fore *be-fore* the autopsy of faith, and by coming into existence before, it can now be spoken of: "The moment came before." Language has indeed come into being, and the language of this coming
into being, which is the "organic" language of an utterly unnatural
faith, is a language of neither propositions nor names but having
suspended the two, a language of a coming-before and passing-on:

> Let us now return to our poem [*Digt*] and to our assumption that the
> god *has* been. . . . It is still an historical fact and only for [*for*] faith.
> Faith is here taken in the direct and direct and everyday sense [*Betydn-
> ing*] as the relationship to the historical; but secondly faith must be
> taken also in the entirely eminent sense [*i ganske eminent Forstand*], the
> sense in which the word can come to the fore [*forekomme*] only once,
> that is, many times, but in only one relationship [*Forhold*]. (86–87,
> modified)

The *digt* whose learning requires no recollection collects the
names that an unknown authority "lets us" pronounce. The dispersion to which the very word *tro* (belief as well as faith) falls prey
does not exclude its uniqueness; on the contrary, the "many times"
of *tro* gives the word its unique characteristic: since it is discovered,

it cannot be counted among the names that Climacus demands and requests with his "let us," but it also cannot function in propositional discourse, since the sense it makes of an object does not let itself be reduced to the meaning expressed in an apophantic sentence. Although no one, by definition, can have access to the sense of the "poem" in which faith, by virtue of its singularity, shares, although the sense is not even its own since it is always only on loan, the sense that the moment has come to the fore and passed on can nevertheless be passed along. The word to which the *digt* reduces, a word in service of an utterly unique reference, is the purely punctual—"thus" (*saaledes*). The believer "no longer has a mere immediacy before him [*for sig*], nor does he confront a necessary coming into existence, but only the '**thus**' of *coming into existence*" (85).

"Thus" is not the elision of a complete proposition, nor does it constitute a name. In the multiplicity of its pronouncements, it is nevertheless a unique reference to the moment *before*—a "before" no longer in service either of the a priori or the priority of causal determination. The absolute historical event comes for the believer, forward to the believer, and before the believer in the singular sense of faith. The one who has a sense for coming into existence says "thus"—the absolute difference came in time—and this enunciation, by making sense in belief, making up the sense of belief, and making belief sense before the absolute historical fact, announces a historical language and constitutes in its brevity the "poem" of coming-into-being, the "poem" that, because it comes into being, has nothing to do with necessity.

"Thus," therefore, is not one word among others. It is the very *digt* that in its concentration shelters language once learned and at the same time exposes this language and its learning to dispersal: to imparting, passing on, and communication. For this sheltering of language is nothing but its passing on. Its explication in propositional discourse is for this reason limitless. But Climacus insists that such explication can never dispense with the force that is concentrated in "thus," and he even offers a means by which one can measure this force. It is *offense*: the greater the offense, the more global the scandal, the more force has been imparted. In every grave articulation the risk of offense is intensified, whereas every attempt to mitigate offense through negligent concentration on extraneous matters results in the "acoustical illusion" (49) that gives the impression that the absolute positing of the "thus" can somehow facilitate transposition into corresponding propositions comprehensible by all disinterested rational agents. And philosophy for Climacus is defined precisely as this curious echo, since in seeking to remove offense, it gets carried along in a forceless language whose very lack of power, its "objectivity," is its distinguishing feature:

> For the believer (and only he, after all, is a disciple) continually has the *autopsy* of faith; he does not see with the eyes of others and sees only the same as every believer sees—with the eyes of faith.
>
> *What, then, can a contemporary do for someone who comes later?* (a) He can tell someone who comes later that he himself has believed this fact [*Factum*]; this is not properly [*egentligen*] a communication at all (that there is no immediate contemporaneity and that the fact is based upon a contradiction express this) but merely an occasion. If I say that this or that occurred, I speak historically; but if I say "I believe and have believed that this happened, *although it is folly to the understanding and an offense to the human heart*," I have in the very same moment done everything to prevent anyone else from making up his mind in immediate continuity with me and to decline all partnership, because every single human being must comport himself in exactly the same way. (b) In this form, he can tell the content of the fact, a content that is still only for faith (*for Troen*), in quite the same sense as colors are only for sight and sound for hearing. In this form, he is able to do it; in any other form, he is only talking nonsense and perhaps inveigles the one who comes later to determine himself in continuity with chatter [*at bestemme sig i Continuitet med Snakken*].   (102)

Chatter (*snak*) does not consist in nonsense; rather, it is the forceless *forstand* that cannot stand before the absolute difference. Chatter is the very medium in which everything makes sense. Although everything goes without saying, speech does not come to an end; rather, it continues, and as it goes on and on, it determines everyone who speaks in continuity with itself. Everyone is as drawn into its speech as every "disciple" is drawn into the *digt* concentrated into "thus." However earnest it may present itself and however seriously it may be taken, *snak* not only falls prey to jest but makes this falling into the principle of *its* teaching: language becomes mere jest; "concepts," by contrast, are said to be serious. And insofar as the various propositions that make up chatter make sense of that which withdraws from propositional discourse, *snak* proves itself to be jest—yet continues to speak in all seriousness. It can determine everything in continuity with itself and thus give rise to Socratic recollection on the one hand and the Cartesian cogito on the other. Philosophy thus draws its sustenance from *snak*. Once *snak* takes over, faith—"I do not exist"—is put off; for this reason, credence is given to self-continuity as the ground on which all discourse finally rests and to which it always implicitly refers. *Philosophiske Smuler* (Crumbs of Philosophy) thus deserves its carefully chosen title: Climacus, whose step-by-step continuity of thought finds its most characteristic expression in his ladderlike name, gives into and gives out *A Philosophical Snack*.[14]

The crumbs on which philosophy snacks are not philosophical fragments. Whereas each fragment, according to the presentation of this "genre" in early romanticism,[15] refers to the whole of which it was once part, no crumb of bread, or of any other food, can claim a referential function, except perhaps the crumbs that fell from the transubstantiated bread of the Last Supper. But even these crumbs, if there were any, would refer to what cannot be incorporated, what cannot be saved, whatever in sum recedes from reference because of its unaccountable, endless insignificance. Climacus never directs attention toward such crumbs, if there were any. Rather, he points toward the crumbs of philosophical discourse, the crumbs Socrates makes when he cuts up arguments and hands them back to whoever handed them out. As the epigraph for the *Concluding Unscientific Postscript* to *Philosophiske Smuler* attests, the word "crumb" is addressed to Socrates: "But Socrates, really, what do you think of all that? It's flakings and clippings of speeches, as I told you before, divided up into little bits [*kata brachu dierēmena*]" (304 A).[16] Little bits of speeches, including epigraphs to books that have already been published, amount to *lēros* and *phluaros*, to "chitter" and "chatter," neither of which will give insight into how to get out of an aporia. The one who wishes to overcome such "difficulties," which is the last word of the dialogue cited in the epigraph, "should give up and abandon all that small-talking [*smikrologias*] so he won't be thought a complete fool for applying himself, as he is now, to chitter-chatter [*lērous kai phluarias*]" (304 B).[17] Tearing the logos into bits therefore constitutes on the one hand the act that communion commemorates and can thus give rise to the community of contemporaneous believers and on the other the conversion of language into "chatter."[18] Tearing the logos to bits creates commemorative communion and anamnesistic "chatter" in turns. Taken together, as one turns into the other, they make up the "argument," the logos of *A Philosophical Snack*: a "poem," namely, that is at once shared and torn to pieces.

Slogans

"The difficulty is in perceiving that one cannot ask such a question" (89). The question to which Climacus refers, "the question of the disciple at second hand," closes *A Philosophical Snack* and at the same time concludes the very process of raising and responding to questions. For everything in Climacus's project in the end bears upon this question, upon the very possibility of proposing this as a question without falling into a "stupidity" so pronounced that it would forfeit "the right to charge one with stupidity who is sensible [*forstandig*] enough not to be able to answer it" (89). The difficulty then lies in abandoning not only one particular question but the very devotion to the process of raising and answering questions, the maieutic movement whose greatest proponent is Socrates. "The question of the disciple at second hand" is simply the question of the source, transmission, and communication of sense.'

When Climacus asks, "Should we not perhaps first consider whether the above question is as legitimate as it lies near at hand?"

(89) he questions the jest that purports to bring the "second hand" near to hand and the pedagogical process that appears to commence with ignorance and distance from the truth and culminate in knowledge and proximity to truth. This utter inability to question further, taken as the very limit of sense, is what Climacus calls "understanding oneself," and the recognition that the question does not conceal knowledge but neglects the absolute difference he calls "knowledge."[19] The unnamed voice that always accompanies Climacus's project responds to such a paradoxical proposal by misunderstanding it:

"For if the question cannot be asked, then the answer causes us no trouble, and the difficulty has become a remarkably easy matter."— "This does not follow, for suppose the difficulty consisted in perceiving that one cannot ask a question thus [*spørge saaledes*]; was this perhaps the meaning [*Meningen*] you expressed in our last conversation (Chapter IV) when you said that you had understood me and all the consequences of what I said, although I as yet had not completely understood myself?" (89)

The difficulty to which Climacus refers in this mock dialogue does not consist in an aporia but an abrupt suspension of questioning. The voice that interrupts his thought understands this suspension as a resolution of the difficulty, for if the difficulty cannot present itself in a question, it cannot present itself at all. It does, however, leaves traces in a strange distortion of the *text itself.* The anonymous voice and the pseudonymous author are, as it were, out of sync. The voice Climacus responds to does not understand the difficulty, but it does understand that the difficulty cannot be asked, and *this* constitutes understanding *meningen* (the meaning). In the preface, just before Climacus begins to dance, he declares that he cannot afford to have a *mening* (opinion), whereas the anonymous voice can afford an opinion to the extent it discovers "meaning" from the words of another.

Every reading of Climacus's "Project of Thought" must thus return to the moment of the text in which it inscribes its *own* discontinuity, its own "pause" (89) in the "dialogue" between the pseudonymous writer and the anonymous voice. The moment of the text, as a disruptive fullness of *mening* (meaning as well as opinion), takes place in a passage where the opposition between the disciple at first hand and the disciple at second hand no longer holds. After having explained that the assertion "I do not know you," when spoken by the teacher to the pupil, does not mean, for instance, "I cannot identify you" but is on the contrary an *action* whereby the student is dismissed, Climacus explains to the unnamed voice that "someone who comes later must receive the condition from the god himself and cannot receive it at second hand, because if that were the case, the second hand would have to be the god himself, and in that case there is no question of a second hand" (69). The single hand of the god, in other words, suffices. And this image of the single hand satisfies Climacus's interlocuter, who immediately gives his decisive *mening* and marks the disruptive moment in the text: "Now that you say it, I certainly do see it" (69).

Speech immediately becomes vision. Such is the precise character of the *digt* concentrated into "thus." It is a dictation that immediately turns into a vision, a "paradoxical" vision, to be sure, but a vision nevertheless. It is the vision of "autopsy." With this saying—"Now that you say it, I certainly do see it"—Climacus arrives at his original articulation of "the *autopsy* of faith" (70), but even after the articulation of this "autopsy," he continues, as though he, but not only he, could not stop speaking:

> If someone who comes later goes on retelling [*fable*] extravagantly about the glory of being a contemporary (in the sense of immediacy) and is continually wanting to be away, then we must let him go, but if you watch him you will easily see by his walk and by the path he has turned onto that he is not on the way to the terror of the paradox but is bounding away like a dancing teacher in order to reach the imperial wedding on time . . .—Only in one respect could I be tempted to regard the contemporary (in the sense of immediacy) as more fortunate than someone who comes later. If we assume that centuries elapsed between the event and the life of the one who comes later, then there presumably will have been a great deal of chatter [*megen Snak*]

among men about this thing [*om denne Ting*], so much loose chatter that the untrue and confused rumors that the contemporary (in the sense of immediacy) had to put up with did not make the possibility of the right relationship nearly as difficult [*vanskelig*], all the more so because in all human probability the centuries-old echo, like the echo in some of our churches, would not only have riddled faith with slogans but would have slain it and turned it into a slogan [*ikke blot vilde slaae Sladder paa Troen, men slaae den hen i Sladder*]. This could not happen in the first generation, when faith must have appeared in all its originality, by opposition [*Modsaetning*] easy to distinguish from its other. (70–71, translation modified)

The grave, life-threatening difficulty is no longer there. Without opposition, there is no longer a unique difficulty but a multitude of difficulties, none of which presents itself as an aporia, each of which, however, departs from the historical "fact" that *the "poem" must be told.* Communication cannot *not* take place. Such is the facticity of communication: the "poem" of coming-into-existence, a "poem" that has nothing to do with necessity and interrupts every claim to necessitation, nevertheless cannot *not* be imparted if it is to save its "poetic"—in this case, salvatory—function. Once all opposition to this "poem" has been suspended, in "centuries-old echoes,"[20] and the speaking of the poem is no longer an immediate vision, the force of this peculiar necessity commits a strange linguistic crime: faith is slain and turned into "slogans."

Not only has all opposition to faith vanished, but the very opposition between the faithful enunciation "thus" and the *snak* of philosophy gives way to their mutual suspension in "slogans." No longer are faith and philosophy opposed, not because a philosophical faith has been justified but because the opposition of one to the other is struck into slogans that are themselves neither faithful nor philosophical. But the very necessity that the "poem" be imparted turns the "poem" into a slogan. For as the entire "Interlude" had tried to argue, necessity precludes a *historical* and therefore *faithful* relation. "Necessity" and "coming-into-existence" are mutually exclusive terms. The impossibility of noncommunication means: not everything is not possible; a "not" of communication is under every condition impossible; the "poem" must be imparted again and yet necessarily again. The necessary poem of "coming-into-existence," a poem whose necessity lies not in its "content" but in its need to be imparted as a "poem," cannot then be a poem of "coming-into-existence." The "poem" is not what it is but is rather its other: altered into a slogan, it becomes boundless *sladder*, a diaspora, not a concentrated *digt*. The autopsy *of* faith thus reads, *slain in and turned into a slogan*.

With this autopsy emerges not only the question of the disciple at the second hand once again but also the question of the disciple at the third hand, at the fourth hand, ad infinitum. The poem of the coming into being of language and its passing on, from hand to hand, cannot be sorted into the simple opposition, the very model of simplicity—source and echo. For the source is always inhabited by its echo at the moment language comes into being, and thus the *digt* that shelters language already carries its own autopsy: "faith—*thus*—does not exist." Spoken in all seriousness before the absolute difference, *ego non sum* reverberates with the sound of a primordially slain language turned into a slogan. "The historical fact that the god has been in human form is the capital matter [*Hovedsagen*], and the other historical details are not even as important as they would be if the subject were a human being instead of the god. Lawyers say that a capital crime [a crime that concerns the head] consumes all the lesser ones—so also with faith" (103–4). But no—they are not finally consumed, since the "historical fact" *has to be imparted*, and in every imparting, the relation of head to body, indeed of all parts to one another, cannot be reduced to one part, without the thought of death, or crumbs. But this thought is of death *as* imparting, not departing, and this imparting takes place without recognition and recollection in the falling down not of heads but crumbs, which, however, are parts of no particular, no "individual" substance.

§ 4 Ordeal of Autonomy:
Fear and Trembling

It is fortunate that *language has a number of expressions for nonsense and drivel.* Otherwise I would have become mad, for what else does it prove except that all that one said was nonsense. Oh, how fortunate that language is so developed in this respect: that way one may yet hope occasionally to hear *reasonable discourse.*

—Kierkegaard, a note to himself

"Indirect Communication"

Communication cannot *not* take place.—This is not a thesis that applies to a specific situation or even to the unique "poem" of "coming-into-existence" projected in *Philosophical Fragments.* It is a singular law of communication. Even noncommunication—whether as silence, muteness, or total passivity—is a negative mode of communication, which, however, remains a matter of communication. Because of the impossibility of noncommunication, a certain necessity accrues to every communication, and this peculiar necessity confounds the ability to communicate and thus communication at every point. Climacus, to say nothing of Kierkegaard's other pseudonyms, tries to void this necessity by projecting a mere possibility, a pure "project of thought," but the very attempt to void the necessity of communication testifies to its force and confirms the singular law of communication: communication cannot *not* take place. It is impossible to avoid communication, even if, and especially when, one attempts to void communication of its necessity by communicating mere possibilities, sheer fictions.[1] For the communication of a void does not avoid communication; avoiding communication communicates a void.

A void of communication is communicated whenever communication is avoided. Making this void into the matter of communication demands that one void communication of its necessity, but this voiding can be done only in part, with a certain duplicity, since communication itself cannot be avoided. The matter of communication, which can no longer be distinguished from its form, is likewise made duplicitous; this "matter" can present itself only as "negative," indeed as the negativity toward which the *Concluding Unscientific Postscript* to *Philosophical Fragments* turns as it submits itself to the law of communication: communication cannot *not* take place; communication cannot be avoided even when the void of communication, its negativity, is communicated. The compulsion of *Concluding Unscientific Postscript* to communicate the incommunicable makes this negativity into the element of its off-putting, offensive "artistry" and the law of its negative performance: "That is how it always goes with the negative; wherever it is unconsciously present, it transforms the positive into the negative. In this case [objective, positive communication], it transmutes communication into an illusion, because no thought is given to the negative in the communication, but the communication is thought of purely and simply as positive. In the deception of double-reflection, consideration is given to the negative of the communication, and therefore this communication, which seems to be nothing compared to that other mode of communication, is indeed communication."[2]

Reflecting on the "negativity" of communication makes "positive" communication impossible and at same time makes "negative" communication, which is communication *simpliciter*, possible—as the communication of the incommunicable. "Positive" communication only *appears* to be communication, whereas "negative" communication, which does not appear to be communication, is communication pure and simple. But "negative" communication is communication pure and simple precisely because it denies the very purity and simplicity of communication. It avoids communication in order to communicate a void, but this void is anything but mere emptiness. The impurity and complexity of communication, which make up its "negativity," therefore cannot be communicated purely and simply; they cannot be communicated as silence, which always retains a certain positivity and directness. On the contrary, the impurity and complexity—in short, the "negativity"—of communication can be communicated only in the breach and breakdown of apparently simple and seemingly pure communication.[3] The most decisive breach and the most radical breakdown take place, however, when the incommunicable, as singular breach and repetitive breakdown, is itself communicated. Such a communication is possible only because communication cannot *not* take place, and the communication of this impossibility, which disorients to the point of total "indirection," constitutes communication in the first place. The "in" of "indirect communication" takes over the "negativity" in which communication always takes place in order to *break* the singular law of communication—in order, that is, to give communication the chance of *not* taking place and to this extent, of communicating the incommunicable.

An "illusion" of communication appears whenever communication sets out to deny its "negativity." It thereafter becomes positive and objective "prattle," the term through which Johannes Climacus understands a Hegel whom no one, as Hegel conceded on his deathbed, understood.[4] By contrast, communication can actually take place whenever it *does not appear* to take place—or since communication cannot not take place, whenever it *appears* not to take place, whenever it withdraws into a self-colloquy or a *communicatio idiomatum*, whenever in sum it appears disengaged, empty, idle, or in vain. Communication cannot escape its illusory appearance any more than it can avoid prattle, emptiness, and idleness. Its element is "negativity," and the acknowledgment of its elemental vanity, not the avoidance of this constitutive void, gives it a chance—but it is only a chance—to break its own law, to break down the appearance of communication by the appearance of noncommunication, to disrupt and interrupt "prattle," for instance, by a "nonsense" that is no longer subservient to the criteria of comprehensibility and that Climacus calls, somewhat misleadingly, "paradox." With the exposition of the algebraic "logic" of such "nonsense" under the rubric "Religiousness B" the *Postscript* comes to an end, along with Kierkegaard's entire "pseudonymous" endeavor.[5] What takes place in these disruptions and interruptions is *another* illusion of communication: the illusion that something other than the incommunicable has been communicated. The *Postscript* submits itself to the task of breaking the law of communication and opening up the possibility of an impossible communication in this breach: a communication, therefore, in which the incommunicable is communicated.

Injunctions on communication always produce secrets, secretiveness, and "mystery cults." Those who participate in such injunctions form the communities that are therein acculturated to secrets and secretiveness. But a secret that can never be communicated under any condition and that therefore breaks every injunction to keep a secret cannot form a cult or a cultic community and cannot to this extent foster communion. Or, the community and communion, without cult and without culture, could have no other place to practice its rites than the void of communication created by the avoidance of communication, an avoidance for which no reason could be given as long as the disclosure of things hitherto hidden constitutes the only reason and the only criterion of rationality. The secret of communication is, however, freedom: "Just as the subjective existing thinker has set himself free by the duplexity [*Dobbelthed*], so the secret of communication specifically hinges on setting the other free"[6]—and emancipating the recipient, in the first place, from communication, above all, from the economic give-and-take of conversation, dialogue, even dialectics. To the extent that Hegelian philosophy claims to conceive of everything and to comprehend everything under its total Concept, it can have no place for secrets other than those that make up the community and communion of Hegelianism, its incomprehensible mantras and phrases. Since it has no place for the "negativity" of communication, it gives up the very possibility of communication, or in what amounts to the same, it gives off only the appearance of communication.

If, however, philosophy ceded a place to the inconceivable and incomprehensible, it could concede a unique moment of secrecy, and by making this concession, it could have a chance to communicate something other than the appearance of communication. The secret of communication is emancipation; the secret of philosophy, as conceived as the inconceivable and the incomprehensible, is freedom. In a late essay on certain religiously motivated writers who misconceive of secrecy as a matter of revelation and therefore try to form a community on its basis—precisely the misconception against which much of the final sections of the *Postscript* were written—Kant concedes as much: "The secret is precisely freedom."[7] Freedom, which according to Kant is so incomprehensible that even its *possibility* cannot be conceived, constitutes the secret, and this secret is put into practice, although never conclusively, as the duplicity of reduplication: in laying down a universal and necessary rule that one concedes for oneself as a particular being; therefore, in applying oneself to a law and yet seeing this application in its relation to one's situation. "Reduplication" therefore designates the operation of autonomy. The "recipient" of communication can never be a mere recipient but must actively give the communication, and the law of communication, to himself. The secret of communication is therefore the communication of the secret, the imparting of freedom as autonomy, which, however, can never be purely and simply imparted but takes apart everyone who tries "directly" to do so. Freedom, as the secret, cannot be communicated, but it alone makes possible communication as the communication of its own impossibility. Since freedom cannot be communicated, however, it becomes an *ordeal* to do so—a trial, a parting, an imparting, a taking apart.

The or-deal of autonomy is its communication. For freedom, as autonomy, cannot be communicated. "Moral education," as the communication of autonomy, not only is not a clear notion; it is impossible and even immoral.[8] Yet the singular law of communication states that nothing, not even freedom, cannot *not* be communicated; indeed, "freedom is always *communicerende*."[9] The impossibility of communicating freedom and the impossibility of not communicating freedom do not amount to a simple contradiction but to a contracommunication: communication against communication, communication crossing itself out. This contracommunication cannot, of course, be represented as a dialogue between two opposing positions over a question posed in common since no *positions* can be sustained without denying the negativity of communication. But the contracommunication in which the ordeal of autonomy takes place can seek out *representatives* of nonpositions and juxtapose them. Two such nonpositions have already been named: a philosophy that conceives of freedom as inconceivable and incomprehensible, and a "writing" that sets out to communicate freedom as the very secret of communication. A contracommunication between Kant and Kierkegaard over freedom can present itself under these terms, and indeed the *Postscript* invites this presentation.

After the supposed completion of philosophy in the Hegelian system, a question nevertheless remains, according to Climacus. That question is how to answer Kant. Hegelianism, since it has no place for the incomprehensible, has never done so: "To answer Kant within the fantastic *Schattenspiel* of pure thinking is precisely not to answer him."[10] Not only Kant's "skepticism" is at issue but everything that arises from his concession to incomprehensibility in the name of freedom. An answer to Kant cannot consist in "thinking through" skepticism; it cannot occur in "pure thought." If Kant is to be answered, the answer can occur only in a *breach* of thought: "It [Kantian skepticism] must be broken off."[11] But a breach of "pure thinking" already takes place in Kant's "answer" to his own "skepticism"—that is, in the thesis of the "primacy of practical reason."[12] A response to Kant's "skepticism" already occurs in Kant, so the "answer" to Kant can take place only in a breach of comprehensibility that Kant has already conceded, a breach that carries over the proper linguistic form of comprehension, the proposition formed into answers and transformed into questions.

Before philosophy "advanced" to the Hegelian position of total comprehensibility, it comprehended the incomprehensible as freedom and sought the ground for human freedom in autonomy. The answer to this "skeptical" position, which is precisely not a position but a concession, cannot be cast in the polemical terms of the *Postscript.*[13] For polemics orients itself toward vanquishing opposition. Nor can a contracommunication assume the form of a "dialogue" with a philosopher, even if "the situation of dialogue" takes away "the whole fantasticality involving pure thinking."[14] For dialogue cannot help but orient itself toward comprehension: "Conversation is the expression for the universal [the general, the ordinary]."[15] The contracommunication with Kant's concession must, on the contrary, deny "the situation of dialogue" in favor of a talking at cross-purposes: a philosophical *program*, which is rooted in the incomprehensibility of freedom, will thus confront the *presentation* of a "secret" that is impossible to communicate but that for this very reason makes communication possible as the impossible imparting of freedom. The or-deal of autonomy, as the setting apart of Kant's grounding of freedom in the self-legislation of the subject, can therefore serve as the title for a contracommunication between Kant's *Laying the Ground for the Metaphysics of Morals* and the shaking of this ground in *Fear and Trembling.*[16]

Kant Comprehending Incomprehensibility

The principle of autonomy states that nothing is to be a law other than a law that is self-legislated. Self-legislation is thereafter the basic criterion for lawfulness, and the constitution of the self in turn lies in laying down the law. The relation of the self to the law poses the supreme philosophical problem once lawfulness comes to define things in general. The principle of autonomy could not therefore appear as the highest principle all at once; on the contrary, the principle of autonomy came into its own only after a complex and tortuous process wherein both the law and the self were held in place on the basis of supposedly higher and indeed self-grounding principles—theological ones, above all, the specific function of which was to relate, as mediators, two distinct *relata*, the self and the law. The principle of autonomy first comes into its own, declares itself to be the highest of principles and thereby turns into an autonomous principle in the ground-breaking work of

Kant, *Grundlegung zur Metaphysik der Sitten* (Laying the Ground for the Metaphysics of Morals).[17] In the central section of this work Kant announces that autonomy is, after all, the highest principle of practical reason, and since practical reason shows itself to be primary in the development of a metaphysical system, it is the highest principle of reason altogether, higher even than those of non-contradiction and reason. For it is these principles put into practice; it is their unique "realization." The demonstration of this "realization" of the twin pillars on which metaphysical knowledge has hitherto rested is the burden of Kant's exposition, a burden so weighty that it requires nothing less than a new, critical grounding for metaphysics in general, and the ground is, of course, to be found in the critical power on which the principle of autonomy draws its strength.

The burden of the exposition is therefore to show that the metaphysics of practical reason rests on the making-metaphysical of practical reason; the latter is to be released from all sensuous content in precisely the same manner that knowledge is made independent of sensuous content in the science of metaphysics. But since metaphysical knowledge is possible only on the condition that its knowledge be subject to critique and that the specific modes in which objects become accessible be rigorously delimited, the metaphysics of morals cannot simply rest content with the disclosure of the ultimate foundation on which morality, as the purification of practical reason, rests. It must also show how this disclosure is itself possible, how therefore the ultimate and highest foundation can show itself. Otherwise a *critical* metaphysics cannot be produced, and the task assigned to the central section of the *Grundlegung* and thus to the principle of autonomy itself—"transition [*Uebergang*] from popular moral wisdom [*Weltweisheit*] to the metaphysics of morals"—cannot be accomplished. And it is the problem of transition that dominates the movement of the work as a whole. The final chapter is just as much a transition, from the "metaphysics of morals" to the "critique of pure practical reason," whose end point is the final station of critique.

Critique is under way until it reaches the point where having gone through so many rites of passage, each of which constitutes an *Uebergang*, it reaches maturity and finds itself at peace. Maturity then marks the final stage of the exposition. Its terms include a moment of insight into the foundation of the entire movement. But the foundation is not then disclosed; instead, one reaches the stage where, as Kant writes at the close of the *Grundlegung*, the student of metaphysics finally "comprehends its incomprehensibility."[18] Gaining access to the inaccessibility of the foundation of practical reason is the last and highest achievement of human reason, the point where transition is termination. This access thus defines the species and at the same time justifies the exposition of a *metaphysica specialis* that is no longer grounded on indubitable insight into the things on which appearances are based.

The last and highest achievement consists in an unlimited acknowledgment of *force*, indeed a force so immediate that the principle of autonomy no longer needs the mediation of sensuous motives or feelings. It is the immediate force in which reason is compelled to "realize" its principles without any regard for sensuous inclinations. The peculiar power and effectiveness of the principle of autonomy do not rest on the effort, however laudable, to make the erstwhile incomprehensible comprehensible; on the contrary, such force and effectiveness reside in the exclusion of the incomprehensible from the very sphere of possible comprehension and the vigilant protection of the former from the all-inclusive encroachment of the latter. The comprehension of incomprehensibility means that the incomprehensible, which consists in the *immediacy* of force, is made accessible by its very inaccessibility and that the specific inability of which it speaks is shown to rest not so much in a "higher" ability as in *enabling* pure and simple—that is, in freedom. Autonomy and incomprehensibility are correlated to the extent that the immediate force of every self-given law lies in the incomprehensibility of freedom, and freedom stands out as the "intermediary" that allows one to speak of autonomy in the first place. It is the attempt to grasp this Idea that compels Kant to conclude the *Grundlegung* by abandoning the search for conclusive resting grounds in favor of an uneasy coming to terms with the compulsion in whose train the entire set of transitions has been written. For this compulsion of reason to seek its ground encounters a mode of necessitation that is all the more powerful because it is immediate, and its immediacy, which like all immediacies eschews conceptualization, assures its incomprehensibility:

> Now it is an essential principle of all employment of reason to push its knowledge to a consciousness of its necessity (for otherwise it would not be knowledge of reason). But it is also an equally essential restriction of this very same reason that it cannot have insight into the necessity of what is or what occurs or what ought to be done, unless a condition under which it is or occurs or ought to be done is presupposed [*zum Grunde gelegt*]. In this way, however, the satisfaction of reason is only further and further postponed by the constant inquiry after the condition. Therefore, reason restlessly seeks the unconditionally necessary [*Unbedingt-notwendige*] and sees itself compelled [*genötigt*] to assume it without a means of making it comprehensible; happy enough if it can only discover the concept that makes peace [*sich verträgt*] with this presupposition. . . . And so we do not comprehend the practical unconditional necessity of the moral imperative, but we comprehend nevertheless its *incomprehensibility*, which is all that can reasonably be demanded of a philosophy that strives to hit the limits of human reason.[19]

With these words Kant closes the *Grundlegung* and defends his effort at laying the ground for the metaphysics of morals from every attempt on the part of disguised metaphysicians to comprehend the foundation on which this metaphysics is supposed to rest. For the absolutely necessary character of moral prescriptions is grounded in the incomprehensibility of freedom. These prescriptions do not simply compel but indeed *outcompel* the power of reason, and the only solution is a contract (*Vertrag*) in which perfect satisfaction (*Befriedigung*) gives way to an uneasy peace. And the entire *Grundlegung*, as the making-metaphysical of practical reason, is guaranteed under the terms of this treaty, this promise to come to a halt after so many "transitions."[20] Not content with such a promise, disguised metaphysicians latch onto all kinds of spurious explanations for the foundations on which the making-metaphysical of morals is supposed to rest. The "interest" taken in the morality, as the name for the inexplicable yet compulsive force, is said to consist, for instance, in its intellectual and sensuous appeal, its "goodness" and even its "beauty," or this "interest" is seen to consist in a *divine* promise of eternal happiness. In all such explanations, unprincipled heteronomy, which finds its mark in mediation, replaces the principle of autonomy, and the comprehension of absolute necessitation in turn undermines its immediacy and thus its absoluteness. Apodictic imperatives turn into contingent ones whose contingency depends upon certain predetermined ends that are supposed to mediate moral practice. The knowledge of those ends can be ascribed to theology or anthropology.

In neither case, however, is metaphysics renounced; on the contrary, its "realization" is forsworn. For it is the absolute force of the imperative, its ability to make practical reason metaphysical, that absolves it of all relation to predetermined ends, confirms its immediacy, and at the same time makes absolution from impure practice contingent upon a radical mode of *testing*: scrutinizing, that is, whether the principles of conduct are based on contingent circumstances (unhappiness) and aim at a contingent situation (happiness) or whether they are altogether necessary and, if necessary, then universalizable. This self-scrutiny, which is not yet an *ordeal* since its terms are at all times available, constitutes the principal operation of autonomy: unless an end accords with a law given in absolution from all worldly relations, and therefore given immediately, it cannot be certified as moral, and the one who makes the law cannot be ascertained at all.

Autonomy is therefore not only the highest principle in which and for which all certification takes place; it is also the principle by virtue of which one can ascertain whether one has absolved oneself of impure practice and has thus achieved a measure of self-knowledge—not, to be sure, self-knowledge itself but its measure, the test for universalization that all subjective principles of conduct must undergo. Once put into practice, the principle of autonomy becomes a means of testing whose medium is nothing less than a measure of self-knowledge. And it is altogether fitting that the principle of autonomy should compel the metaphysics of morals, otherwise content with disclosure of its highest principle, to critique. This critique does not concern the conditions of objectively valid knowledge but the fragile constitution of subjectivity:

Autonomy of the Will as the Highest Principle of Morality

Autonomy of the will is the constitution [*Beschaffenheit*] of the will by which it is a law to itself (independently of the entire constitution of the objects of willing). The principle of autonomy is therefore: choose in no other way than this—the maxims of your will are in the same act of willing at the same time co-comprehended [*mit begreifen*] as a universal law. That this practical rule is an imperative, i.e., that the will of every rational being is necessarily bound to it as a condition, cannot be proved by a mere analysis of the concepts occurring in it, because it is a synthetical proposition; one must go beyond the knowledge of the object and on to a critique of the subject [*Kritik des Subjekts*], that is, to pure practical reason, for this sentence, which bids apodictically, must be able to be known completely *a priori*. But this business does not belong in the present section.   (4:440)

Nothing less than the relation of critique to metaphysics and as a result the very fate of philosophy are implied in the last statement. If it is the business of critique to determine the validity of synthetic a priori propositions, then surely the justification of the apodictic character of moral imperatives does not belong in a section devoted to a "transition" from scattered notions to metaphysics, since the sole task of the latter consists in the analysis and systematic presentation of already ascertained a priori judgments. But matters are significantly more complicated if the highest principle of metaphysics is itself *critical* and indeed aims its critique, its effort to delimit and determine, at the subjective principles, as those rules or "maxims" on whose basis subjectivity motivates itself and therefore moves in the first place. And such is the case with the principle of autonomy. It not only operates in the metaphysics of morals but also lays down its groundwork. This double task cannot be dissociated from a certain disarticulation of metaphysics and critique. For the critical character of the principle of autonomy, as the basis of the metaphysics of morals, is not only supposed to bring about the transition to a critique of pure practical reason; it is this critique itself, as Kant almost acknowledges at the conclusion of the preface to the *Grundlegung* (4:391). A critique of pure practical reason is "synthetic" to the extent that it engages a "third thing"—precisely not a thing but rather the utterly insubstantial and yet no less "real" Idea of freedom—in order to ground the *ability* of the subject to act solely on the basis of a self-given law. Only the mediation of the Idea of freedom, as the "third thing," lets the law turn into an immediate force and outcompel all other compulsions, including the one to seek the grounds of all things. This "synthesis" whereby the Idea of freedom grounds the subject is enacted every time a subjective principle of action, a *propositio maxima* or maximum proposition, is scrutinized according to the principle of autonomy. For subjectivity is thereby placed into the space of its own freedom, and the disclosure not of this space but of such pure placement-with, as *syn-thesis*, takes place in an *imperative*: the positing, that is, of entirely new "things"—obligations and duties.

Critique and metaphysics are so closely interrelated in the space of this positing that they can show themselves to be one, and a critical metaphysics can now be won, on the sole condition that the *basis of the maxim itself* go untested. The basis of the maxim itself is not its aim, nor is it the subjective process of its emergence; it is the *medium* in which maxims are articulated in the first place. This medium mirrors the Idea of freedom insofar as the latter mediates all action in order to make the law apply immediately to action. The least one can say about the medium of maximization, however, is that it is linguistic. To say more would require an entirely different test than that of autonomy, and the most that could be said, the limit of language conceived as a medium of propositions, would under no condition make *itself* known on its own and according to its own laws but would have to rely on another: a presentation no longer subordinated to the exposition of the argument as it goes from one transit point to the next. And the articulation of this difference would in turn constitute precisely that ordeal, that taking apart and communicating the part thus taken

(*Mit-teilung*), which the highest, most independent, and most inviolable principle of critical metaphysics undergoes the moment access to a *maxima propositio* is no longer taken for granted.

Taking the access to maxims for granted generates the transition of a metaphysics of morals to a critique not of *pure* practical reason but merely practical reason. Pure practical reason, as Kant will proceed to declare in the preface to the *Critique of Practical Reason*, requires no critique and, as the treatise aims to show, is finally made possible on the basis of a quite special fact: the fact of reason.[21] In the *Critique of Practical Reason*—and with increasing determination in all of Kant's subsequent writings—the fact of reason, as the *Faktum* the subject makes for itself in the form of an a priori consciousness of the binding power of the law, operates on already fabricated maxims: an "already," to wit, that cannot be understood as a restatement of the a priori character of transcendental consciousness. This operation on the basis of such maxims constitutes the putting into practice of the principle of autonomy. The medium of the maxims is to this extent entirely forgotten, whereas in the *Grundlegung* the possibility of a critique of *pure* practical reason, and therefore autonomy itself, was for a moment disclosed only to be foreclosed with the concluding term of peace, that is, "comprehending incomprehensibility." Incomprehensibility not only accrues to the source of the absolute necessity of moral imperatives but also, and in a more disconcerting because less determinate manner, to the medium of the maxims themselves.

Critiques of Kant almost invariably cite his statement that one can neither know oneself nor ever be certain under precisely which maxim one operates; it is therefore impossible to know if any conduct has ever been moral (4:406–7). But the lack of insight into intelligible character does not in itself condemn the project of the *Grundlegung* to duplicity; duplicity, or reduplication, resides, rather, in the uncomprehended if not incomprehensible accessibility of maxims on all occasions, even the most extreme. A *propositio maxima* tested for its ability to be altogether maximized and thus "universalized" is not, to be sure, a "copybook maxim" that children read in schoolbooks or the empty maxims with which one presses forth an argument,[22] but the originality of the "maximum propositions" in a "practical syllogism" is as unfathomable as the ability to become a subject of morality and thus to "learn" the meaning of obligation. Being able to retrieve a maxim under which conduct falls is, however, the very condition of articulateness and moral subjectivity: in short, the condition of "maturity." Kant's unwillingness to examine this condition is all the more striking in a work whose *structure* is pedagogical to the core: "transition" after "transition" leads from unarticulated conviction to the summit of articulate insight, whereupon one articulates the terms of the journey already taken and rehearses the entire exercise in dutiful order. The origin of maxims, of maximization and thereafter universalization, remains so unexamined that it takes on the character of utterly unoriginal facts: maximized but not yet universalized according to an unknown procedure that in turn makes it impossible to return to the site of their manufacture and goes on to confirm this inability under the title *Faktum der Vernunft.*

No appeal to "psychological" processes is warranted if the written and indeed *rote* character of maxims is remembered. However much Kant's maxims are distinguished from those found in schoolbooks, they cannot be altogether withdrawn from the provenance of pedagogy and reading.[23] Without an exposition of how a maxim comes to light, the structure of the *Grundlegung* lacks an indispensable "transition." For it is this transition that conditions the application of practical reason to the principle of autonomy and thereby makes morality metaphysical in the first place. As the ground on which the entire dynamics of autonomy takes place, this condition cannot simply be consigned to incomprehensibility, not even to the incomprehensible Idea of freedom. It is, rather, the medium of comprehensibility, the strange double of this Idea, that inevitably leads to a certain duplicity. Those elements of a synthesis that Kant sought to investigate so thoroughly in empirical knowledge are left entirely untouched when the synthesis is not one of knowledge, or judgment or even propositions as mental entities, but language.

The tests of universality canonized in the formulae of the Categorical Imperative apply only to maxims, so the mode of access to the universally accessible medium of maximization itself remains untested. Under no condition should freedom be confused with the origin of maxims, since freedom is an a priori presupposition, whereas the temporality of the "origin" of maxims is at the very most indeterminate. And yet it is precisely the conflation of these two conditions that makes possible the altogether smooth operation of the principle of autonomy, its ability to make a transition from metaphysics of morals to a critique of practical reason. Just as incomprehensibility rescues the principle of autonomy from spurious foundations, the comprehensibility of its own language, as already fabricated maxims, rescues the subject from being exposed to an ordeal in which the superlative character of its "highest" principle is itself tested.

"A Dangerous Standpoint"

This ordeal does not go entirely unnoticed in the presentation of the *Grundlegung*. Nowhere does it receive conceptual elucidation, nor does it appear in one of the many images Kant develops to "illustrate" the concepts under examination. On the contrary, the ordeal of autonomy enters into the *Grundlegung* at the very moment one such image breaks down—falls to the ground, more precisely, but not to the foundation secured in the ground-laying operation of the *Grundlegung*. The latter foundation, of course, is reason as the faculty of principles (*Grundsätze*). The breaking down of the image of groundlaying brings into view the very ability of this faculty to absolve itself of all relations to the grounds for conduct as they have hitherto been represented. Philosophy distances itself from theological representations of the basis for human conduct being in God's will on the one hand, and it removes itself entirely from representations of this foundation in earthly desires and goals on the other. Philosophy hovers, therefore, without any support other than the support it gives itself, and the image of hovering breaks down the groundlaying image.

If, then, the very being of philosophy is being in between, *inter-esse*, it escapes the aporia with which the *Grundlegung* ends: the aporia of having to presuppose a purely rational "interest," even though this interest is impossible to represent and thus to conceive: "I will concede that no interest [*Interesse*] impels me to do so [that is, to subject myself to the moral law], for that would then give no categorical imperative. But I must nevertheless take an interest in it" (5:449).[24] In order to resolve this aporia and make way for moral progress, Kant lays the foundation for a metaphysics of morals *in* this very interest, and without conceding as much, he *presents* this groundlaying in the air—in between heaven and earth, in between all substantial being, *inter-esse* itself—as the being of philosophy and of the finite rationality it exposes to critique:

> Here we now see philosophy in fact placed on a dangerous standpoint [*mißlichen Standpunkt*] that should be firm, even though it neither hangs on—nor is supported by—anything in heaven or on earth. Here philosophy should demonstrate its purity [*Lauterkeit*] as the self-sustainer of its laws [*Selbsthalterin ihrer Gesetze*], not as the herald [*Herold*] of those which an implanted sense or who knows what pre-articulate nature whispers [*vormundschaftliche Natur einflüstert*]; these whispers in their entirety, which may be better than absolutely nothing, nonetheless can never give principles that reason dictates [*diktiert*], and these dictations must have their source completely a priori and at the same time thereby acquire their commanding visage [*gebietendes Ansehen*]. (4:425–26)

Philosophy achieves its autonomy and grounds itself on the principle of autonomy when its speech ceases to be that of a messenger who amplifies inarticulate whispers but instead lets the dictations of reason to the rational subject be heard at full volume. The loudness of these dictations corresponds to their *Lauterkeit* (purity), just as the softness of prearticulate whispers testifies to their impurity.[25] But a prearticulate whisper—what is that? Certainly every whisper is already articulated and articulate, already a matter of a mouth (*Mund*) that has been weaned of its natural source of nourishment; it is already mature enough to speak on its own and is thus confirmed in its *Mündigkeit*. Indeed, no speech is more its own than a whisper since whispering, which is usually reserved for the communication of secrets, already communicates a limit to its own communicability. It is critical from the start. The self-dictation of reason, by contrast, presupposes precisely that condition of which whispering speaks: a linguistic medium in which dictation, as *Dichtung* and dictatorial speech in one, is first made communicable, even if the ground of such speech, absolute freedom, is assigned to incomprehensibility.

Nothing is more contrary to philosophy than being simply a mouthpiece, an amplifier of softly spoken messages, but this fundamental antipathy of philosophy to playing the part of the exalted medium, its supreme antiangelic pathos, does not in the least absolve it of an ordeal in which its absolute communication with itself, its inescapable *communicatio idiomatum*, is nevertheless exposed to the limits of communicability. And that means: *presented*. The proof of this inability of philosophy to carry out this final absolution can be found in the "image" of intimacy to which Kant is drawn: a mouth, once weaned, wishes to return through soft speech to its former source. But Kant could think of those limits and this intimacy only in terms of pathos. Determining the limitation on the communicability of *feelings*, not communicability itself, poses the final task of critique, and so the critique of the power of judgment, as the basis of universally communicable feelings, assumes the position left open when the critique of the power to make maxims and therefore the critique of the linguistic medium of maximization fails to materialize. Exposed to the language of feeling and the feeling of language—what else speaks in a whisper?—Kant could do nothing but proscribe the enabling conditions of the aesthetic on the one hand[26] and on the other, decry as deranged those who like Abraham in binding Isaac, could not distinguish pathos from discourse, *Stimmung* from *Stimme*, for long enough to grasp the danger to which they exposed themselves when they distanced themselves from the intimacy inherent in the principle of autonomy.[27]

Critique, Ordeal

Critique is not, however, unfamiliar with the role of medium. Kantian critique excuses itself from this role, to be sure, but textual criticism has often proclaimed its task to be that of heralding, transmitting, and amplifying the words spoken by another speaker—above all, when that speaker is, as a genius, so close to *natura naturans* as to imitate its creative activity. Critical elaboration then consists in raising the *Lauterkeit* of the text to an audible level, and it *can* do so for the precise reason that the text on which it operates is said to be autonomous; it follows its own laws, and the task of critique is to bring those laws to light. Once illuminated, the whisperings of the text, which were beforehand prearticulate, are so fully articulated that its meaning and significance are everywhere apparent. Criticism is thus enabled on the basis of autonomy, even if critical labor itself is heteronomous. Its specific mode of testing a text consists in attesting to its purity, its power to give itself its own rules. But for this very reason, criticism can achieve its own autonomy, indeed a higher one than the texts it tests. Its task turns out to be purification after all: it is the medium in which the autonomy of a text makes itself known through the progressive distillation of its heteronomous elements, and this process of coming to knowledge constitutes the Idea of criticism and confirms its autonomy over against the work criticized.[28] Autonomy therefore determines the dimension of critical labor. And never more so than when "external factors"—be they historical, economic, or political—are laid out to make the text significant in ways that it could never have been on its own; its "ownness" is then founded in criticism itself. Perhaps nothing is less likely to put the principle of autonomy to test than the declaration, as an underlying methodological principle, that such factors are decisive in the determination of significance, since autonomy then takes up residence in an Idea—as the Idea of a total array of factors in which the stringent laws of "meaning-manufacture" operate so successfully on their own that in their overdetermination of every fabrication, the "self" to whom facts are meaningful is said to be nothing outside these laws, this "nature" thus constructed.

No more extreme antipode to such a conception of critique could be found than *Fear and Trembling*. For the presentations of the binding of Isaac to which the text again and again returns do not aim at purification: neither the self-sufficient and self-given laws of the text are presupposed, nor do they pose the Idea of a lawful ordering of factors, however overdetermined, by means of which a text achieves its—perhaps only historically determined—identity and significance. On the contrary, *Fear and Trembling* disposes of such conceptions of critique to make room for precisely what Kant missed: a critique of *pure* practical reason, a critique of the medium in which maxims are articulated. But this new "critique" does not rest there, for this medium must be taken apart, communicated in part, delivered over to an or-deal in which the principle of autonomy, as the foundation of the Idea of purity, is exposed and presented. Communicating the "ordeal" (*Prøve*) of Abraham is the locus of this exposition.

The conception of language, moreover, cannot remain unaltered, and the direction of its alteration is already indicated in the citation of Hamann that serves as the epigraph to *Fear and Trembling*: "What Tarquinius Superbus said in his garden with the poppy heads, the son understood but not the messenger."[29] The messenger cannot understand the message and is therefore incapable of its communication, but this incapacity is communicated in the very act of communication: the cutting of poppy heads. For this cutting, as a de-cision devoid of all discussion, is incomprehensible to the extent that it excludes every maxim under which it would fall as a case: it means nothing to the messenger since he not only cannot comprehend the language of flower cutting but cannot even comprehend flower cutting as a language. Messenger and medium therefore exclude each other. This mutual exclusion means that a particular language has emerged in which no maxims can be articulated, for the reason that this language, which messengers cannot understand even as a medium of communication, *minimizes*; it reduces words to gestures until only a breach, a cut or a scission, is communicable. Johannes de Silentio, pseudonymous author of *Fear and Trembling*, everywhere reduces the articulation of concepts to decisive, incisive, and mute gesticulation, thereby giving the impression that he communicates a message from father Superbus to a no less superb son as deftly and imperceptibly as the harvested poppy plant communicates its intoxicating effect.

But matters are significantly more complicated when messenger and medium do not exclude each other with such vehemence. And this is the case in *Fear and Trembling*, however much the pseudonymous author, and the entire edifice of falsified messengers who make up the Kierkegaardian corpus,[30] may wish to give the impression that conceptual articulation can be so reduced to decisive gesticulations that only certain chosen individuals, as newly recognized sons, can understand them. Johannes may descend from a region entitled Silentio, but as the text itself bears witness, he has abandoned his homeland and ventured into the foreign region of discourse, into the domain of writing, to be more exact, as long as writing encompasses a complex medium in which articulation and gesticulation, if only as a tracing motion of the hand, are indissociable.[31] The movement from homeland to alien domain is moreover the very topic of the text, and it is one undertaken as an ordeal whose specific terms of comprehension are utterly inaccessible to Johannes himself: these terms belong to silence, his estranged provenance. In the repetitive presentation of an incomprehensible ordeal, that of Abraham binding Isaac, the text therefore enacts the scene of its own origination.

Not only is it as a result obsessed with issues of generation and regeneration, endlessly bringing pedagogy, as the "leading of children," into its purview; its status as *critique* necessarily resolves into ever more incisive testings of the biblical passage whose aim is to see if it measures up not precisely to its own laws or a set of external rules in which it can be made meaningful but to its very origination: the passage, that is, from silence to writing. Under no condition should this origination be organized according to the axis of organic time; it need not belong to the "beginning" of life but could quite easily be its "end." What marks the moment of transition, however, is the utter inaccessibility of a maxim. For no subjective principle of conduct, as *maxima propositio*, could be articulated before the "transition" itself took place. The ordeal, in sum, is that of autonomy, and it is a double one. The or-deal of the author, as the imparting of his communication, cannot present itself as an unambiguous articulation of philosophical concepts whose aim is the confirmation of an argument. It can take place, if it does so at all, only in the act of presenting *another* ordeal, that of Abraham, which far from being straightforwardly "fictional" or even "lyrical," is in fact relentlessly critical. This critique is, of course, altogether different from biblical "higher" criticism, not only because it does not aim to "purify" the text of all extraneous additions and emendations to which it has been subject on account of its historicity but above all because it does not attempt to discover the historical axioms through which its meaning, purified of all subsequent exegeses and interpretations, can be ascertained at last. Critique is, rather, *lowered*, indeed lowered to the point where it consists in nothing but presentation after presentation.

The object of critique is the presentation of an event that goes by the name "the binding of Isaac," a binding in which the re-binding of *re-ligio* is itself tested. This event is not relegated to the unpresentable; least of all is it unpresentable because it belongs to the "past" and is therefore incorporated into some nostalgic longing. Nostalgia doubtless plays into the opening section of *Fear and Trembling* since it gives an account of childhood and takes place under the dispositional heading of *Stemning*, "mood" or "attunement." But it is equally indubitable that the "mood" of the presentations is not one of nostalgia since the doubt to which it gives witness could not be resolved through a return to the security of childhood. If the *Stemning* is implicated in a return, it is to the *stemme* (voice) in which the event first came into existence:

> Once upon a time there was a man who as a child had heard the beautiful story [*skjønne Fortælling*] of how God tempted [*fristede*] Abraham and of how Abraham withstood the temptation, kept the faith, and, contrary to expectation, got a son a second time. When he

grew older, he read the same story with even greater admiration, for his life had fractured what had been united in the pious simplicity of the child. The older he became, the more often his thoughts turned to that story; his enthusiasm for it became greater and greater, and yet he could understand the story less and less. Finally, he forgot everything else because of it; his soul had but one wish, to see Abraham, but one longing, to have witnessed the event [*Begivenhed*]. (9)

As the written text replaces the spoken story, the complexity of a fractured life replaces simplicity. And the text appears on all counts to be the locus of the fracture; its comprehension, the argument runs, would restore wholeness in fragmentation, and something like maturation, unity in self-division, would thereby be accomplished. But such is not the case, for the anonymous subject of this story, whose existence is defined solely in its terms, does not long after a lost childhood, nor can the event whose presentation he desires be understood as a displacement of this longing since the event dissociates itself from every narrative other than the bare "thus, it has been." The witnessing of such an event consists in its presentation, and this presentation, whose *conditio sine qua non* is a radical amnesia, removes his desire from the domain of storytelling, including the retelling of that story whose comprehension was apparently able to lead him back home and therefore the one that would relate his homecoming, his nostalgia. Since he wants nothing to do with the spoken story of his childhood, nothing in the end to do with the narrative as memorial, he everywhere renounces the anamnestic element of beauty in favor of a thought that cannot be thought through: "His craving was not to see the beautiful regions of the East, not the earthly glory of the promised land. . . . His wish was to be present in the hour when Abraham raised his eyes and saw Mount Moriah in the distance, the hour when he left the asses behind and went up the mountain alone with Isaac—for what occupied him was not the artful tapestry of the imagination but the shudder of the thought" (9, modified).

If the story as it was first spoken lies in a beauty whose telos is the intricate texture of imaginative art, its estrangement in the desire to be present at the hour of mountain climbing can hardly avoid being assigned to sublimity. And all the more so when the hour is understood to be one of elevation, of *hupsos* in which terror negates pleasure only to end up in the liveliest of negative pleasures: Isaac returned intact. On the basis of the apparent incomprehensibility of this event, "the sublime" emerges as a term, perhaps even the preeminent term of peace. For it terminates the search for grounds as it names the highest point. Less and less comprehension, more and more pleasure in suffering, until the shuddering of the mind, which designates negative pleasure as much as the negation of pleasure, discovers rest in incomprehensibility itself.

Comparisons with elements of Kant's "Analytic of the Sublime," or any other consideration of sublimity, are unnecessary here. For the phenomena of fear and trembling are, to be sure, integrated into the dynamical sublime to the extent that they attest to an overwhelming power,[32] but *Fear and Trembling* overtakes this dynamical character in the name of another sublimity, or something other than sublimity, a downward movement: "To be able to come down in such a way that instantaneously one seems to stand and to walk, to change the leap into life into walking, absolutely to express [*udtrykke*] the sublime in the pedestrian—only that the knight can do it, and this is the one and only marvel" (41). The "pedestrian sublime" not only is not a new mode of sublimity but is its undoing: "to be able to come down" designates the power under examination, but this power is not at all implicated in the apprehensive-comprehensive functions of the faculty called the imagination, so this examination is not interchangeable with the scrutiny of subjectivity to which Kant devotes his analysis of the "feeling" of sublimity. If the latter aims, with whatever hope of success, to probe not only the origin of subjectivity but also the "culture" through which this origin takes root, the pedestrian movement of *Fear and Trembling* in which sublimity, as it walks along the street, is brought down consists entirely in its *expression*, and that means its articulation and gesticulation, its mute yet communicative presentation.

Whereas the sublime refers every one of its moments to the unpresentable and therefore makes the unpresentable into the term of peace through which its most radical aspirations are mediated, presentability defines its lowly, pedestrian challenge. The ability to come down from the summit of sublimity, which is also the culmination of autonomous subjectivity, is nothing other than the ability to present oneself, but at the very moment of this descent the "self" of this self-presentation undergoes an ordeal unlike anything encountered in the affective judgment of sublimity. For the distinctive terms of this presentation are absent, so the entirety of its self-presentation appears to be a self-absentation in which absolutely nothing strikes the eye: the "knight," whose power is in no way limited by Common Law, makes his appearance in the form of a peripatetic, non-noble if not ignoble, thoroughly "bourgeois" tax collector (38–41). And instead of an affective judgment, an *Urteil* based on the ability to feel as well as a feeling based on *Urteilskraft* itself, there emerges in the breach of universal communicability a "passion."

The universal communicability of the feeling of sublimity demonstrates for Kant that communicability is not altogether subordinated to comprehensibility, but it just as surely turns this insubordination into the final proof for the order of reason and its ultimate terms of comprehension. The faculty of feeling preserves this order to the extent that certain feelings are able to be communicated universally. The or-deal of sublimity as the highest achievement of autonomy cannot therefore consist in the *Mit-teilung* of certain feelings but rather in the interruption and reinscription of such potentially universal im-parting. Communicability of certain "emotions," whether they be fear or trembling, does not designate the telos of the movement from which *Fear and Trembling* is written; rather, the concept of "communicability" to which Kant takes recourse in his last critical exercise is a final term of peace by means of which the issues of presentability, and therefore absentability, are systematically elided. Since feelings are held to play no part in presentation and are denied all relation to language, their "universal" communicability can go hand in hand with the most radical "illustrations" of groundless, ateleological incomprehensibility. Exposing "universal" communicability to articulation and gesticulation does not divorce it from the "faculty" of feeling but makes the latter into something linguistic, a *stemning* over which no ascertainable *stemme* has control. Such an exposition brings into play an "affective" language without rules, without precedents, and indeed without specific laws to which every speaker is indebted for the privilege of "expression": language, therefore, without natural or conventional language; language, in sum, *without language* insofar as language is understood to be "the universal" (60). Articulating such a language, which at this point cannot be dissociated from presenting it in writing, is a "problem" for Johannes de Silentio as well as for the one who is presented—namely, Abraham on his way up and down.

Problems, Promises

To articulate any language other than this "other" of rule-bound and law-defined language is the temptation to resign oneself to the unpresentable on the one hand or to "express" oneself in universally applicable terms on the other. That problem is addressed in the last of the *Problemata*: "Was it Ethically Defensible for Abraham to Conceal his Undertaking from Sarah, from Eliezer, and from Isaac?" (82) But this problem, as something thrown onto the path of progress, already manifests itself in the beginning—that is, in the *Stemning*. And it does so there entirely as a matter of presentation, not as a question open to discursive discussion. The exposition of the *Stemning* in this way takes precedence. The difficulty is not how Abraham raises himself up the mountain but on the contrary, how he is able to *come down*, and it is a *difficulty*, never an articulate "problem," precisely because Abraham is unable to arrive at a propositional or categorial formulation for his appalling conduct. Instead of articulating a problem, the *Stemning* exhibits a difficulty of articulation, a difficulty that cannot be expressed as a problem and thereby be reduced to an aporia.

Whereas an aporia constitutes an impasse to movement, a difficulty propels one into motion. The difficulty exhibited in the *Stemning* sends Abraham in particular on his journey outward. The emptiness around which all aporetic discussions are organized, and therefore the emptiness that organizes philosophical discourse since its inception in Socratic interrogation, gives way to an infinitely more incisive emptiness: the nullity not simply of human speech but of the divine, the absolute word, given that there is one. For God gave Abraham His word, and the gift of this word is, one supposes, as good as the accomplishment of the deed it promises. The "things" vouchsafed by the divine word should therefore be as good as the original things created in the one and only speech act that makes the actual entities—and not merely certain debts, obligations, or problems—to which it refers. In giving Abraham His word, God as good as created the thing He promised. But in taking back this word, which marks the difficulty, God puts into question the goodness of His word. And if His word cannot be considered good, none can. Each word is as vain, empty, and idle as the one that promised Abraham and Sarah a belated progeny.

To say that Abraham is "tested" thus begs the question. It is not only Abraham whose faith is tested but, more exactly, the word is tested for its ability to be given, and thus for its goodness. And no word is better able to take this test than a divine, absolute one. If the word of God isn't good, none is, and that means: no word can be given; words cannot be trusted; nobody can have faith in anything spoken; language in sum is as disreputable as an outright philanderer. The question of Abraham's testing is thus absorbed into a necessarily anonymous, but not for that reason indifferent, ordeal. Faith in language, which anyone who believes in the immediate accessibility of maxims must accept from the outset, is tested at the precise moment God takes back His word. The words left behind, including the Biblical and Koranic narratives, are in turn tested, "critiqued," in every presentation of Abraham's outing. By giving in to this divine revocation, Abraham gives up—or, better said, nullifies, makes inert, freezes—the one, absolutely active, altogether creative word. Henceforth, each word is at bottom inactive, inert, in vain. From this perspective, Abraham's silence is not a "problem" at all: speaking and acting are mutually exclusive. Instead of speech acts, there is "fear and trembling," and each presentation of Abraham's action, or "passion," in *Fear and Trembling* takes its point of departure from the absolute, unimaginable deactivation of discourse.

Conducting a son up a mountain is no doubt natural for a father, particularly one who is accustomed to pedagogy, and under certain circumstances it is doubtless moral. But the very possibility of calling such conduct either natural or moral depends upon an ability to formulate its principle, the *propositio maxima* on which every scrutiny of this conduct, whether in the form of causal rule or moral law, must begin. Such a beginning is denied the *Stemning*, and for this reason it becomes a presentation in which the very ability to arrive at a maxim for the conduct of conducting, to say nothing of inducing or seducing, undergoes an unprecedented and yet repetitive critique. This critique then presents an ordeal of autonomy to the extent that both the criticized text, a passage from Genesis, and the topic of criticism, Abraham's walk, cease to rest on a law they lay down for themselves. So little can Abraham legislate to himself the conduct he undertakes that he is even barred from bringing this conduct under a maxim, which could be scrutinized according to universalizability, and it is this inability to comprehend the conduct under a maxim that motivates the presentation. The latter takes over at the exact place where the alliance of language to proposition, and in turn the accord between speech and "maximization," no longer hold, although it was this alliance and this accord that underwrote the treaty whose terms are contained in the acknowledgment of incomprehensibility.

This collapse is not unmotivated. On the contrary, it has a powerful motor in the breakdown of promising: the idleness of this speech act sends Abraham off. The son whom he was promised in his and Sarah's old age is now to be destroyed. If all promises are somehow unintelligible, none is more unintelligible, none more incomprehensible, than this one. Hume, a thinker with whom Kierkegaard would have made contact through the medium of Jacobi and Hamann, had undertaken to demonstrate that "a promise is *naturally* something altogether unintelligible, nor is there any act of the mind belonging to it."[33] The natural unintelligibility of the promise consists in the power of language to create something altogether new, namely, an obligation or a debt; and this creational power of language is as unintelligible as that of the traditional God of creation who, not surprisingly, has been invoked as the guarantor of such newly created things in order to give this power of language a ground and thus to make it intelligible.

The principle of autonomy in Kant revokes such a secure guarantor as it discovers in freedom, whose incomprehensibility makes it inviolable, a new guarantee for the power of promises to deliver an obligation every time one is uttered. Kant thus answers Hume by letting the incomprehensibility of freedom underwrite every promise. Freedom alone—not, as Hume thought, a community of the naturally like-minded—can draw obligations altogether outside the domain of nature and deposit them, according to Kant, not in language, nor in writing, least of all in gesticulation, but in the "spontaneity" of propositional, categorial thought. Since, moreover, language is conceived according to the model of the proposition whose meaning consists in the judgment that thought composes, it is no surprise that Kant conceives of broken promises as a certain class of "lies"—propositions, in other words, that do not correspond to an intention (*Vorsatz*).[34] Nothing is therefore more problematic for the principle of autonomy than a promise that is at once irreducible to a false proposition and yet still breakable. Such a promise would present the natural unintelligibility of promising without making the incomprehensible domain of freedom into the ground of its new "creations," its variously specified obligations. This presentation need only shift the position of the negative; instead of natural unintelligibility, it departs from unnatural communicability. And if the "natural" is understood to be the rule-bound and the lawful, the unnatural, far from simply naming the "supernatural," designates that unavoidable moment in promising that escapes maximization and generalization.

Once the promise in its very unnaturalness is shown to be breakable, it motivates the collapse of the hitherto solid alliance of language and judgment expressed in the form of the proposition and articulated in the form of a problem. Repetition alone, however, breaches singularity. The singularity of the situation and repetition of its presentation go hand in hand. Whereas the promise to Abraham of a late-born son is comprehensible because of its unnaturalness, its breach, which threatens to make even the divine word idle and inert, is not merely incomprehensible; it thwarts the very comprehension of incomprehensibility in which freedom as autonomy is supposed to ground itself. If the incomprehensibility of freedom grounds the intelligibility of promising, then the breach of the most well founded promise of all, the breach of the promise made by the being that is supposed to ground itself, destroys the schemata of intelligibility and the concepts of comprehensibility through which meaning is secured. The promise of intelligibility that belongs to every proposition and every problem is in turn undermined, so the alliance of language with propositions—and with already maximized ones at that—comes to an end. The implicit terms of peace, including those of incomprehensibility and "skeptical" unintelligibility, terminate in repetitive presentations of breach after breach until nothing is left of either "natural" or "conventional" language. At such extreme points, presentation after presentation, each of which constitutes a breach of promise and its implicit terms of peace, takes place.

Abraham's Outings

Each presentation brings Abraham's outing—his movements out, up, and down—into view. However, the versions are less modes of seeing an event than modes of critique. For the "event" is textual throughout. Critique consists in presentation after presentation as long as the "content" represented, Abraham's conduct, cannot be described under a rule, a generality, a common saying— in short, a maxim—that could then be criticized according to the criterion of universalizability. This "content" therefore cannot be represented in the strict sense of the word, and such unrepresentability gives rise to a critique composed entirely of presentations. Since every attempt to describe the conduct under a common saying is of no avail, the terms of its testing are from the beginning unavailable. The attempt to do so can then appear only as a temptation.

The breach of promise on which the outing is motivated robs thought of its alliance with an already constituted, hence already "naturalized" language. Without a maxim on which subjectivity can rest its critical activity and therefore its very conception of thought, however, the principle of autonomy itself is scrutinized, tested; having been taken apart, *auto-nomos* undergoes an or-deal in which it departs from its secure foundation. The presentation of Abraham's outing progressively inclines toward the moment of collapse in which all terms of peace, including that of incomprehensibility, are broken for the precise reason that the absolute promise—the promise of grounding itself, the promise of a God *or* a ground laying—is breached. Broached in the *Stemning*, as the critique of a passage from Genesis, is thus the breakdown of generation. The fulfillment of the promise, which occurs in the maturation of the child, is emptied of all significance. At the core of the presentation, therefore, is *infantilism*: "immature" conduct to the extent that the criterion of maturity has been established as the ability to act on maxims articulated into propositions.

Infantilism, as is natural, strikes the infant first, so the first version of the event presents the child's earliest lesson in language, his "growing up." For the upward movement is precisely the promise in its fulfillment. In this version, Abraham comprehends his conduct, but so little is this comprehension capable of communication that Isaac is unable to understand. Incomprehensibility and a corresponding incommunicability determine the terms of movement, and the incommunicable, as a secret Abraham cannot divulge, is located in a very specific break in communication: the breach of promise and therefore, as expected, the destruction of the promised one himself. Once this breach is communicated, all communication, even the most intimate, threatens to collapse, and the incommunicable communicates itself *in a feeling*, indeed the uplifting sensation of terror by virtue of which the child makes himself independent of the father, releases himself from all relations other than those he decrees on his own.

Abraham's conduct thus proves to be the peda-gogical in the most precise sense, conducting the child to the point where he, no longer "dumb," can speak on his own and in so speaking name his own father, his own cause, his own ground. And this speech is all the more mature since he understands his own ground to be *necessarily* incomprehensible. All speech before this point—and Isaac is not bereft of it—is of no significance, for it is still immature and inarticulate. Thus, the ordeal of autonomy at first presents the arduous trial dumbness undergoes as it comes into mature speech: speech, that is, that will proclaim its own roots in incomprehensibility. And since this speech expresses the peculiar passion (*Ledenskab*) Johannes de Silentio calls "faith" (67), the final moment of pedagogy consists in the communication, without transition and thus without comprehension, of a horrible "feeling," that of breaking with all hitherto established natural and legal relations:

> Abraham said to himself, "I will not hide from Isaac where this walk is taking him." He stood still, he laid his hand on Isaac's head in blessing, and Isaac kneeled to receive it. And Abraham's face epitomized fatherliness; his gaze was gentle, his words admonishing. But Isaac could not understand him, his soul could not be lifted. . . . Abraham climbed Mount Moriah, but Isaac did not understand him. Then Abraham turned away for a moment, but when Isaac saw Abraham's face again, it had changed: his gaze was wild, his whole being sheer horror. He seized Isaac by the chest, threw him to the ground, and said, "Dumb boy [*Dumme Dreng*], do you think I am your father? I am an idolater. Do you think it is God's command? No, it is my desire." Then Isaac trembled and cried out in fear: "God in heaven, have mercy on me, God of Abraham, have mercy on me; if I have no father on earth, then you be my father!" (10)

Only in sheer terror can the child lift *himself* up, for absolute terror expresses the dissolution of all relations other than those the child himself proclaims. And the child who makes this self-emancipation proclamation for the first time stands on his own; he is no longer related to his supposed father since the latter, who is himself "lost" once he is no longer "the father of faith," admits his own bareness: " 'It is better that he believes me a monster [an inhuman, *et Umenneske*] than that he should lose faith in you' "

(11). If Isaac *could* lose faith, he was never related to *its* father, and the recognition of this lack of relation, this freedom, rests on the power to decree for himself a new and utterly incomprehensible foundation.

Abraham in turn goes incognito: he absents himself from the presentation under the guise of an "idolater," thereby making room for his son's confession of a faith founded on incomprehension. And freedom, whose incomprehensibility makes every message from father to child equally incomprehensible, presents itself not simply as the ability to create something by oneself—an obligation, a promissory note—but as the power to create and destroy in the same gesture, to bequeath and to breach faith in the same speech act, to make and to break the groundlaying promise in the same inscribing motion. At the pinnacle of the presentation, the principle of autonomy shows its limiting condition: not freedom pure and simple but a linguistic medium in which creation and destruction, resolution and dissolution, making and breaking, are so closely bound to one another as to nullify all extralinguistic, natural, as well as legal relations.

Such nullification, not the father's despair or the son's anxiety, is the "thing" presented in the presentation of the event. If every word participates in creation and destruction at the same time by virtue of its linguistic medium, nothing spoken can even hope to confirm an obligation, offer consolation, maintain a relation. So Abraham is struck dumb. His infantilism does not, however, look forward to the emergence of articulate discourse but on the contrary commemorates the nullification of every relation other than those created and at the same time destroyed in the medium of language. Every movement down the mountain will thereafter explicate the character of this medium. The second version of the event does not, like the first, leave out this movement downward. On the contrary, it presents Abraham's muteness on the way up and his blindness on the way down. This muteness does not indicate that Abraham has regressed to an "earlier" stage of development, before he has integrated himself into the laws of language ruled by the conception of language as "the universal" (60); rather, he articulates the breakdown of the ability of rule-bound language to express the up-and-down movement in which his "passion" is tested: "They rode along the road in silence, and Abraham stared continuously and fixedly at the ground until the fourth day, when he looked up and saw Mount Moriah far away, but once again he turned his eyes toward the ground. Silently he arranged the firewood and bound Isaac; silently he drew the knife" (12).

No longer is Abraham given to understand what he is to do, and he even ceases to speak with his son. Comprehension and incomprehensibility are inapplicable terms for the presentation of Abraham as he, with eyes cast down, absents himself from the language in which various "views" of the same thing are represented. For the ability to comprehend consists in the power to discover the rules that govern those relations whose nullification marks the pinnacle of the presentation. On the way downward these terms are no longer of service. Instead of incomprehensibility there is *unforgettability*, and instead of comprehension there is *command*—a command, moreover, that Abraham can as little issue on his own as he can beget Isaac alone. And this impossibility makes it both unspoken and unforgettable. Whereas comprehension and the incomprehensible exclude each other, unforgettability so little precludes forgetting that an act of forgetting is itself the unforgettable: such an act takes place when Abraham no longer remembers his relation to Isaac, and its linguistic medium is called, and recalled as, command: "From that day henceforth, Abraham was old; he could not forget that God had commanded him to do this. Isaac flourished as before, but Abraham's eyes were darkened, and he saw joy no more" (12). *Aging* occurs at the precise moment everything appears in remembrance, especially for one who was once promised a new youthfulness. Thus, the absolute end to infantilism—not simply the end to childhood, or even the end of every relation to generation and regeneration, but above all, an endless absorption into the language as a *medium*—takes place when the ability to forget is itself lost.

Yet the second version of the event does not altogether convert issues of comprehension and incomprehensibility into those of forgetting and unforgettability. The very ability to understand the unforgettable *as a command* implicates the presentation in comprehension and incomprehensibility. For the command is not the linguistic medium itself but only a certain modality of speech. To the extent that the ordeal Abraham undergoes is shown to be grounded in a command, its presentation cannot do without the inexhaustible terminology of comprehension. Once the point of the departure for the entire ordeal is no longer presented as a command, the very terms "comprehension" and "incomprehensibility" are progressively absorbed into ever newly posed relations of forgetting to the unforgettable. Such an alteration should not be understood as the replacement of "conceptual" operations for "psychological" processes since it is not at all certain that forgetting is a matter of psychology; the forgetting on which the presentation turns has nothing to do with the phenomenon of "losing track of a train of thought." Abraham still "remembers" his relation to Isaac as he conducts him upwards, yet this relation has been forgotten. For reference to Isaac, as the linguistic mode of this relation and the medium of remembrance, proves impossible. Abraham attempts to refer to Isaac by means of certain superlatives—"the best," "the most loved"—but even the uniqueness of the superlative case does not sufficiently single Isaac out. For this reason, superlative after superlative has to be invoked, each new one denying the singularity claimed by the previous one. The superlatives do not single Isaac out but only signal how the referential relation, the relation that singles language out, has been suspended.

Abraham, in turn, no longer speaks with anyone who could claim a superlative status, least of all with God. The ordeal of autonomy comes to reside in an exposure to an unsuperlative other who is bound up with self-critique, and self-critique soon presents itself as incessant "thought":

> And Abraham rode thoughtfully down the road; he thought of Hagar and the son, whom he drove out into the desert. He climbed Mount Moriah, he drew the knife.
>
> It was a quiet evening when Abraham rode out alone, and he rode to

Mount Moriah; he threw himself down on his face, he prayed God to forgive him his sin, that he had been willing to sacrifice Isaac, that the father had forgotten his duty to his son. He often rode his lonesome road, but he found no peace. He could not comprehend that it was a sin that he had been willing to sacrifice to God the best that he had, the possession for which he himself would have gladly died many times; and if it was a sin, if he had not loved Isaac in this manner, he could not understand that it could be forgiven, for what sin was more terrible? (13)

It hardly suffices to say that Abraham cannot grasp the maxim of his conduct. His conduct takes place "before" any maxim could have been formed, and therefore it appears under the rubric of sacrifice: a "sacrifice" that immediately crosses itself out since nothing could have been gained. For this reason, Abraham's conduct does not constitute an exchange but an or-deal. His self-critique is endless, since there is no substantial self to subject to critique. Critique cannot arrive at a foundation for his conduct precisely because it cannot even bring this conduct into propositional terms or view it as a problem, and this impossibility finds its expression in the *repetition* of the "same" conduct now emptied of the "content" that would let one judge it to be the "same": no one is conducted; only the conducting "itself" takes place.

Having driven out his first son, Abraham drives out his second; having driven out his second, he drives out on his own. He then drives *himself* out, and the presentation of this drive is seen as endless self-critique in which the "self" under scrutiny is driven out and becomes in turn a void. Repetition is so little opposed to the unrepeatable, the singular, that the unrepeatable *alone* undergoes repetition. In repetition, the identity and indeed the ideality of the "thought" with which the critic shudders (9) is enabled and disabled at the same time.[35] The impurity of repetition then plays itself out as the constant concern with impurity, with "sin." The repetition of the unrepeatable as the repeated presentation of what again and again escapes the power of the self to conceive characterizes the medium in which worried thought erupts: the medium, that is, in which selfhood itself is "tested." In this medium, movement is not undertaken on its own; on the contrary, motion, which alters only in its presentation of the other, takes place when the conduct of the self undergoes an "emotion"—call it regret, remorse, repentance, or repetition "itself"—over which it has no control. Whereas Abraham once conduced Isaac, he again and again conducts *and loses* himself in such remonstrative "emotion."

The first version of the presentation left Isaac uplifted on the basis of decreeing a new "father" as a newly disclosed, although still incomprehensible foundation. When this version repeats itself and he comes down, it is as repetition "itself." No longer is there the slightest indication that the ordeal is based on a divine command. The critique of the biblical text has reached a point where the very concept of command has been absorbed into that of repetition. For a command is comprehensible as a command only to the extent that it can be *followed*, and that means: repeated. Conduct occurs in the train of repetition. The other to which the conductor is exposed as he both pulls and is pulled apart is none other than the one conducted, namely, Isaac, who "is" repetition "itself." When Abraham receives Isaac back, he learns the ways of repetition *because Isaac "is" repetition*. Abraham's familiarity with repetition does not thus consist in a familial relation with Isaac but in its nullification. And this nullification is the "content" of repetition "itself," the event that occupies Isaac and that Isaac therefore cannot forget. Not, however, because it is incomprehensible nor because it is comprehensible but because it is presentable and absentable in turns:

> They rode along in harmony, Abraham and Isaac, until they came to Mount Moriah. Abraham made everything ready for the sacrifice, calmly and gently, but when he turned away and drew the knife, Isaac saw that Abraham's left hand was clenched in despair, that a shudder went through his body—but Abraham drew the knife.
>
> Then they returned home again, and Sarah hurried to meet them, but Isaac had lost faith. Not a word is ever said of this in the world, and Isaac never talked to anyone about what he had seen, and Abraham was unaware that anyone had seen it. (14)

Abraham's gesture articulates an ordeal in which he is not only torn apart but also, and without his awareness, imparts this apartness from himself to the one who understands his gesture. So little does this understanding show father and son to be of like mind, despite their remarkable "harmony," that it disposes of the very thesis of universal like-mindedness toward whose basis comprehension and incomprehensibility are both oriented. By being torn apart, Abraham imparts his apartness from himself to his son, who is likewise torn apart but, unlike his father, cannot impart this being torn apart to anyone else. The or-deal im-parts, in short—without judgment, without *Urteil*, without the decision one would have expected from an ordeal. Least of all does Isaac carry out a judgment on, or sever himself from, his father. Although he cannot impart his own apartness to anyone else, he nevertheless communicates this apartness with a gesture, perhaps even an original writing, which does not present itself as a gesture or a writing, or even a language—the gesture, namely, of "losing faith": losing the faith of the father who in his ordeal becomes the father of faith; losing, therefore, the father in the breach of natural piety that broaches piety *simpliciter*; losing the faith of the father because the father has proved to be without faith and therefore not a father at all; losing the faith and the father, which are indistinguishable, without, moreover, decreeing a new father and thus fathering a new faith; losing both past and future when father and faith are gone; losing oneself, in sum, to such an extent that one is just this "loss" of self, this ever-present nonentity, this repetition of "now-point" after "now-point" without continuity, without anteriority, and without posterity.

Since, finally, Abraham is defined as the father of faith, this "loss" is not even possible. The loss is a loss so impossible that it *has to be forgotten*: there was never any faith to lose; there was never *anything* to lose. Forgetting unforgettability—not comprehending incomprehensibility—designates the mode of access to the "thought" of repetition, and it makes sure that it is a closed one at that. The "loss" of faith leaves Isaac on his own, closed up "in himself," but such "ownness" constitutes the demonic, ghostly otherness to which Abraham is exposed in his "own" house *without the slightest awareness.* Otherness of this character is altogether unfamiliar, yet it is precisely not divine; it is far closer to the inhuman—a monster, *et Umenneske*—whose role Abraham assumed when in the first version he had denied all familiarity with Isaac.

The monster is no longer a role presented on stage; the presentation is, rather, articulated in the monster itself. Not, however, because the inhuman, like an angel, whispers some message to a subject. Its muteness consists in gesture and articulation, the "writing" of an impossible loss. Nothing can be represented; only a presentation of the void of communication takes place. Isaac is exposed to the self-division imparted to Abraham through his ordeal, and this exposure makes his ordeal double: he cannot communicate his ordeal because the ordeal is not even understood to be *his.* Likewise, the secret he keeps is not *his* to keep; in sum, nothing he says *cannot* speak of the ordeal because every word he speaks or suppresses, and especially suppresses, marks the double self-division to which he is at every instant exposed. If "every language calls you [Abraham] to mind" (23), then all the more so for the language of the last Isaac: a language of neither "childhood" nor "maturity" but endlessly repetitive pre- and after-lives, nowpoint after now-point.

By avoiding the communication of an ordeal that he could not communicate, he communicates *another* ordeal, or the ordeal of the altogether other, in his very avoidance. That no one imparts this communication is of no significance. For the Isaac of the last version makes the singular law of communication his own, as he loses his selfhood, his ownness, and his home to this law. A singular law, however, is as little a law as an altogether emptied promise— and Isaac is this too—is a still promise. Isaac in turn is never himself but again and again another, an "un-human" whose infantilism does not lead to greater maturity and more controlled articulation but without the slightest lead, conductorless, repeats its impossible loss over and over until the age-old, ghostly infant is, insofar as it exists at all, just this singularity, this loss *of* repetition. Not a divine voice, even less a command from on high, but this loss—

without corresponding gain, without response or correspondence altogether—sets the ordeal of autonomy into motion.[36]

Allegory, Meaning, "Weaning"

Isaac loses his particularity and comes to stand for a concept. Such is the simplest recipe for allegory. Isaac could then "personify" repetition. But not only must "personify" seek refuge in quotation marks; so too must every word of this "recipe." For nothing like "particularity" over against "conceptuality" survives the "allegory" in which Isaac "loses" his "particularity," not only because "repetition" thwarts the constitutive continuity of "personification" but above all because the concept of "repetition," like that of "anxiety," cannot be represented according to a rule and therefore cannot stand for a concept. And yet all these "not"s do not add up to a determination, destination, or even definition that could do without quotation marks.[37] Quotation marks themselves cannot withstand the temptation to present Isaac in terms of allegory; this temptation is so strong that it dominates the predominant, although by no means unchallenged interpretation of his birth and his binding.

In the only reference to "allegory" in the biblical Testaments, both "old" and "new," Paul of Tarsus relates the "old" to the "new" and thus the "promise" of the latter to reveal the meaning of the former by means of this word. From his letter to the Galatians, the "allegorical" interpretation of Isaac, and not only Isaac, receives its impetus:

> Tell me, if you want to be under the law, do you not understand the law [*tōn nomōn ouk akouetē*]? For it is written that Abraham had two sons, one from the slave woman and one from the free woman. But the one from the slave woman was born according to flesh, while the one from the free woman through the promise [*di epangēlias*]. These things are allegorical [*allēgoroumena*]. For these [things, women; *autai*] are two covenants; one from Mount Sinai, giving birth into slavery—this is Hagar. Now Hagar is Mount Sinai in Arabia, but she also stands for the present Jerusalem, for she lives in slavery together with her children. But the Jerusalem above is free; this is our mother.[38]

To be free, then, is to be Isaac, born of Sarah. For Isaac's birth takes place in the logos, as promised, not in the bonds of mute physicality. Every language may perhaps, as Johannes de Silentio states in *Fear and Trembling*, call *Abraham* to mind (23), but every *free* language, every language of freedom, would recall the one to whom the birth of freedom is promised, namely Sarah, who becomes "our"—allegorical—"mother." To the extent that one speaks freely and speaks of freedom, to the extent that "our" language is related to liberation, the speaker "is" Isaac and owes the faculty of speaking to Sarah, "our mother." The only *nomos* to which speech then addresses itself is a freely given one, and no speech can demonstrate its freedom more than one that means something other than—and in the end, the nullity of—what it represents.

Isaac, born of Sarah, means freedom. The representation of Isaac means something other than it says: it speaks otherwise, *allō agoreuein*, and therefore communicates "indirectly." The "indirectness" of the communication arises from the incomprehension of those who, living in a "worldly" Jerusalem, claim to be descended from Sarah but are allegorically born of Hagar. Only those born of the free woman, "our mother," would comprehend communication if a birth into freedom were itself comprehensible; otherwise, "indirect" communication would not communicate something indirectly but would communicate a void that owed its origin to the avoidance of communication, not to any intention to communicate clandestinely. The void of communication leaves no room for comprehension or incomprehensibility. And such is the case with the very term through which Paul represents Isaac and his, or "our," mother—namely, "allegory." As a *hapax legomenon*, it defies comprehension as fiercely as the singular outing of Abraham, and it defies incomprehensibility to the extent that it, like Abraham's outing, sets the stage for an endless series of presentations.

In his *Epistolam ad Galatas*, Johannes Chrysostom thus declares this one-time word to breach the terms of comprehension and incomprehensibility; it constitutes, according to John "Golden Mouth," a case of catachresis.[39] Catachrestic allegory, however, is "allegory," a word that is not only *kata chrēsin* (against usage) but against any *common* usage, including the common usage of "direct" communication. It can then become an "uncommon" term: an aberration on the one hand or a *terminus technicus* on the other. From this either-or of "uncommon" usage arises the criterion of autonomous philosophical discourse, a discourse that neither serves theological purposes nor abandons itself to rhetorical aberration. The autonomy of philosophical discourse, which makes possible a discourse of autonomy, owes its origin to an interruption of "common" usage, and this interruption makes the inception of philosophy into a free and therefore incomprehensible "origin."[40] Each of its terms is born in freedom, conceived by "our mother," Sarah. Philosophy thus speaks the language that "we," each of "us" being one more Isaac, have learned to speak. Speaking of an autonomous philosophical discourse is, as a result, speaking of its allegorical origin and speaking "indirectly"—in quotation marks, through citations of direct speech—its mother tongue.

Contestations of the very idea of an autonomous philosophical discourse, which began in earnest with Hamann's response to Kant,[41] try to show the origin of this idea in a language over which philosophy has no control and from which it cannot be freed. Attacking the establishment of an all-encompassing but entirely abstract "encyclopedia of philosophy" is one attempt to do so. Testing the range and applicability of philosophical discourse according to the standards of the natural, the everyday, and the ordinary is another such attempt. Testing the autonomy of rationality according to the standard of unenforced reconciliation between the *ratio* and its other is still another attempt. Common to each of these critiques of the idea of autonomy and autonomous philosophical discourse is the conception of incomprehensibility, which can go by the arbitrary name "Isaac" and which, because of its ordinariness or its extraordinariness, escapes the terms of philosophical discourse and the determination of philosophy to comprehend everything. *Fear and Trembling* could easily be enlisted into each of these critiques. But it *also* undermines their effectiveness insofar as its presentations of Isaac progressively break down the dialectic of comprehension and incomprehensibility with which every one of them operates.

If comprehension and incomprehensibility still determine in part each version of Abraham's outing, the same cannot be said of the *subscriptiones* against which all the versions have to be set. These subtexts function as names for the various versions of the ordeal and by thus marking them, make them into allegories of their own incomprehensibility: allegories, therefore, that suspend the dialectic of comprehension and incomprehensibility with which each version begins and to which each remains in part indebted. Not without reason, then, do the subtexts speak of an original breach, an ur-parting—the departure, that is, of a child from its mother's breast, the departure of mouth from its first source of nourishment, a departure that makes possible all "mature," articulate, and "cultured" uses of the mouth, including that of speaking and whispering. The *subscriptiones* do not pose the question of the meaning of "weaning" as long as meaning owes its origin to a dialectic in which incomprehensibility grounds and guarantees comprehensibility. A graphic separation from this dialectic—graphic by virtue of the setting of the presentations into print—makes "weaning" into a name for whatever separates itself and thereby escapes, at least in part, from the meaning captured, lost, and recovered in the dialectic of comprehension and incomprehensibility.

Whereas the name of the father—it is always Abraham—is spoken, that of the mother is not. Nowhere are the mothers who appear in the various *subscriptiones* identified with Sarah, Hagar, or any other woman. Yet the anonymity of these mothers cannot be attributed solely to their total absorption into the function of which they are the allegorical representatives. Arbitrarily superimposed, or subimposed, onto the various versions of Abraham's outing, the subtexts are themselves names for their texts, names that do not make sense of these texts or secure their senselessness but suspend the dialectic of sense and senselessness already presented in the texts themselves. The "origin" of this allegorical naming, this allegory of allegoresis, its "mother," goes without a name, but the mothers represented in these allegories are not for

this reason allegorical figures of origination. They—and the plural
is important—do not mean something other than they represent,
without, however, meaning precisely what they present. The meaning of these mothers escapes such a disjunctive judgment to the
extent that any judgment on their meaning already presupposes the
unavoidable or-deal they undergo: the or-deal of imparting the
apartness, or the void, from which subjectivity, whose principal
function is judgment (*Urteil*), originates. This "void," as an apartness to which communication no less than judgment is indebted,
becomes the "matter" of each *subscriptio*.

Whereas the first presentation of Abraham's outing has him alter
himself into another—into the other of humanity, into "the inhuman"—the first of the *subscriptiones* leaves the mother, in the
eyes of the child, unaltered, even as she alters herself. Under no
condition, therefore, can the mother *represent* father Abraham; on
the contrary, her unaltered identity, from the perspective of infantile eyes, undermines the function of representation, which would
otherwise have secured its roots in the constancy of unaltered
identity. The anonymous mother therefore means something other
than father Abraham, whom she apparently "represents," a father
who for his part represents himself as other than he is and in the
end nullifies himself. She *would* represent this very nullification of
himself if representation did not collapse with the nullification of
self-presence. The mother does not represent the absence of the
father. She does not mean the lack of what she represents. "Weaning" runs counter to meaning; it is the separation of meaning from
the terms of its comprehension, representation, and nullification.
Such an allegory of traditional allegorical representation, which
is no longer allegory and no longer communicates "indirectly,"
makes the first of the subtexts into a superscript, a name or a title,
for every text in its train: "When the child is to be weaned, the
mother blackens her breast. It would be hard to have the breast
look inviting when the child must not have it. So the child believes
[*troer*] that the breast has changed, but the mother—she is still the
same, her gaze is tender and loving as ever. How fortunate the one
who did not need more terrible means to wean the child!" (11).

The child "believes" not so much that the breast has changed—it has indeed changed—but that the mother remains the same, that her identity persists, no matter how her parts appear. The or-deal of autonomy, its imparting, is made less "terrible" as long as the mother elides herself in part. The "faith" in identity may thus mitigate the "terror" of autonomy, but its own unmitigated arbitrariness is proclaimed in the *maxim* on which this, and every other, *subscriptio* concludes: "How fortunate!" The arbitrariness of the "means" to which "faith" owes its existence, "indirect" communication at its origin, no doubt constitutes a retrieval of incomprehensibility, but the fortune expressed in the maxim "How fortunate!" does not simply defy comprehension; it suspends the dialectic of incomprehension and incomprehensibility to the extent that "How fortunate!" bespeaks the fortune of being able to speak *simpliciter*, although the speech *itself* is never simple: it always involves the complication of comprehension and incomprehensibility, one grounding the other. The fortune of "How fortunate!" is, by contrast, not a ground, foundation, cause: it is, if anything, an *occasion*, a voiding of necessity in favor of the random and the utterly fortuitous. All of the subsequent *subscriptiones* make the various "images" that loom above them incomprehensible according to the terms of their own incomprehensibility, and they do so by drawing first *identity*, then *existence*, then *grief*, and lastly *death* into maxims that are of no practical, theoretical, or even "existential" meaning. Nothing fortunate is ever spiritual.

The ordeal of autonomy is "weaning." But "weaning" does not mean something other than it represents: it does not mean "autonomy." For the child who is to be weaned in each of the *subscriptiones*, regardless of whether the child is seen to represent Abraham or Isaac, is to be weaned *away from* autonomy. The meaning of "weaning" cannot be separated from the generation of meaning— and comprehension and representation—in substitution. "Weaning," as ur-substitution as well as ur-separation, generates meaning as long as one substance is substituted for another, and each one can be interpreted as a substitute or representative. However, if "weaning" does not succeed in substituting one substance for another, nothing becomes meaningful, not even the nullity of meaning represented in allegory. The possibility that substitution fails finds its suppressed expression in every invocation of "How fortunate!" but this very failure only makes itself legible in the last of the *subscriptiones*, the *subscriptio* that serves as the subterranean attack on Isaac's—and not only Isaac's—martyred silence: "When the child is to be weaned, the mother has stronger food at hand so that the child does not die. How fortunate the one who has this stronger food at hand" (14, italics added).

How poorly does the word "fortune" fit this maxim, for not only is the image of the mother with food at her hand, not at her breast, a categorial declaration that allows for neither choice nor fate, nor even fortune in its customary sense. The loss of all "stronger food" would not result in an unhappy child, or a happy one, but the one delivered over to its "eternal happiness" or its eternal unhappiness, neither of which is a matter of happiness at all. "Stronger food" may replace some other food, but it is not a substitute for another substance; indeed, no substitution of one substance for another takes place. Such is the "deal," a deal—or gift of fortune—without decisive points of division and therefore without the possibility of an ordeal. Food is food. The terms "stronger" and "weaker" are relative to the same substance, the same indifferent, undifferentiated stuff. "Stronger food" thus marks the space of a banality, a linguistic null-point, not a point of incomprehensibility, meaninglessness, or unrepresentability, where words cannot even mean the nullity of what they represent. For they "are" the nullity. The communication of the last maxim could not as a result be more "direct": "How fortunate the one who has stronger food at hand." The directness of this communication does not give any directions, least of all for meaning or weaning. Out of the breach of the divine promise, which makes all words idle and inert, there arises this maxim; it communicates nothing other than a banality, a banality so extreme that no voice in the text will claim it as its own. For perhaps nothing is more certain in *Fear and Trembling* than that neither "we," Johannes de Silentio, nor "the man of whom we speak" (14) interject this banality into the tragic presentation of an Abraham and an Isaac who are at decisive moments struck dumb.

§ 5 Notifying the Authorities:
A Literary Review

> Up until now I have made myself useful by helping
> the pseudonyms become authors. What if I de-
> cided from now on to do the little writing I can ex-
> cuse in the form of criticism? Then I would put
> down what I had to say in reviews, developing my
> ideas from some book or other and in such a way
> that they could be included in the work itself. In
> this way I would still avoid becoming an author.
>
> —Kierkegaard, a note to himself

Fortune

Kierkegaard's reviews of literary works take their point of departure from the concept of fortune. A fortuitous and by no means
calculable dispensation from "the Muses," or from some other
spirit, gives literary "works" their worklike character. The critical
review of Johan Ludvig Heiberg's transcription of Scribe's *First Love*
that makes its way into the first part of *Either/Or* sets out the rules
for such dispensations: fortune knows no rules, or to use the term
in which the review casts the dispensation of literary fortune, the
rules of fortune are those of "the occasion," and the oc-casion, since
it simultaneously gives and denies grounding, nullifies every rule.
From the concept of the occasion, moreover, the contradictory—
and therefore inconceivable—character of anxiety, faith, and even
the prodigious paradox of the Parousia presents itself: "It has
pleased the gods to link together the greatest contradictions in this
way. This is a secret implicit in actuality—an offense to the Jews
and foolishness to the Greeks. The occasion is always the accidental, and the prodigious paradox is that the accidental is absolutely
just as necessary as the necessary."[1] The necessity of contingency,
which gives rise to fortune and constitutes the secret of "actuality,"
makes itself known in specifically literary works precisely because

literary works are of no significance unless they are occasional, and that means: unless their "actuality" implies a *secret,* which by definition cannot be communicated but cannot nevertheless *not* be communicated. The necessity of communicating whatever cannot be communicated makes every communication of this necessity into an accident, into an occasion, into the noncausal, abyssal ground of any work that presents itself as literary: "The occasion, therefore, is of the greatest significance for every literary work."[2]

Literary works, however, do not exhaust the significance of the occasion. Not only does the contradictory character of the occasion make it into a representative of everything that communicates in a contradiction, including the "sign of a contradiction" upon which Kierkegaard "exercises" his exegetical ability in *Training in Christianity,*[3] but the occasion also, and to a greater degree, determines the terms in which reading itself takes place. Without a recognition of the significance of the occasion, the review of literary works is impossible since the reviewer has no other task than an immersion in the occasions for reviewing, that is, in the works under review: "The disregard of the significance of occasion has had the result that reviews have generally been so bungled, have been such downright hackwork. In the world of criticism, the occasion acquires a heightened significance."[4] Raising the significance of the occasion above its significance for the literary work, which is already decisive, cannot escape the risk of opening up a void in the very concept of significance, a void, however, that "the world of criticism" cannot avoid. For—and here is the distinguishing characteristic of the reading that takes place in the space of a review—a review has nothing to say *about* its "object" since the actual significance of that "object" lies in the secrecy of its occasion. Without being able to speak of something and nevertheless unable to make something of itself, a reading of literary works has no choice but to expose the void of communication without, however, being able to fill this void, to give off the illusion, common among literary *works,* that something has been *done* about the unavoidable void of communication.

"The world of criticism" does not name a world of its own but only a void to which reading refers—and fails to refer insofar as it "is" this void. For this reason, a literary review does not concern itself simply with the work under review but also with the very status of occasional language and occasional communication. Since, however, the word "occasional" in the phrases "occasional language" and "occasional communication" names the "negativity"— the unruliness, groundlessness, and vacuity—of language and communication, literary reviews take as their common concern the status of language and communication pure and simple: language and communication insofar as they cannot be pure and simple but must always be occasional and therefore *historical,* or to use another term, *effective in their very vacuity.* The status of historical language and effective communication are to this extent the unavoidable, although empty, topic of a literary review that neither gives in to mere paraphrase nor claims for itself the status of a new literary work.

The latitude of "the world of criticism" is measured according to two extremes of literary productivity: the generalization of the occasion on the one hand and its outright denial on the other. The first extreme expresses itself in trivial interruption: "Any literary productivity in the category of triviality—and, worse luck, this kind of productivity is most of all the order of the day—overlooks the occasion just as much as it overlooks inspiration. . . . Therefore, it completely overlooks the significance of the occasion—that is, it sees an occasion in everything. It is like a talkative person [*snaksomt Menneske*] who in the most opposite things sees an occasion to bring up himself and history, whether one has heard it before or not."[5] The other extreme expresses itself in an uninterruptible flow: "Those who do not even suggest the necessity of an occasion may be regarded as less conceited but more demented. Without looking to the right or the left, they spin out indefatigably the thin thread of their babbling [*Passiars*], and they produce the same effect on life with their chatter [*Snak*] and their writings as the mill in a fairy tale, of which it says: And while all this was happening, the mill went klip klap, klip klap."[6]

Overlooking the significance of the occasion, which arises from a vision that sees occasions everywhere, produces "talkativeness," whereas overlooking the occasion altogether produces the incidental "babbling" of a machine. Looking over, or surveying, the significance of the occasion for the literary work, by contrast, constitutes the task of the reviewer, but the execution of this task does not protect the reviewer from "talkativeness" or "babbling." On the contrary: since the significance of the occasion lies in its insignificance, its retreat from the generalities and rules upon which meaning depends, the reviewer can only hurl himself into the extremities of "the world of criticism" and by doing so, *interrupt* his own discourse and *continue on* without the slightest regard for his own interruption. Such is the course of Kierkegaard's review of Heiberg's transcription of Scribe's *First Love* as it breaks off the "introduction" in order to begin its "survey," which, however, also serves as an "introduction" to the play:

> Very fortunately, it so happens that I have already said what I wanted to say, for the more I deliberate on this matter, the more I am convinced that there is nothing in general to be said about it, because there is no occasion in general. If so, then I have come just about as far as I was when I began. The reader must not be angry with me—it is not my fault; it is the occasion's. He might perhaps think that I ought to have thought the whole thing through before I started to write, and then I ought not to have begun to say something that later turned out to be nothing. Nevertheless, I do believe that he ought to give my method its due, insofar as he has convinced himself in a more satisfying manner that the occasion in general is something that is nothing. Later on, he perhaps will come to think about this again when he has convinced himself that there is something else in the world about which one can say much under the impression that it is something, and yet it is of such a character that, once it is said, it turns out to be nothing. What is said here, then, must be regarded as a superfluity, like a superfluous title page that is not included when the world is bound. Therefore, I know no other way to conclude than in the incomparable laconic manner in which I see that Professor Poul Møller concludes the introduction of his excellent review of *Extremerne* [Thomasine Gyllembourg's novella *Extremes*]: With this the introduction is concluded.[7]

The occasion of the literary review is the literary work, but the literary work is itself occasional, so the significance of the occasion for the literary review lies in its out-occasioning occasionality itself: it drives toward the extremes of the occasion, to its generalization and its denial, to "talkativeness" and "babbling," to language no longer elaborated into a "work" but language languishing in its own void—in the absence of work, in idleness, in all those varied traits of the "aesthetic" that make up and mark out the section of *Either/Or* devoted to committed indecisiveness. Each time an occasion gives rise to speech and each time one speaks of an occasion—and this exhausts the possibilities of language to the point of languishing in its own impossibility—the speech turns out to have nothing to say. "The world of criticism" has its home in this "nothing" and for this reason cannot avoid speaking of its own constitutive void. After Kierkegaard had given up his "authorship," each work of which tried to guard itself from this void by projecting pseudonym after pseudonym, he once again throws himself into a lengthy literary review, the inescapable topic of which turns out to be "talkativeness" itself.

Occasions for *A Literary Review*

Having given up his "authorship," Kierkegaard could nevertheless write—as a reviewer. Such writing after "authorship" cannot help but refer itself to an occasion, more specifically to the good fortune of finding a new work published by the author of "A Story of Everyday Life." The occasion for the renewal of writing after the possibilities of "authorship" had been extinguished and the "secret" of this "authorship" was out—Kierkegaard, namely, was the author—is the possibility of writing, once again, papers "from one still living": living, that is, after the death of the "authorship," living out, therefore, the death that was before only a figure of speech. After the death of the "authorship," Kierkegaard can live in the space of the literary review and re-view himself *becoming a dead author*: "Fortunately, my reference to 'A Story of Everyday Life' is to me"—"me" here denotes the one who can finally sign the name Søren Kierkegaard as he had done "against his will" on the title pages of *Papers of One Still Living*—"Fortunately, my reference to 'A Story of Everyday Life' is to me not a detestable occasion for a reviewer's officious importance in directing attention, superimposing viewpoints, demonstrating the necessity of the development, showing how the author at this particular point had to be a dramatist, here a natural scientist, etc. but for me is a choice occasion for a happy repetition of a beautiful recollection."[8]

A Literary Review thus owes its origin to an occasion in which repetition and recollection are no longer opposed to each other but on the contrary are superimposed one onto the other. The repetition of *Papers from One Still Living*, as the papers from one still living after the "life-views" of the "authorship" have played themselves out, does not simply recollect Kierkegaard's favorable presentation of Thomasine Gyllembourg, author of "The Story of Everyday Life," for it constitutes the repetition of a recollection that had already taken place in *Papers* and thus empties the recollection of its putative "content." The repetition of the recollection erases the very pastness of the "things" recollected, so the literary review occupies a strange temporal position: neither in the past nor the present, but perhaps reserved for a future of repetition. The occasion of the review consists, then, in the fortuitous possibility of reading not only Thomasine Gyllembourg but also rereading himself before he became an author. Nothing could be more fortuitous for one who wished to relinquish the very idea of "autonomous" authorship. Bound to the language of Heiberg's mother, who is doubtless also Heiberg's "first love," Kierkegaard, who never once writes of his mother, can concede his inability to speak on his own and at the same time read the words he wrote before he dared declare himself a mature, self-legislating author. The occasion of the review, as the repetition of a recollection, gives Kierkegaard a future insofar as this future consists in a past Kierkegaard could never otherwise retrieve: a past without pastness, a past without content, a past as occasion—not cause, not ground, not even expression—for the future.

But the occasion for the review, which is in fact a re-viewing of the review, does not simply consist in the repetition of a recollection. The occasion is also *not* "a detestable" one, an occasion for "superimposing one's views" and for taking these views from observations of the author's *life*. This "indirect" occasion cannot be ignored if the occasion for *A Literary Review* and its own occasional character is to be delineated in detail. At its limit, the "indirect" occasion, as an occasion to shy away from every other occasion, is always a *scandal*: not simply a stumbling block to understanding but also, and especially in literary affairs, a stumbling block to an understanding that, once revealed, makes a work altogether comprehensible as a representation of the author's secret "lived" experience. Reference to "lived" experience is of a piece with every literary *skandalon*, and very specific references to Kierkegaard's "lived" experience in a literary review of his pseudonymous writings constitute an "indirect" occasion for *A Literary Review*, an occasion that Kierkegaard does not mention by name but that for this very reason gives rise to the specific way he re-views his *Papers* and sees again the "life-view" of Thomasine Gyllembourg's anonymous literary production.

This other occasion is an anonymously published review by P. L. Møller that accuses Kierkegaard of the same failure that Kierkegaard had diagnosed in Hans Christian Andersen, namely, that he had failed to attain a "life-view" and was therefore condemned to interrupt his literary work with references to "lived" experience—in short, that he had a tendency to chatter: " 'Yes, that's just it,' said another. 'What I have against all these books [*Either/Or, Stages on Life's Way*] . . . is that every time one feels able to surrender to pure literary enjoyment the author gets in the way with his own personal ethical and religious development, which no one actually is asking about, which privately may be very respectable but does not have the mark of detachment of the Langelinie [the Long-line, a promenade along the Copenhagen harbor] of objective literature; he [Kierkegaard] commits the same error for which the poet Andersen had been taken to task, for exposing his whole inner [and, one might add, newer] development to the public eye.' "[9]

But P. L. Møller does not simply denounce Kierkegaard's pro-
clivity for prolix treatises, especially those written in the guise of an
overtalkative and unpersuasive Father Taciturnus, nor does he
simply seek out the root of this talkativeness in his tendency to
interrupt his literary writings with references to "his own personal
ethical and religious development": he even refers to one very
specific "lived" experience that serves as the crucible of Kierkegaard's life, if not his "life-view." This one "lived" experience
constitutes the very experience of experimentation: an experience
in which Kierkegaard doubtless experiments on himself—such are
his "autopsies"—but also on other, and this time *live*, bodies:

> If you regard life as a dissecting laboratory and oneself as a cadaver,
> then go ahead and lacerate yourself as much as you want to; as long as
> you do not harm anyone else, the police will not disturb your activity.
> But to spin another creature into your spider web, dissect it alive or
> torture the soul out of it drop by drop by means of experimentation—
> that is not allowed, except with insects, and is there not something
> horrible and revolting to the healthy human mind even in this idea?[10]

Since Kierkegaard does not practice reflective autopsy entirely
on himself, an appeal to the authorities is warranted: the innocent
should be protected from his "experiments." Such an appeal calls
for a judgment to be made on Kierkegaard: "Guilty–Not guilty."
And this judgment is, quite clearly, literary as well as civil. Without
such a judgment, a review would lose its critical character. Since,
however, this judgment is *both* literary and civil, since therefore the
disjunction either-or is suspended under a both-and, critique does
not simply consist in aesthetic evaluation; it is eminently "political." It calls for the police to protect the city from those who
perform "horrible" experiments on its citizens. Kierkegaard then
takes the "political" character of this critique to heart, for he turns
the always prolix Father Taciturnus, pseudonymous editor of the
last section of *Stages on Life's Way*, into a "literary policeman" who
makes out a report on a literary "police action."[11] The report,
however, is also an appeal to the anonymous literary reviewers of
The Corsair to exercise their putative "irony" on him. "The Dialec-

tical Result of a Literary Police Action," signed by Father Tac- iturnus, makes self-abuse into the "dialectical" solution to the problem posed by the "prostituted" publications like that of *The Corsair*: "I cannot do more for others than to request to be abused myself. . . . I say for my whole life, or at least for a long time—until *The Corsair* is ruined by the dialectic of one person's order to be abused."[12] This appeal to self-abuse constitutes a "dialectical" solu- tion to this situation since it tacitly accepts and enlarges the accusation of self-torture on the one hand and explicitly sets out to ruin every "satire" by outdoing its abusiveness on the other.

"The Dialectical Result of a Literary Police Action" does not, therefore, report the result of an actual "literary police action" but carries out its own police action on the basis of a result, the ruin of a literary journal, that has not yet taken place. Father Taciturnus, as a literary policeman, suspends the distinction between police, pros- ecutor, and judge just as he traverses the distinction between civilian and cleric. From the future destruction of a literary journal, the agent of which is the dialectical self-abuse Kierkegaard had practiced in order to become an author, the "results" of Father Taciturnus's "literary police action" can be envisaged, and a new kind of police force emerges in kind: a *literary* police force that does without the claim of law as it likewise "reports" only what *will have taken place*, never what has already occurred. The "indirect" occa- sion of *A Literary Review* comes down to the future itself: a future without precedent and without presence, a future that "results" from its own report.

Persuasion

The policy with which Kierkegaard begins *A Literary Review* is simple: refrain from making appeals to the police. No authorities will be invoked. The occasion for the strictly interpretative sections of the review, and therefore its "direct" occasion, is a new literary production by the author of "A Story of Everyday Life." This is a joyous occasion, and not a little of the joy comes from its ability to pull everyone away from the dangerous situation of mutual recrimination; it gathers everyone together without letting this gathering turn into a place of accusation, defense, and appeals to the police. This occasion for reviewing would not therefore be an occasion at all if it were not for another, "indirect" occasion to which the opening of *A Literary Review* refers in the abstract. By keeping the reference abstract, the review extracts itself from the frightful scene of mutual recrimination:

> Complaining about disloyalty and faithlessness between man and man is not uncommon in the world, and frequently enough the situation borders on the comic: the relation is not one of difference but, regrettably, of a faithful image of mutual resemblance, two changed ones who in new misunderstanding continue to relate to each other, each as the accuser of the other, instead of each one separately accusing himself and finding understanding. However much and however justifiably one person upbraids another for disloyalty, he still guards against accounting for his own instability on those grounds, because he thereby declares himself as one who has the law of existence outside himself—but what is changeableness if not that?   (7, modified)

To submit to a law of existence "outside" oneself, which is the very definition of heteronomy, indicates a state of instability, and every declaration of disloyalty and faithlessness amounts to a submission to such a law. Kierkegaard will therefore forswear accusation; his "world of criticism" will have no place for mutual recrimination because the accusation of criminality already shows latent criminality—that is, changeability—of the one who appeals to a law of existence "outside" himself. The novel under review, as its very title indicates, places the issue of changeability at its center. But Thomasine Gyllembourg's *Two Ages* is even more closely integrated into these opening lines. For it presents itself as two *images*, and it is from these images that accusations of unfaithfulness are produced. In the prefatory "review" of the novel that is to follow, the author declares that *Two Ages* aims at "what I would call domestic reflection (*huuslige Reflex*)."[13] The images of a house as it changes according to certain laws "outside" itself, laws of the "two ages," make it unnecessary to *voice* an accusation of unfaithfulness;

the characters of the unfaithful present themselves to the eye, or to the renewed eye of the reviewer. So Kierkegaard can speak of the "indirect" occasion of *A Literary Review* without having to raise his own voice; the accusation of unfaithfulness will rather arise from the "domestic" images of the novel itself. To this extent, the novel "reflects" the situation of Kierkegaard: it communicates "indirectly" the accusations against those who are swayed by laws "outside" oneself without having to make an appeal to those laws and thereby fall under them. Author and reviewer can maintain their mutual autonomy—and that is a literary miracle.

Without such a miracle, the literary world would be condemned to ever-intensified scenes of mutual accusation until "literary patricide" (9) becomes the law. For the very structure of the house of literature, ruled by Herods, is one of disrespect and faithlessness, where the review of recent literary works shows itself to be the most faithless force of all—the force, that is, of anonymous, amorphous, always accusatory and never stable aesthetic judgments. That Kierkegaard, and the entire Danish literary world, should be blessed by an author whom no one can accuse of literary faults or critical unfaithfulness makes her newest novel into a miraculous event, an occasion for joyous celebration. As Kierkegaard underlines in his introduction to *A Literary Review*, "The author remained faithful to himself" (13), and at the same time "the reading public has been faithful to the author" (16). A literary faith makes it possible to give witness to a work, to "review" it, without having to make this witness into an accusation of any sort. It allows for an autopsy, as self-review, in which one nevertheless reads word for word the work of the author; it lets one read and write at the same time, and to make this simultaneity of reading and writing into the contemporaneity of a literary faith, a faithfulness of reader to writer, even when the text is devoted to the very changeableness and unfaithfulness whereby one "age" turns into another.

A literary faith takes its point of departure from a "life-view," and each "life-view" marks the closure of the "lived" experiences to which reader and writer could refer. Kierkegaard therefore makes his introduction into an exit: an exit from life and into the "life-view" of the author whose earlier "life-view"—but it was always the same, hence the literary faith—was his entrance into life as an author: "Every life-view knows the way out [*Udveien*] and is recognizable by the way out it knows. . . . The life-view is the way out, and the story is the way" (15). Since the "life-view" leads out of life via the story, the ultimate point of reference for each story must be its own extremity, the point at which it ceases to be simply a story. This point of reference Kierkegaard calls "pain" (*Smerte*). "Unlived" pain, pain to which no one can refer except as the extreme point of a story, serves to ground a "life-view" in life itself, not in the particular life of an empirical author. The "pain" to which each story refers, as long as the story is written and read from the perspective of the "life-view," belongs to no one in particular: it is to this extent a "public" pain, a pain of de-privation, the pain that makes possible "persuasion," *overtalelse*. Persuasion takes place in common reference to a pain over which no one will henceforth speak: "All this is not discussed—it just happens—and for this reason the persuasiveness is so great if one gives oneself to it" (19).

Persuasion, as *overtalelse*, outdoes discussion and yet does not do without speaking: it out-speaks every possible discussion and leaves speech with no "lived" experience over which conversants could speak: "Here it [persuasion] is not a matter of a relationship between two individuals" (20). The pain to which each persuasive story owes its persuasive power goes without saying. For this reason, a story written and read from the perspective of a "life-view" emancipates itself from speech while nevertheless being a matter of speech—as outspeaking, as *overtalelse*. So unstable is this situation that it marks the limits of language devoted to conversation, discussion, discursivity. Persuasion "just happens," and the historical character of each story of "everyday life" resides in its happening as persuasion. It belongs neither to subjectivity nor to objectivity, neither to author nor to reader; rather, it is an entirely *literary* affair, as the point where the literary no longer has anything to do with discursivity and the affair of literature is this neither-nor: "Here persuasion is not a matter between two people but is the path in the life-view, and the novel leads one into the world that the view creatively supports. But this world, as a matter of fact, is actuality; thus one has not been deceived but simply been persuaded to remain where one is" (19–20).

Persuasion does not involve the "transport" (18) that defines poetic imagination; it alters nothing, and yet an alteration does take place—an alteration in place, the alteration of repetition. Every moment in Kierkegaard's review is then dedicated to such repetition: the author repeats herself, the reviewer repeats himself, and *A Literary Review*, which repeats *From the Papers of One Still Living*, is supposed to demonstrate to the author that the reviewer has remained "unchanged" (23)—or since persuasion has taken place, "changed in the repetition" (23). However, since the category of persuasion has no place in the *Papers*, "persuasion" names the change in place: it concentrates into itself the impasses onto which the *Papers* had stumbled. Persuasion, which "presupposes a difficulty, an obstacle, an opposition" (20), designates the dissolution of all oppositions: "It starts with this [opposition], and then persuasion clears it away" (20). To the extent that persuasion dissolves all oppositions—and does so without discussion, without consensus built on discussion, without conviction based on consensus—it dissolves the very oppositions through which it comes to be defined: the oppositions to aesthetic "translation" into "the medium of the imagination" on the one hand and religious "translation" into "eternity" on the other. Nothing stands opposed to persuasion, but persuasion cannot do without opposition.

Persuasion, if it lives up to its name, clears away its own presuppositions, including the oppositions in which it is set and its function determined. Even "spiritual jolting" (22), which is supposed to oppose the healing power of persuasion, cannot withstand persuasion. "Faith" and "persuasion" replace each other and never more so than when "faithfulness" and "faithlessness," devotion and philandering, are under discussion. For persuasion leaves nothing but the space of repetition, the very space in which spirit is supposed to become spirit in the first place: "Persuasion is a movement on the spot, but a movement that changes the then and there" (20). Persuasion names a limit function of discursive language: speaking that "outspeaks" speech and at the same time goes without saying, speech that therefore removes itself from the concepts and categories of comprehension and incomprehensibility: "It just happens" (19). The persuasive—and one might say rhetorical—function of language, as outspeaking discursive speech, delivers language over to an event, a "happening," in which comprehension and incomprehensibility play no part. Persuasion thus presents itself as the historical character of language, and it is this character that a reading of *Two Ages* engages over and over.

Surveying *Two Ages*

The very title of the novel under review, *Two Ages*, gives an indication that repetition is more than an incidental concern. The "two times" to which the novel refers are defined by persuasion: movement in place, and the place of this movement is the house. Such at least is the core of Kierkegaard's careful "Survey [*Udsigt*] of Contents in Both Parts." As a survey, it lays down no theses; rather, it shows the repetitive structure of the novel in a double image of the "same" house. It is not, therefore, nature that changes, nor is it precisely culture; the house, as a place of acculturation, mirrors the eruptive event of history *as* natural cataclysm. Thus, as the author explains in her preface, the novel does not depict the "great events that so violently shook the close of the previous century" but shows the "domestic reflection [*huuslige Reflex*]" of that "raging storm" in *both* ages.[14] One storm, one house, two reflections. Each reflection then reflects itself in repetition, and so the novel ceases to represent anything but this repetition.

Kierkegaard's faithfulness to the author does not stop with his survey of the novel's contents; it goes down to the very word "reflection" through which she, like Kierkegaard, represents the novel's form. Certain discontinuities, however, disturb the surface of reflection, and it is from these hardly invisible disturbances that Kierkegaard re-presents, or re-writes, the novel. Everything Kierkegaard "surveys" assumes the shape of this invisibility to the extent that his "vision" of the novel is organized by the writing and the reading of a doubly fictional book, a book within a book. Kierke-gaard shows this book, a volume of revolutionary poetry, to be the staging ground for both revolution and restoration, the "two ages." *Primulae veris*, the title of the volume, brings an end to the "artifi-cial" house through its promotion of "natural" passion and thereby brings on the "first" age, the age of revolution: it is an age of revolutionary poems that by their very nature transport writers and readers outside themselves—and back into nature, *primulae veris*.

Primulae veris, as the image of nature in its deracination, under-mines the apparent naturalness of the house. Each member of the house in which this book appears finds in the book a repulsive force; some are repulsed into undomesticated, "natural" emotion, others into deracinated, "acculturated" domesticity: "Already iso-lated by her solitary knowledge of her relation to Lusard, Claudine becomes more and more isolated. Ferdinand Waller saddens and worries his father when he writes a small book of poems (*Primulae veris*) containing revolutionary ideas and then goes abroad" (26). Once Claudine, heroine of the first part since she "renounces" her passion, is left entirely without a home, she can reflect the storms to which she is thereby exposed: "yes, the age of revolution reflected in a poor abandoned woman's secret seclusion out in the country" (26). Homelessness, whose image is exile into the wilderness, brings to light the "meaning" of the revolutionary age. The author of *Primulae veris*, Ferdinand Waller, then turns into the very image of the wanderer, the homeless one. The agent of this homelessness is his ever-circulating volume of poetry. When the house is cleared out and its emptiness appears as seclusion in the country, natural passion replaces domestic bonds: the novel mirrors not certain events but their "meaning," whose vehicle is a book one only reads about. Not only does Claudine remain faithful to her lover even though she is given every opportunity to legitimatize her child through marriage; the poem that transports her along with the poet out of the house is dedicated to Jeanne d'Arc, a figure of sexual destabilization on the one hand and the defense of the domestic borders on the other.[15]

The restoration of domesticity depends on the domestication of the poet. The unsettling image in which nature and artificiality no longer stand in opposition but are in complicity must give way to a domestic establishment in which the house *appears* to be natural, with the proviso that this appearance show itself to be an illusion. The possibility of a domestic reflection whose image is as artificial as the house then emerges. The image in which the novel casts "the present age" is an artificial house built on the ruins caused by "vicious" natural passions. After Ferdinand abandons poetry, renounces *Primulae veris*, and settles down in his restored house, he becomes the character on which the repetitive character of the novel depends: he makes possible Claudine's "repetition," that is, her return to her onetime and renewed lover. No longer in transport, the poet stands in the middle and without moving from his place *persuades*. His mediation—and here Kierkegaard the reviewer figures himself as the one who has renounced "authorship"—can demonstrate that Claudine, his onetime reader, had indeed remained faithful to herself and to her lover. The faithfulness of the author, as he abandons poetry for persuasion, and the faithfulness of the reader, who has remained the same, give rise to the reconciliation of the poet to the household, of author to reader, of novelist to reviewer: "Ferdinand Waller, who in the meantime has married and is a partner in a big company in Switzerland and upon coming home has learned of her [Claudine's] whereabouts. . . . Ferdinand in turn brings news to Lusard, who believes Claudine is faithless and is married and living in Germany. Ferdinand communicates his news as sensitively as possible so that the reunion might not be a poor, reluctant acquiescence but an enthusiastic *repetition*" (27–28, italics added).

　　Ferdinand, no longer given over to poetic transport, makes possible "enthusiastic repetition" insofar as he communicates "sensitively," indirectly. His volume of poetry in turn indirectly communicates the closing repetition of the novel—the repetition whereby his grandson receives back the woman whom he abandoned for lack of money: "At a book auction Lusard had bought the little volume of verse, *Primulae veris*, for twenty-five dollars, and his curiosity was awakened to find out who was the second bidder at this excessive price. From the arbor he now recognizes the lover by his voice and signet ring—it is none other than Ferdinand Bergland [grandson of the poet], the one being sought" (29–30).[16] The value of *Primulae veris* comes to lie in its price, not its "content," and this hollowing out of its content in favor of its sheer exchangeability makes it into an "indirect" means of communication: it does not speak to anyone of anything but gives away whoever tries to make it into a possession. Poetic ecstasis has turned into prosaic circulation, and this movement returns again and again to the place of origination: to the house as the "reflection" of "two ages," the first age being the one in which poetry transported poets and readers out of the house, the second one in which a book draws them back to its reestablishment. Kierkegaard concludes his survey with a recapitulation of the various moments in which Ferdinand's poems were recited. Each moment reflects nothing more than the "nothing more" of recitation itself: movement in place, without excitation, progress, or regress.

Repetition

Kierkegaard's survey of the "contents" of the novel does not take up the revolutionary volume of poetry as a particularly striking motif; it makes this volume, which has no "existence" outside the novel, into its *occasion*: the moment of its "inspiration." The novel in turn replaces such inspiration with prosaic "persuasion," and this very replacement becomes the occasion for novelistic production. The absorption of the occasion into the novel repeats itself in the review, since Kierkegaard absorbs the novel into his reading, and this absorption of text into review has its own name—repetition. *A Literary Review* "repeats" *Two Ages* to the extent that *Two Ages* already constitutes a repetition—of Kierkegaard's *Repetition*. For the novel takes up the issue of this "novel": faithfulness, namely, takes place and shows itself in repetition. Indeed, *Two Ages* reworks *Repetition* to the point where it appears precisely as a repetition of *Repetition*. It is as though the author of "A Story of Everyday Life" had read *Repetition* and the result was a "review" of this "novel" under the title *Two Ages*—"of everyday life."

Thomasine Gyllembourg had, of course, "lived" experiences of both the age of revolution and the age of restoration, but even if one left aside Kierkegaard's assurance that the author has a "life-view" and has therefore transubstantiated her "lived" experience, the resulting literary "hieroglyphs"[17] would prove inconclusive: Thomasine Gyllembourg's biography has little to do with the structural principle of the novel and even less with Kierkegaard's survey of its content.[18] She, who never achieved "repetition," cannot therefore be confused with Claudine, heroine of the first part of the novel, but Claudine—and what is more, her repetition in the present age, Mariane[19]—cannot be easily dissociated from the Young Man with whom Constantin Constantius corresponds in *Repetition*. For all three learn what it means to repeat: having renounced everything, Claudine, Mariane, and the Young Man come to understand that comprehension and incomprehensibility have nothing to do with the reception in which one spontaneously, freely receives everything back.[20]

The relation between *Repetition* and *Two Ages* is mediated by a review of the former by the only one whose name stands on the title page of the latter—Johan Ludvig Heiberg, who in his "literary review" commends the pseudonymous author of *Repetition* for drawing attention to an important concept but condemns his inability to sublate it into a higher category: "Repetition that is not mediated through subjectivity into something higher than itself is boring and devoid of spirit."[21] Heiberg further criticizes the author of *Repetition* for his "experiment" with repetition, that is, his attempt to repeat an earlier trip to Berlin: "The author, who was merely seeking repetition, should not have repeated his journey to Berlin. On the other hand, the repetition of the reading of a book . . . can heighten and in a way surpass the first impression, because one thereby immerses oneself more deeply in the object and appropriates it more inwardly."[22] Heiberg thereafter returns to Goethe, since he was able to "embrace the whole dialectic of repetition."[23] Yet it is precisely such immersion in the *entire* dialectic that repetition, according to *Repetition*, thwarts. Thus, in one of Kierkegaard's many drafts of a counterreview to Heiberg's review, he shows how Heiberg fails to apprehend the only sense of repetition whose possibility *Repetition* aims to examine: "It is repetition in the pregnant sense."[24]

Such repetition has no precedent, no natural insemination, but is given over to a pure anteriority and an equally pure futurity: modes of time, or ill timing, that are inconceivable but are for this reason the "times" of repetition, its "two ages." Although the mother of Heiberg, author of *Two Ages*, could not have known of Kierkegaard's counterreview,[25] the novel she wrote has no other concern than the issue of a nonsublatable, "magical" repetition: renunciation in which the two heroines receive everything back. And it concludes precisely with the scene of repetition that Heiberg wishes to see replace Constantius's trip to Berlin, a scene of reading over and over again: " 'Ah!' said Lusard. 'At the moment you are saying this I am gripped by the thought that everything in life so strikingly repeats itself. We are sitting here on a September evening in the moonlight . . . and reading this book which according to my parents was celebrated in this very same way when it came out, in an arbor such as this, on an evening such as this.' "[26]

This repetition of reading makes *Two Ages* into a repetition of *Repetition*, an altered repetition, to be sure, but one altered by a reading of repetition undertaken by the "editor" of *Two Ages*. Who wrote *Two Ages* is therefore more than an idle question. A name will not suffice so long as the name is understood as the mark of identity and self-recognition. The anonymity of this novel—and of its review, which Kierkegaard published under his "own" name, as if he had a name he could call his own—is so pervasive, so interwoven into its repetitive structure and repetitive occasion that nothing like the famous slogan "Truth is subjectivity" does justice to the truth of this novel. It is a nonsubjective, anonymous, *typical* truth, the very "truth" against which the *Concluding Unscientific Postscript* was directed.[27] And "the amazing thing about the novel is that everything is categorically true" (58), true because it expresses the "totality of the age" down to its smallest detail.

Kierkegaard's "Esthetic Interpretation of the Novel and Its Details [*Enkeltheder*]" wants nothing to do with "that single individual" (*hin Enkelte*). On the contrary, details and individuality are absorbed into the repetitive anonymity of "two ages" as each character of the novel—such is the manner of "interpretation"—shows how it reflects "the totality of the age." While extolling the author's talents, Kierkegaard proceeds to destroy the unity of the novel in favor of this anonymous "totality." Interpretation as destruction, destruction as the demonstration of the occasional nature of the novel's characters—these are the rules to which Kierkegaard's review adheres as he shows how the novel represents "two ages":

> A novel in general has only the pictorial background [*Grund*], similar to the outline an illustrator sketches over when he draws the figure; the drawing itself is the product, while the outlined background merely hinders the eye from seeing the sketch as hovering in the air. But here the novel is more universally grounded [*grundet*] in something that is more essential even than the production itself, although the production intends only to provide the afterglow. The novel has as its presupposition the distinctive totality of the age, and the representation is the reflection in domestic life; the mind turns from the representation to totality of the age, which has been disclosed in this reflexion.   (32, modified)

Each character disappears into the outlines that with this disappearance reveal the ground. Such self-erasing figures constitute the matter of Kierkegaard's "Esthetic Interpretation." This interpretation is "aesthetic" not only because it eschews ethical evaluation but because it makes every character into an occasion for reflection on the age it represents and thereby draws every character into an illusion as its ground: the illusion, that is, of "the totality of the age." If this totality does not constitute a determining ground—and everything in Kierkegaard's introductory remarks on demands of the age, to say nothing of his conclusion on "the present age," supports this contention—then each character does not so much reflect or "represent" something as *nothing*, and this reflection of "nothing," which is no longer reflection and no longer concerns discernible characters of the novel, becomes the matter to be reviewed: an "empty" matter, to be sure, but a matter that nevertheless presents itself as "ground." At its limit, "aesthetic interpretation" gives way to a *literary reading*, a reading of the empty "matter" of interpretation, a reading that *appears* to do without a written work. For the work, if there ever was one, has so completely disappeared into the repetitive, idle structure and repetitive, idle occasion of the review that this disappearance gives off an illusion of nonreading, of mere "evaluation." Taking "aesthetic interpretation" to its limit, Kierkegaard reduces the work to its empty matter, begins to read what no one, not even an anonymous one, has written and writes what the first translator of *A Literary Review* called a "critique of the present."[28]

Critique, Mudslinging

Kierkegaard appears to emancipate himself from the novel under review in order to turn toward the "things" represented in the text: the two ages. But this appearance is an illusion to the extent that these two "things" are not things at all but, rather, non-things, abstractions, illusions in their own right. Translations of the final section as "Kritik der Gegenwart" (critique of the present) or as "The Present Age"—or even a translation of the entire text as *Two Ages*—register a certain disengagement at work in the review, but this disengagement is not from the category of "the literary." On the contrary, *A Literary Review* lives up to its literariness only when it gives up "aesthetic interpretation" in favor of a mode of reading that breaks down the illusory unity of "the aesthetic" with the same degree of thoroughness as the "aesthetic interpretation" breaks up the unity of the novel. Kierkegaard does not shy away from the demands literariness makes on the literary review: every fragment of the work becomes an occasion, not a ground for interpretation or an effect that requires causal explanation. The work stands in pieces, but these pieces do not even add up to a whole work; they are incidents of reading, each of which is, as an incident, unruly and unauthorized.

Kierkegaard therefore criticizes the author on one very special count: she prefaces her novel with her own "review" and therefore gives guidelines for reading. By doing so, she makes the novel, quite literally, unreadable: no one will *read* it. Instead, they will read her prefatory "review," and in the place of a reading there will emerge "chatter." Unreadability threatens any work that sends out advance guards for reading because these guards *authorize* a reading, but an authorized reading is not a reading. By giving her own reading of her novel, the author opens herself to *two* modes of critique: the "chatty" commentaries of the "literary world" on the one hand and Kierkegaard's critique of her exposing herself in this way to the "chatty" commentary of the "literary world":

> *Conclusion for Observation* [*Udbytte for Iagttagelsen*] of *Two Ages*

> I now come to the final section and face the difficulty the author has posed for a critic by his own leveling [*levere*] of a criticism. I wish the author had not done it. I certainly do not say this on my own account, for in another sense it would be to my advantage to accept the clues offered, but nevertheless I will not copy them and pass them off as my own criticisms. But in my opinion the book has been harmed by this preface, precisely because it can prompt rash and impulsive people and loose tongues to say: 'Is that the whole?' 'The whole can be said on a page.' It is certainly true that what a chatty person [*snaksomt Menneske*] or a sassy, degenerate child says makes no difference whatsoever, but when it comes it concerns a book by a reputable, distinguished, and established literary figure [*Firma in Literaturen*], something else is manifestly more desirable, something which we, who perhaps are too accustomed to malice, almost forget, that the chatty person or the degenerate child should simply have kept quiet. Something that may be insignificant if it happens to others proves to be all out of proportion when it happens to a person of importance, and what is tolerable when it concerns [*angaaer*] oneself distresses one when it concerns someone of distinction.   (60, modified)

Kierkegaard criticizes the author's critique, reviews the author's review, because it exposes the author to impurity, to being sullied by critical commentaries. Purity is, as usual, the aim of critique, and Kierkegaard wishes to purify the novel of its own critique to keep critique pure—of a determinate "object." The purification of critique, as the reduction of its "object" to nothing, is then played out in its conclusion. Just as Kierkegaard's sole critical comment in the conclusion to his "Esthetic Interpretation" concerns a slightly dirty remark addressed to a not entirely spotless woman (59), he opens the conclusion with a scene of defilement that by its very nature turns the "review" into something else: an appeal to—or more exactly, a *notification* of—the authorities. Hidden and yet altogether apparent in *En literair Anmeldelse* is *anmeldelse*: not "review" but "announcement," or better still, "notification." A literary review turns into a notification to certain unnamed authorities that literary reviews, which sully the works under review, *happen*. An observation of a scene of defilement, which constitutes the communicative character of "chatter," thus begins the "Concluding Observation":

> When someone is wearing rubbers because of the muddy roads, he cheerfully takes his chances, but when the same person sees a young girl, for example, who has solved the difficult task [*vanskelige Opgave*] by walking a rather long way from her home without getting muddy at all and blissfully conscious of this trips merrily along—and then along comes a boor who in passing splashes her with mud, the person wearing rubbers is distressed. It seems to him to be an injustice of existence [*Tilværelse*] to raise absurdities at the same time; he feels the enormity [*Uhyggelige*] that the street is for everybody instead of everybody's going out his way for the young girl—and in Danish literature at this moment there is no right of way and no police whatsoever who at least could keep the street-corner loafers and porters and louts off the sidewalk. (60–61, modified)

Whatever other name the young girl bears, her first name is Kierkegaard, whose writings were recently the occasion for a literary smear campaign in the pages of the inhuman *Corsair*. Kierkegaard cannot, however, present the image of defilement as the horrible fate to which "genius" is exposed on the streets of Copenhagen. For he would then show his unfaithfulness to himself; his attack on Andersen in *Papers* would suddenly strike back at him and demonstrate his complicity in those specular accusations of unfaithfulness that he takes pains to avoid. No one in particular will be attacked in the space of *A Literary Review*, except, it turns out, the *author*, for exposing herself to critical attacks that defile her just as much as the mud of the street sullies the "young girl." Kierkegaard's review becomes in turn a notification of *possible* defilement that is, however, immediately made "actual" in his very own critique: it solicits the attention of the "loafers and porters and louts" without being able to bring *them* instead of the "young girl" to the attention of the authorities. For there are no authorities, "at this moment," that could attend to this defilement; there are no "police whatsoever" that could, *for entirely aesthetic reasons,* reorder the streets to serve the enticing "young girl" alone. The absence of an aesthetic authority, which would hold back the "talkativeness" and "chattiness" of critical reviews, including Kierkegaard's own, defines "this moment." Defining it in terms of "two ages" then replaces the critique of *Two Ages*, as *Two Ages* disappears under the prospective leveling of its very distinctiveness. At the precise spot where the seducer first determined his victim[29] the reviewer notifies "no one" of the "leveling" to which *any* word, even the ones that are "categorically true" (58), is exposed once it makes its way onto the open spaces of the streets.

The Aesthetic Validity of Revolution

The image of a *lapsus* informs the "Concluding Observation." The "young girl" falls because *she fails to leap*, which in this case means that the author does not restrain herself from writing a preface to her work. To leap would mean to trust in the work without having to support oneself by an authorized reading. It would be to trust in the aesthetic integrity of the novel without having to send out advance guards to protect the novel from misunderstanding. The aesthetic integrity of the novel—without prefatory comments, without criticism, without "chattiness"—then gives the image of an age from which the novel is removed, an age therefore "prior" to the novel in which each work, no matter how insignificant, could do without prefatory comments precisely because each one was *expressive.* The cleanliness and propriety of expression show themselves in the purity of form, a purity that has no place for "content" or any space for prefatory reviews or critical commentary:

> The age of revolution is essentially passionate, and therefore it essentially has *form*. Even the most vehement expression of an essential passion *eo ipso* has form, for this is the expression itself, and therefore also has in its form an apology, an element of reconciliation. Only for a completely external and indifferent dialectic is the form not the alter ego of content and thereby the content itself, but rather an irrelevant third something. For example, every letter that bears the mark of inwardness in the expression of an essential felt passion *eo ipso* has form. But whether the letter is folded formlessly could occupy only a totally external dialectic with the apparent importance of being a question of form. (61)

The age of revolution, as the age of form, represents the aesthetic insofar as the aesthetic is defined by its absorption of all content into form. The justification for the revolution does not reside in an "ethical-philosophical evaluation" (61) but in its own aesthetic validity. "Passion" acquires its proper form to the extent that it "expresses" itself *immediately*, and the immediacy of its expression underlies its aesthetic character. For the aesthetic validity of revolution justifies every passionately written expression, no matter how hastily prepared and no matter how its "folds" distort its outward form. An ill-composed letter, as an expression of "passion," is more formally correct than a meticulous but expressionless composition. The very formality of the expression includes a moment of "reconciliation," not simply of one lover with another but in the end of "nature" with "culture."

For this reason, "the age of revolution is essentially passionate and therefore has *culture*" (61), even though the culture of revolution is precisely nature; its cult is in turn the natural, and the most natural expression for this cult is, of course, walking the streets au naturel. As "reconciliation" makes opposition into equality, it undoes the opposition of each "age" to the other and as a result presents itself as a return to the original "age," the natural one, and a natural culture appears in the image of uncovering nakedness:

In the relation of father to son, reactionary immediacy wants to do away with the inexplicables of piety and make nature the only determinant: thus dependency should be abolished on coming to maturity, and parents and children should be equals and friends. In fact this idea, yes, even the idea of freedom and equality, is not without form as long as the idea itself is the essential truth inspiring the enthusiast [*den væsentlige begeisrende Sandhed i de Begreistrede*], for then the inwardness is not abolished. When the religious idea inspires the Moravian Brethren to express equality by being brothers and sisters, this is not formlessness at all, for uniformity is the essential form; nor is it empty abstraction as long as inwardness is implicit. Formlessness is simply the absence of content. For example, if a woman in a fit of boredom got the notion of dolling herself up and dressing in all her finery, this would be formlessness for the simple reason that there would be no idea behind it. The naked Archimedes is adorned with joy over his discovery and is therefore essentially dressed.   (65–66)

The progress of the revolutionary age therefore consists in regression. Its every movement aims at the restoration of the nature so long as "nature" means reconciliation. No more perfect image of such restoration could be found than a body insusceptible to defilement: the naked body of Archimedes leaping out of a bathtub, washed and refreshed. The beauty of bodily disclosure, like that of certain impious as well as incestuous relations, finds its justification in this immediate expression of "passion." No matter how perverse a relation might appear, its image in the revolutionary cannot be sullied, for it means nothing but natural form, newly cleaned and in possession of the new measure of the bathed body. Indeed, the most passionate moments of discovery, the intimate expression of which is doubtless eureka, "I have discovered," reveals to all that the revolutionary age stands *in truth* and everywhere radiates this truth outward. The aesthetic validity of revolution appears in an uncovered body and finds its motto in uncoveredness and "dis-covery." Enwrapped in himself and yet exposed to every other, Archimedes never runs the risk of defilement, even as he runs through the streets of his city naked.

Every modification of the revolutionary age is implicated in a process whereby things are not discovered or uncovered but are instead exposed to dirt. Yet for all its naturalness, the age of revolution does not constitute a ground; it is not a "nature" of which a succeeding age would be its "culture" since its cult of nature constitutes "culture" in the proper sense. The only "justification" for the age of revolution is its aesthetic character, but this is nevertheless *a* justification. Nothing of the kind could be said of the aftermath of the revolution, the age of ages, or "the present age." Not only is the age of revolution not its basis; it is denied its own aesthetic validity, and so it can claim no ground, no validity, no justification whatsoever. "The present age" is, rather, an occasion: the occasion to reflect on undoing of the schema of ground and consequence that is reflected in each occasion for reflection. *A Literary Review* throws itself into this undoing and thereby abandons every reason for being, including its apparent reason for being—as a "response" (61) to a novel.

The exposition of "the present age" takes the review to its limit: the constellation of occasions, both direct and indirect, to which it owes its origin presents itself as the ungrounded, unjustifiable set of contingencies that make up "the totality of the age." Fortune, or misfortune, does not simply give rise to the review but is its "content," and the impossibility of bringing such fortune into the generalities of language expresses itself in a potentially endless series of "generalizations" (61) on the "present age." The persuasive character of the novel, which gives one the chance to "remain where one is" (20), is likewise taken to the limit, with the result that it is impossible to say "where one is"—or each saying constitutes an oversaying, an *overtalelse* in which too much and yet not enough is said.

The unwieldy review, as it grows to match the size of the novel, presents the "present age" as an overdressed woman. She—not the distinguished novelist, mother of Johan Ludvig Heiberg, or a "young girl"—comes to embody an age in which the coincidence of too much and not enough assumes the unique form of deformity and reveals its content to be emptiness: "Just as an overgroomed woman fails to look well-dressed because that demands tasteful proportion, so the present age seems to have so decked itself out in the multifariousness of reflection as to preclude the development of harmonious balance" (110). This "overgroomed woman" takes over the exposition of "the present age" because her clothes, which express nothing of her body, represent the expressionless character of "reflection" itself. No "passion" is expressed; the immediacy of expression does not make content into form; nothing exposes itself to view other than the *expressionless*, and this makes up the matter of an ever-reflective, overblown "review."

The Swamp

The groundlessness of "the present age" removes the background from which each of its characters could be interpreted; only the inexpressivity of these characters can be read. The ghostly presence of those who overdress matches that of the age—"ghostly" presence because everything in "the present age," including its authors, breaks down form to such an extent that the very form of life no longer holds. Mortality, in other words, ceases to give discourse its "passion" and expressivity; no stories originate from a death sentence, or, what amounts to the same, a "life-view": "But it is one thing to save one's life by the enchantment of story-telling as in *A Thousand and One Nights*; it is something else again to shut oneself from the enchantment of enthusiasm over an idea and the rebirth of passion—by talkativeness [*Snaksomhed*]" (63–64). Storytelling, narrative in general, no longer takes its point of departure from the certainty of death; rather, language survives in another mode of negativity: a pre-death or a post-death; in any case, a death of lively speech, of all speech in which "lived" experience forms itself in a "life-view" and storytelling can find its reason for being. In place of such talk, there is "talkativeness," *snaksomhed*.

"Talkativeness," unlike talk, does not express mortal subjects in whom "passion" is "reborn." But "talkativeness" is the very being of talk: talk *by itself*, without mortal subjects, each of whom addresses the other. To this extent, it cannot be easily distinguished from

"persuasion" (*overtalelse*), the very mode of speech in which oppositions vanish and which is never "a matter of a relationship
between two people" (20). "Talkativeness" shuts everyone up in
itself; its communication, without expression, is a *communicatio
idiomatum* in which substances do not communicate with one
another but a substanceless nonentity, a mere abstraction, draws
every supposed substance into itself.

That nonentity, which is neither mortal nor immortal, is likewise anonymous; it is "the public." *The public presents itself in "the
present age."* Authorship does not die—and indeed cannot die, since
death makes it possible in the first place—but in place of the mortal
author, who expresses "passions" and in whom the "rebirth" of
"passion" spells revolution, there arises a monstrosity that suspends
the opposition of life to death without, however, giving rise to a
higher category, including that of rebirth. On the contrary, this
"monstrous nonentity [*uhyre Intet*]" (91) shuts itself up as it spreads
itself out. No longer is there a place for spirit; a "phantom," which
Kierkegaard does not hesitate to call a "spirit [*Aand*]" (91), takes
over the place of spirit and thereby confounds spirit and spiritlessness.[30] The presence of "the present age" is defined by the publicity
of the public, the very nature of which makes presence to oneself,
whether conceived as "life" or "death" or "rebirth," impossible.

The public cannot present itself in an image, not even in the
image of utter groundlessness. For an image of the public would be
readable against a background, and the public denies access to all
such grounds. Without a secure ground yet without the assurance
that comes from an ascertained groundlessness, the public nevertheless comes to present itself in an image of a receding ground—in
a *swamp*. The swamp, more than the "sea" or the "sand," washes
everything away and therefore makes *character*, as "something
engraved" (77), impossible to sustain. This swamp is the confounded place into which *A Literary Review* disburdens its persuasive flow. The swamp is just as little groundless as it is grounded,
just as little fertile as it is infertile, just as little finite as it is
undefined, and it responds in the most curious ways to the peculiar

"logic" of "talkativeness": *too much life* implies *too little life*; death does not leave a graveyard, a "kierkegaard," in its wake but gives rise to fetid rebirth. Not the baroque graveyard, as has sometime been suggested,[31] but the swamp oversees Kierkegaard's place of residence. The mud of the swamp, which, as *bysnak*, stands by every speaker, washes his streets:

> Gossip [*Bysnak*] and rumor and chimeric significance [*Betydningsfuld-hed*] and apathetic envy become a surrogate for each and all. Individuals do not in inwardness turn away from each other, do not turn outwardly in unanimity for an idea, but mutually turn to each other in a frustrating and chimeric, aggressive leveling reciprocity. The avenue of the idea is blocked off; individuals mutually thwart and contravene each other; selfish and mutual reflexive opposition is like a swamp [*Hængesæk*]—and now [*nu*] they are sitting in it.   (63)

"The present age" is on the way to presenting itself in the image of the swamp, but the way is blocked—by the swamp itself. As the image of the impossibility of presenting the presence of "the present age" (*Nutiden*) in an image, the time of the swamp is "now" (*nu*), but this "now" never takes place: it is nothing more than now-point and yet again another now-point, without past, present, or future. The swamp is the place of "reflexive opposition," but every opposition, once reflected upon, loses its positional character and falls back, without position or opposition, into the swamp. The reflective opposition with which *A Literary Review* began, the opposition engendered by claims of "faithlessness" (7), generates a swamp, and once generated, the swamp spreads, closing down each exit. Least of all does a "leap" let one out. For a "leap" depends on solid ground, precisely what swamps everywhere deny.

By virtue of its reflexivity, *A Literary Review* is thus an "expression" of the swamp: an expression of its own inexpressivity. Kierkegaard does not shy away from the verdict delivered upon his writings by the anonymous reviewer of his work who occasioned this review; instead, without so much as saying so, he abuses himself in disabusing the "age" of its swampiness: "Nothing is fresh and direct, everything has to be reflected on. . . . Despite all his

intelligence, reflection for him has become a severe sickness. . . .
[He] is a nonentity who can find a place neither in heaven nor in
hell but only in the thin air of reflection, where no creature can
live."³² These statements are not signed by Kierkegaard but by one
who has reviewed Kierkegaard's work; in return, Kierkegaard gives
these accusations a firmer footing by naming the place that is
neither "in heaven nor in hell": it is the swamp, the place for
reflection, abstraction, nonentities. *A Literary Review* does not
therefore oppose this review of Kierkegaard's "authorship," nor
does it defend it from attack, but takes its abuse to its limit. It
plumbs the depths of the swamp, to reflect—without expression, as
the expressionless—the nonabyssal bottomlessness of abstraction,
reflexivity, nonentitiness.

The opposition of direct to "indirect" communication likewise
fails. For *A Literary Review* does not set out to communicate
something or to communicate the incommunicable but suspends
this opposition in its monumental yet occasional inexpressivity.
"The initial expression," to say nothing of "the essential expression" or "the decisive expression"—three expressions from the conclusion to the *Concluding Unscientific Postscript*³³—is always found
in the image of the "leap." But this image will no longer do; it
cannot stand against the swamp. Without this image, however, the
"indirectness" of communication loses its own expressivity; it no
longer means something other than, or in the end the nullity of,
what it says and can therefore no longer generate "irony," "humor,"
or pseudonymous productions. Into the swamp, then, communication falls, regardless of the "direction" it takes. Perhaps this is
what Kierkegaard's reviewer meant when he closed the review with
Kierkegaard standing "like an ironization of irony."³⁴ In any case,
the swamp undercuts transcendence into another "stage of life" as
much as it undermines progress into another "sphere of existence."
Jumping up is not a way out. But *the swamp grows*, and woe accrues
to whoever tries to hold back its progress. The swamp grows, yet
unlike the desert of which Nietzsche speaks,³⁵ its growth is not
ongoing drainage and death. Its destructive growth, true to the
"logic" of "chatter," is overgrowth; its nature is excess.

"That It Is Not"

The excessiveness of the swamp does not constitute a secret; it does not make communication possible by denying, "dialectically," the communicability of whatever is supposed to be communicated. Regardless of the "direction" of its communication, the overgrowth of the swamp grows and makes it impossible to distinguish growth from nongrowth, life from death. For the "life" of the swamp is *communicerende*: not of course the communication of a communion in which the community shares and thereby constitutes itself as a community but also not entirely the defilement of the exceptional by the common and the profane; rather, the *communicerende* that makes up the "life" of the swamp suspends the opposition between these two interpretations of "making-common." Such is the force of "leveling": not only is the sacred denied, but so too is the profane, since the profane needs the sacred to show its essential commonness. The generalized profanity of "the present age" cannot even be called profane without this call generating a more general profanity.

"Leveling" undoes the distinctions through which "the age of revolution" revealed and justified itself: form and content, nature and culture. "The present age" has neither form nor content, neither nature nor culture. Nothing like a "restoration of natural relationships" (65, modified) can take place in a swamp, especially since "natural relationships," as excessive, overgrown, and unnatural, constitute the swampiness of a swamp and make every communication of this situation murky. The very relation of "the present age" to "the age of revolution" thereafter defies representation according to any schema of succession. Not only is the "the age of revolution" not a ground for "the present age," but conversely, "the age of revolution" is a projection of "the present age" as the illusory fulfillment of its presence to itself. "The age of revolution" shows itself in turn to be at bottom *regressive*, and "the present age" turns out to be progressive precisely because of its swampiness: its lack of foundation does not amount to a secure groundlessness, a sublime "abyss."

Nothing is more revolutionary than this muddy situation, even as it denies anything like a revolutionary moment, a leap into another age. The secret of "the present age"—that which because of its noncommunicability would allow for its "indirect" notification—is that it is, after all, revolutionary, indeed more revolutionary than any other age. Its revolutionary character does not consist in a return to nature, albeit fully cultivated, but to an interminable turning *in place.* Its perversity no less than its persuasiveness takes its roots from this incessant turning. The "two ages" of Kierkegaard's review, if not of Thomasine Gyllembourg's novel, belong to an asymmetrical structure of historicity, the articulation of which is not causal, certainly not "developmental," but instead *repetitive*—progressive regression repeating itself as regressive progression:

A passionate, tumultuous age wants to *overthrow everything, set aside everything.* An age that is revolutionary but also reflecting and devoid of passion changes the expression of power into a *dialectical tour de force: it lets everything remain but subtly drains the meaning out of it; rather than culminating in an uprising, it exhausts the inner actuality of relations in a tension of reflection that lets everything remain and yet has transformed the whole of existence into an ambiguity* [Tvydighed] *that in its facticity is, while entirely privately a dialectical fraud interpolates a secret mode of reading—that it is not* [medens dialektisk Sviig privatissime underskyder en hemmlig Læsemaade—at den ikke er]. (77, modified)

If it were not for a certain fraud—the linguistic crime par excellence, the crime whose means and medium is communication—"the present age" would give up its secret, to wit, that it is "revolutionary" after all. Thus a dialectical tour de force would come full circle, as the tour of the revolution from beginning to end; the opposition between the two ages, and perhaps even between *Two Ages* and *A Literary Review,* would give rise, according to the dialectical schema of sublation, to a higher age of mutual reconciliation. The speculative philosopher who recognizes this transition would in turn already have arrived home (*bei sich*). But such is not the case, at least not in *A Literary Review* or in "the present age."

For a certain fraud defrauds dialectics of its tour, which is always from beginning to end. The determinate negation of the negativity of "the present age" does not take place; instead of a negation, there is "drainage," and this clandestine draining of meaning includes the draining of meaning from "negation" itself. "Negation," as the active operation of dialectics, does not mean negation anymore. Such is negativity of "the present age"—a linguistic negativity, which, however, does not leave language alone but "interpolates" into every discourse a "mode of reading" that denies language the very meaningfulness and expressivity through which it is defined.

A "dialectical fraud" can defraud dialectics of its negativity only insofar as the language of this fraud is older and more powerful than that of dialectics itself: it is a language that denies its own meaningfulness, its own ability to measure up to the task dialectics assigns it. Such a language breaks up dialectics as much as it undercuts every work in service of dialectical concepts. Under no condition, however, could this language then appear on its own, as a "natural" language or an artificially constructed one; it is, rather, a derivative language, "a secret mode of reading." The "secret mode of reading" interpolates itself "privately" and by making everything public, puts an end to privacy. This "secret mode of reading" makes it impossible to communicate a secret and therefore to communicate in the first place, unless the communication be "that it is not." The "not" here does not negate "the whole of existence" since "the whole of existence" remains as it is; it does not simply negate the univocity of "existence" since the "ambiguity that in its facticity it is," as the word "facticity" indicates, is already ambiguous. No. The "not" of reading—or of "the secret mode of reading," which is reading, strictly speaking—does not make "the whole of existence" ambiguous but drains it of the "meaning" that determines whether something is univocal, ambiguous, or polysemic. "The whole of existence" is not, but the "not" still does not negate "the whole of existence" and does not negate its meaning. The "not" interrupts negation and the affirmative negation of negation to the extent that it "entirely privately" makes both negation and affirmation into utterly linguistic matters, matters of language "itself."

Reading "that it is not" is not therefore an easy matter; it is the very matter of reading insofar as a mode of reading interrupts each discourse and leaves in place of seamless continuity an awkward phrase—"that it is not." This phrase is, to the extent that it marks a "secret mode of reading," unreadable; as little as "character," which is "something engraved (*charassō*)" (77), leaves behind a trace in the sea, the sand, or the swamp, so little does the phrase "that it is not" leave any statement of meaning untouched. On the contrary, the secrecy of "the secret mode of reading—that it is not" makes it impossible to determine when and where such reading takes place without, however, making this secret into the ground and guarantor of communicability. A "secret mode of reading" interpolates every claim to succession and leaves in its place the phrase "that it is not." This remainder is therefore, to resurrect a term found in a section of *Either/Or* on the ghostly presence of the past, an *anacoluthon*. It does not follow, it does not obey. No rules of grammar or logic underlie the sequence that makes up a sentence.

Whereas *Either/Or* calls on an "anacoluthic thought process" to enable a melancholic aesthete "to evoke an enjoyment that is never present tense but always has an element of the past and is thus present in the past,"[36] the observation on "the present age" undertaken in *A Literary Review*, which could henceforth be called "Neither/Nor," has no place for the evocation of enjoyment. Enjoyment, if it has a place at all, resides in the mimetic, "reflective" power of the novel. Anacoluthon annuls such reflection, and with it, enjoyment. Under the suspended rule of anacoluthon—"that it is not"—the absence of the present tense does not signal delicious melancholia but rather deprives presence of its expression. Presence without expression is then understood as the absence of inwardness, interiority, insight, privacy, secretiveness, and these terms of absence become the ones through which critique determines the negativity of the age. But in place of this very understanding, and as a replacement for this critique, *A Literary Review* interpolates into its observations and critical operations a "secret mode of reading" that by virtue of its secrecy undoes the terms in which the understanding of expressionless presence or the critique of "the present age" have been cast.

The "secret mode of reading" thus deprives speculation of its foundation in the grammar of the present-tense proposition. Such is indeed a "dialectical" fraud, the defrauding of determinate negation of its power to determine anything, including the nothingness of death. Since the phrase "that it is not" does not yield to the force of dialectics, it will always already have been overlooked in any speculative survey. Not reading this "secret mode of reading," which implies an inability to read the specific "privative" in which all reading takes place, constitutes the act of omission whereby *A Literary Review* makes its appearance as a free-floating "critique of the present age"—a critique, not surprisingly, that has been seen to emphasize the *inconsequentiality*, as ineffectiveness and indolence, of this age.

Inconsequentiality, however, is meaningful as the negation of significance, effectiveness, justification, and succession; the anacoluthon—"that it is not"—escapes the dialectic of meaningfulness and meaninglessness, as it likewise escapes the distinction of past and present or private and public: "After all, the single individual who reads is not a public, and then gradually many individuals read, perhaps all do, but there is no contemporaneity" (91). The "secret mode of reading," which is "entirely privately interpolated," does not take place in private, nor precisely in public, but by suspending this distinction, gives rise to inconsequentiality incarnate, namely, "the press" (90). The press, in its turn, does not generate its own public, which could perhaps be conceived as "strong communal life," but institutes "this abstraction 'the public'" (91): "the public" suspended in quotation marks, the "public" without a *forum* in which it could speak, "the public" without a *res publica* but only certain privative "modes of reading."[37] The specter of the Cartesian "ghost in the machine" reappears in the press as a mode of reading and writing in which sequentiality disappears into endless, nonnarrative anacolutha, a string of interruptive and disruptive suspensions, a random series of neither-nors. Nothing can be present to the press, although—or rather for this very reason—it makes everything "current" and "topical." Everyone and everything is distracted, defrauded of the sequential horizon of past, present, and future. "The present age," therefore, says precisely what it is *not*—namely, "present." A "secret mode of reading" has so drained "presence" of its meaning, and drained it into the swamp of "the present age," that the age of self-absence, the age of the press, can be characterized by *this* word without anyone other than a *reader*—and not even a good one—noticing it.

A Literary Review notifies the authorities of the absence of "the present age," and it does so in an image of the house into which its "secret" (*hemmilighed*) has sought refuge. This image, unlike that of the swamp, throws light on what draws the "secret mode of reading" into the secret of "the present age." The undoing of the schema of sequentiality makes possible something like "contemporaneity," but the distention of "presence" into distraction concomitantly makes "contemporaneity," the only saving mode of time, unsalvageable:

> Allow me to illustrate with an entirely simple image [*Billede*] what I mean. I once visited a family with a room-clock that for some reason or other was out of order. But the trouble did not express itself in a sudden slackness of the spring or the breaking of a chain or a failure to strike; on the contrary, it went on striking, but in a peculiar, abstractly normal, but nevertheless confusing way. It did not strike twelve strokes at twelve o'clock and then once at one o'clock; rather, it struck one stroke [*slog eet Slog*] at definite intervals. It went on striking this way all day and never once gave the hour. So it is in an enervating tension: the relations remain, but in a state of an abstract unbrokenness that prevents the breakdown [*en abstrakt Uafbrudthed, som forhindrer Bruddet*]; something expresses itself, which one could call the expression of the relations, and yet the relations are not only indicated imprecisely but meaninglessly.   (80, modified)

The image is not one of time nor, as is clear, good timing, but the image is also not one of timelessness or timeliness; rather, the image is of a stroke that strikes down each mode of time and therefore time "itself." The strokes of the clock interrupt the temporal interruptions whereby each mode of time, including that of contemporaneity, is measured. The interruption of interruption appears as the impossibility of interruption; no breakdown can take place because the constancy of the breaks makes every breakdown meaningless, less a breakdown than a repetition of the incessant interruptions of time. The strokes then express the expressionless, the loss of time that, however, gives no image of eternity. Each stroke, rather, kills time. And so Kierkegaard goes underground, or into the swamp, to find the culprit of this unheard-of killing: "Reflection is not the evil" (96), nor are the public or even the press. The image of the clock gone wrong makes the search for the one who struck time down all the more difficult, for it seems as though it happened all by itself, automatically. To seek out the culprit, Kierkegaard discards the image and poses to himself the question of the forces at his disposal: "Force can be used against rebellion, punishment awaits demonstrable counterfeiting, but dialectical secretiveness [*Hemmlighedsfuldhed*] is difficult to root out; it takes relatively finer ears to trace the soundless [*lydløse*] stratagems of reflection through the sneaky ways of ambiguity" (80, modified).

No oppositional forces can be gathered against the "secretiveness" in which the very distinction between direct communication and "indirect" communication vanishes. Force, therefore, cannot be used to bring out the culprit that struck time down. Indeed, nothing brings the *culprit* to light; only the *strokes* are heard, and they can be heard only by those "ears" that have refined themselves through unbroken reflection on hearing oneself speak to oneself, which is, however, reflection itself.[38] Even if a massive philosophical tradition supports the displacement of reflection into an aural register, this displacement does not make the task of hearing any easier for the most refined ears. For the strokes are still "soundless" (*lydløse*). If they, and therefore the culprit, are to be detected, the ears of the detective have to accustom themselves to hearing nothing, yet this "nothing" cannot be simply silence. The ears of the detective have to be able to hear the "less" of soundlessness: a negativity that drains words of meaning without changing a single one.

Literary Soldiers

"The time is out of joint"—this line of Hamlet's stamps the character of "the present age" with the same force that the Danish prince's advice to give "an understanding but no tongue" determines the exposition of the demonic.[39] The becoming unhinged of time is not a matter of course; it does not happen according to a natural cycle or any sequence whatsoever. It is, rather, the expression of an attack on time whose monstrousness demands that someone, or "no one," be notified. Such a notification can only be expressionless; it gives no directions for the search after struckdown time. These strokes are as little against the law as they are against nature. To seek them out, certain emergency laws have to be laid down, and the one who lays these emergency laws down erases the distinction between legislation and execution through which laws are legitimized and thus legitimate force is distinguished from coercion. From such an emergency law, or countermanding of legitimacy in general, the character of the strokes against time can be more precisely determined: "Suppose a law were passed and could be maintained that did not forbid people to speak but merely ordered that everything spoken about had to be spoken about as if it happened fifty years ago—that would be it for all the chatterers [*Snakkerne*], they would despair" (100, modified). The strokes against time are, to be sure, not simply representations of "chatter" for the sake of an image since they cannot represent anything in particular, but the strokes and "chatter" are indistinguishable: a law against the presence of "chatter" would put an end to the crime committed against time. "Chatter" would come to an end under this law: "no more present tense!" And this law, if it could be enforced, would mean: no more "present age."

If an authority in whose name the enforcement would take place could be identified, the address of the notification—"time is out of joint"—could finally be determined. But such is not the case. Each law of "the present age," in order for it to be itself, must maintain the present tense; none can regress back "fifty years," and even if one did so, the very terms of Kierkegaard's review would make this law illegitimate. For "the age of revolution" occurred fifty years ago, and this age abandoned law in favor of "passion." Only in the name of the "the public," that "monstrous nonentity" (91), could the law be enforced, but "the public" is not a name; it is as anonymous as the author of *Two Ages*. The enforcement of the law cannot then take place under a name or even under a pseudonym.[40] If, therefore, emergency laws alone allow for the detection of what emerges as "the present age" and these emergency laws cannot be legislated and executed in the name of anyone, they can be enforced only by an illegitimate force: a "private" militia, a militia as private as the "secret mode of reading" through which meaning is drained and small talk is struck. Such a militia seals Kierkegaard's response to the question that *A Literary Review*, to say nothing of his "authorship," has incessantly raised—"What is chatter?":

> What is it *to chatter*? It is the annulment of the passionate disjunction between being silent and speaking. Only the person who can remain essentially silent can speak essentially, can act essentially. Silence is inwardness. . . . The law manifest in poetic production is identical, on a smaller scale, with the law for the life of every person in social intercourse and education. Anyone who experiences anything primitively also experiences in ideality the possibilities of the same thing and the possibility of the opposite. These possibilities are his legitimate literary property. His own personal actuality, however, is not. His speaking and his producing are, in fact, born of silence. The ideal perfection of what he says and what he produces will correspond to his silence, and the supreme mark of that silence will be that the ideality contains the qualitatively opposite possibility. As soon as the productive artist must give over his own actuality, its facticity, he is no longer essentially productive; his beginning will be his end, and his first word will already be a trespass against the holy modesty of ideality. Therefore from an aesthetic point of view, such a poetic work is certainly also a kind of private talkativeness and is readily recognized by the absence of its opposite equilibrium. For ideality is the equilibrium of opposites. For example, someone who has been motivated to creativity by unhappiness, if he is genuinely devoted to ideality, will be equally inclined to write about happiness and about unhappiness. But silence, the brackets he puts around his own personality, is precisely the condition for gaining ideality; otherwise, despite all precautionary measures such as setting the scene in Africa etc., his one-sided performance will still show. An author certainly must have his private personality as everyone else has, but this must be his *aduton*, and just

as the entrance to a house is barred by stationing two soldiers with crossed bayonets, so by means of the dialectical cross of qualitative opposites the equality of ideality forms the barrier that prevents all access. (97–99)

The *aduton* with which *From the Papers of One Still Living* begins reappears at the close of *A Literary Review* as the sign and seal of its repetition, its "persuasiveness," its "movement in place."[41] This secret chamber not only protects "authorship" from the failures of Hans Christian Andersen's novel but more importantly guards speech itself from condemnation under the category of "chatter." But—and this is decisive—the secret chamber *cannot protect itself*; its very nature is to be vulnerable to attack, which means in this case: to disclosure, to being divulged, to vulgarization, to being made public, to publicity, to communication, to being made common. To guard against this threat, something must stand guard; some stand-in must be discovered; some representative for this secret chamber in the open spaces of the profane must keep watch. *Papers* discovered a stand-in of this sort in the "editor," who, as a medium for the "author," instituted communication as *communicatio idiomatum*. The pseudonyms of Kierkegaard's "authorship" were similar stand-ins; each pseudonym was at least a *vigilius*, if not a Vigilius Haufniensis who as a guard oversaw Copenhagen.

But the stand-ins, as literary "soldiers with crossed bayonets," do not derive their power from the people of Copenhagen, from the king of Copenhagen, from a divine inspiration or any power whatsoever. The power of these stand-ins to enforce the law of exclusion—"No entrance!"—derives entirely from the exclusivity of the *aduton*. By keeping the *aduton* free from foreigners, the stand-ins make it possible to understand "existence" as "inwardness." For without these literary soldiers, the communication of "existence" would immediately become its defilement; everything could be interpreted as referring to "lived"—not transfigured, internalized, retrieved—experience. The stand-ins therefore make it possible to communicate without such communication making "existence" common to all and thereby making it into something other than ex-istence, namely, a standing-in without "inwardness." Every stand-in insists on this: it does not exist.

Such is indeed the insistence of the editors and pseudonyms who try to reclaim "existence." The "soldiers with crossed bayonets," however illegitimate they may be, cannot *not* take their place before the door of the *aduton* if the *aduton*, and therefore "existence" as well as "inwardness," is to be itself and not immediately an abstraction, a nonentity. The stand-ins cannot *not* take their place, and this impossibility, which gives rise to a peculiar necessity, makes "authorship" and speech in general dependent on their illegitimate, *unauthorized* power. If the possibility of "opposites" is an author's "legitimate literary property," it is not a property that properly belongs to the author but derives from *possible readings*, and the literary "soldiers," of course, represent these readings. For this reason, Kierkegaard criticizes the author of *Two Ages* for prefacing her novel with its own review and therefore sending out an advance guard—that is, an "authorized" reading. No reading can be authorized without its immediately exposing the author to "chatter," which the authorization was intended to prevent. If, however, every reading is unauthorized, so is every "soldier."

Standing opposite the house, standing opposed to each other, standing in for the speaker, *the soldiers are themselves the suspension of the disjunction between private and public.* They are not the agents of "chatter" and are not simply representatives of possible "chatterers" but stand for "chatter" itself, even as their duty consists in keeping "chatter" at bay. Neither one nor the other can be understood as an authorized reading, so they *both* stand for neither-nor, and these neither-nors interpolate every text, every discourse. The communication of orders to such soldiers—"Keep the doors crossed," "Make these things known"—countermands these very orders, since no order can stand without its own soldier. No communication, therefore, escapes the unauthorized power of this literary militia, which means that communication cannot escape the suspension of the opposition between private and public, privacy and publicity, "indirectness" and directness. Communication cannot escape "chatter" without itself becoming more—and not qualitatively different—"chatter."

Prophecy, "Police"

"Chatter" is pure language. Purified of meaning as well as intentionality, expressionless to the point of standing in for "inwardness" itself, "chatter" is precisely the defilement of the difference through which Kierkegaard sought to secure communication from the threat of making the exceptional and the unique into the common: the distinction, namely, between direct and "indirect" modes of discourse. "Chatter" even escapes the suspension of opposites, speech and silence, into a higher conceptual unity: "What is it *to chatter*? It is the suspension [*Ophævelsen*] of the passionate disjunction between being silent and speaking" (97, modified). Nothing could be further from Hegelian *Aufhebung* than this *ophævelse* since the former conceives of opposites in terms of the concept that annuls the principle of noncontradiction whereas the latter annuls the disjunctive judgment—"either/or"—and makes the very conceptuality of every concept, its ability to single things out, undecidable.

"Chatter," as a result, does not raise speech and silence into a speech that includes its own silence; such a speech would in fact correspond to "indirect" communication, the communication of the incommunicable. "Chatter" is not "indirect" communication, yet it cannot be distinguished from it by any means. Certainly no reading can discover the criteria for this distinction, for each reading is exposed to a modification in which *it*, and not the *aduton* and therefore not "existence," goes underground and comes out as a "secret mode of reading." The secrecy of speech against secret reading: no one can decide on this altercation, without opposition; no one can even say that each cannot do without the other, "essential speaking" (97) generating "chatter" and "chatter," in reverse, generating "essential speaking."

An intention toward "chatter" is self-defeating. Under no condition can one *try* to "chatter," since "chatter" is then cited, and speaking, if not "essential speaking," once again takes over. Such speaking can then, of course, revert to "chatter," but this reversion, which no conversion can forestall and no conversation guard itself against, is not a matter of intentions, plans, attempts, or experiments. The nonsubjective character of "chatter" does not, however, imply its objectivity. "Chatter" is, rather, the permanent displacement of the terms through which language has been grasped, including the terms "subject" and "object" as they have been deployed in philosophy, logic, and grammar: "What does it mean *to be loquacious*? It is the suspended [*ophævede*] passionate disjunction between subjectivity and objectivity" (103, modified). The suspension of this disjunction displaces the subject and object of logic, grammar, and philosophy; it therefore undoes the terms of opposition through which Kierkegaard had cast his polemic against the "objectivity" of Hegelian philosophy. Dialectical *Aufhebung* (sublation) suspends its operation in the *ophævelse* carried out by a colloquial loquacity.

With the suspension of the disjunction between subjectivity and objectivity, all other terms of opposition collapse, including those of sexuality. Kierkegaard's "Concluding Observation" crystallizes the collapse of disjunction in one characterless character of *Two Ages*, a character without the constancy of character who by always altering, "represents" the anonymity and presentlessness of "the present age." It is, as could be expected, a certain overdressed woman, a Mrs. Waller. She is not simply an overdressed woman; by virtue of her age and position, she represents the author, whom Kierkegaard never fails to call "he," even when he recognizes his "feminine resignation" (16). But Mrs. Waller does not simply represent the author; she speaks of "the demonic" in a way that repeats the author of *The Concept of Anxiety* and thereby disrupts the criteria of identity to the point where the demonic loses its distinction from the mechanical:

> Mrs. Waller's comment on the demonic is very true, and yet as she says it she gives the impression of being an anonymity, a hand-organ [*Positiv*], a music-box. Utterances become so objective, their range so

all-encompassing, that eventually it becomes accidental who says
them, a situation which in terms of human speaking corresponds to
acting on principle. And just as the public is a pure abstraction,
eventually human speech [*menneskeligt Tale*] will become such; no one
will speak any longer, but an objective reflection will gradually deposit
a kind of atmospheric something, an abstract sound that will render
human speech superfluous, just as machines render workers superfluous. (104, modified)

Language as such, "chatter," displaces subjectivity and thereby
takes away the once secure position of the *worker*, the one in whose
labor spirit is uplifted and for whom love, as "works of love," is
manifest. Therein lies the threat as well as the promise of "chatter."
Kierkegaard assigns chatter to "objectivity" but has forgotten that
this cannot be the case: "What does it mean *to be loquacious*? It is
the suspended passionate disjunction between subjectivity and
objectivity. . . . The loquacious man chatters about anything and
everything" (103). "Objectivity," which is nothing more than a
paleonym for a mode of being not yet named, resides in a certain
positivity: in a *positiv*, a hand organ, a talking machine. Its irregular
resistance to the manipulation of subjectivity releases its spiritless
sound, including the spiritless sounds wherein the specter of the
demonic is heard. Nothing could be further from the invocation of
the genius-artist to whom Hans Christian Andersen dedicated his
novelistic energies than such a *positiv*. And Mrs. Waller, as hand
grinder, who spins out statements on "the demonic," is so thoroughly integrated into this machine for making noise that one
cannot even say that she is talking; talkativeness goes on, and its
goings-on are ghostly, "spiritual," repetitious, and demonic.
    Mrs. Waller thus emerges as the precise counterpart to that
image of the tortured artist whose cries of torture are turned into
the song with which Kierkegaard introduced the opening fragment
of *Either/Or* and thus opened his vast but short-lived "authorship."
In that first fragment, the address of which is *ad se ipsum*, it is "a
reviewer" who, overhearing the sounds, has no ear for their origin
in torture: "Now of course a reviewer resembles a poet to a hair,

except that he does not have the anguish in his heart, or the music on his lips."[42] No subject suffers within the confines of the *positiv*; the hand that turns it exerts pressure, to be sure, but it has nothing to say, and so the hairline distinction between poet and reviewer, which defines the aesthete and aesthetics in general, is itself suspended, leaving no place for the indecisive aesthete or aesthetics as a site of indecisiveness. Neither/nor overtakes *Either/Or*.

According to *The Concept of Anxiety*, the word "demonic" is "rare in our day."[43] Mrs. Waller makes it common, defiles it, but in doing so undoes its definition: it no longer serves to define the willful turning away from the salvation faith alone can grant. The opposition of faith to faithlessness, like that of spirit to demonism, is absorbed into a category of all-inclusive sexual disorientation, namely, "philandering." Mrs. Waller repeats what she has heard about the demonic character of philandering[44] and thereby makes "philandering," as a phrase, into a suspension of the polemical relationship between faithfulness and faithlessness with which *A Literary Review* began. Philandering names a mode of sexuality that knows no opposition and for this reason cannot distinguish between two sexes; it is in fact nonsexual, as long as sexuality is defined by "passion" and "passion" expresses itself in overcoming, or coming over, opposition. Otherness, as opposition, means nothing to the linguistic philandering that speaks of the philandering as demonic. Philandering accepts therefore no position; it abandons language to an "objectivity" without positions, theses, or statements, a language of sheer *positivity*: language as *positiv*, pure language.

When chatter takes place, language itself, and not an "existing" subject, speaks. But this speech is immediately broken off because the purity of language is confounded in such speech. Language thus interrupts and disrupts every organic development, every claim to succession, every well-ordered machine, but its punctual yet untimely strokes are not without a certain promise. Indeed, Kierkegaard ends the review with the promise that any reader who in rereading *Two Ages* is able to distinguish the claims of the author from those of "the present age" on the one hand and those of the reviewer on the other will experience a distinctive joy. The condition for the fulfillment of this promise is a "critical" ability to distinguish Fru Waller from Fru Gyllembourg, to distinguish, in other words, philandering "chatter" from faithful "authorship." On this condition, reflection on "chatter" can give rise to an almost vertiginous glee. Kierkegaard's giddiness when speaking of Fru Waller's fleeting reflection on herself before the mirror (54) has less to do with critical appreciation than with the ecstasis of a reflection that is allowed, for a moment, to reflect on reflection without having to add, "Reflection itself is not the evil" (96). It is pure pleasure once it is domesticated into "domestic reflection," and repetition is therefore reduced to mimesis. The "persuasiveness" (*overtalelse*) of the novel, as opposed to the talkativeness of its principal "character," is a function of this domesticating operation.

But this operation cannot be protected from the corrosive character of "the present age," an age in which the disjunction between domestic and foreign, private and public, the work of the subject and the play of language, is as thoroughly suspended as that between subjectivity and objectivity, silence and speech. The oversized review is proof of this. Neither the "decisive" category of the religious nor the "indecisive" one of the aesthetic can make "persuasiveness" give up its tendency toward loquacity, its own "overtalking." Persuasion talks too much, or not enough, or neither, but never just enough and never "essentially." Another category is therefore needed to speak of the persuasive without having already ruled out its talkativeness. Such a category punctuates *A Literary Review*: it is the literary—the literary no longer subservient to "aesthetic interpretation," no longer in service of surveying a novel; the literary as breaking up, without reserve, of words into broken, inexpressive letters: "But when the context has become meaningless, it is futile to make large-scale surveys; then the best thing to do is to scrutinize the particular parts of what is said. When the mouth strikes slogans [*slaaer Sladder*], it is futile to deliver a coherent discourse; it is better to take each word by itself—and so it is with the situation of individuals" (106). Isolated words, forced out of propositional contexts, struck into slogans, give themselves up;

they are no longer significant words but letters held together by quotation marks, mere "words."

These counterstrokes to the strikes against time grant Kierkegaard a certain profane prophetic power. From the striking of words into slogans, from this shattering, or "chattering," of language, there arises a mode of speaking in advance that does not appeal to natural or cultural regularities or even to the divine ruler of the world. Speaking in advance of cognitive, aesthetic, or religious criteria, Kierkegaard takes his cue from "chatter" itself: "Chatter anticipates essential speaking [*Snakken anticiperer den væsentlige Talen*]" (97). The profanity of Kierkegaard's prophecy consists in precisely this anticipation. It does not wait for "essence" but stands out in the mode of permanent preliminariness; it gives up its effort to guard the "sacred" *aduton* and makes public not precisely the "secret" of Kierkegaard the man but a "secret mode of reading" to which the secret of communication, its freedom, falls prey. Speaking the *fatum* of communication then occasions a prophetic *phēmē* (rumor).

When language is "chattered," slogans are struck. One such slogan absorbs all the others: it is POLICE. Anxiety converges on this alarming word. As name and call, it appeals to public—not "aesthetic" and not "religious"—authorities whose absence, or inexistence, is made apparent in the de-privation to which the very word "public" attests. No authority is "public" except that of the phantomlike, spiritless spirit of the "press": an authority without authority, an authority in whose train a monstrous series of phantomlike "authors" appears. To this authority *A Literary Notification* must turn, and it does so in order to denounce itself, to renounce "the literary." With this slogan—"police"—the literary crosses itself out and opens the space for anticipatory speaking:

> The following changes will also occur. Whereas in older structures (relations between individuals and generations) the non-commissioned officers, company commanders, generals, the hero (that is, the men of excellence, the men prominent in their various ranks, the leaders) were *recognizable* . . . , now the men of excellence, the leaders (each

according to his respective rank) will be without authority precisely because they will have divinely understood the diabolical principle of the leveling process. Like civilian, plain-clothes policemen [*som Politiet er civilt*], they will be *unrecognizable*, concealing their respective distinctions and giving support only negatively—that is, by repulsion, while the infinite uniformity of abstraction judges every individual, examines him in his isolation. (107)

The street clothes of the policeman bear no mark of distinction, not even those that might indicate whether the policeman is a man at all. The assignment to which these "police" are committed, in contrast to those of the prophet, judge, scientist, or "author," has no support whatsoever; least of all do "the police" have the support of a polis or a *civis* whose border they would patrol. Their "agents" are "secret" (107), not because their actions take place in secret but because they cannot *not* hide the secret that they are "agents" and therefore somehow, perhaps unbeknownst to themselves, *act*. But the action of this police force consists of nothing other than this; it notifies the authorities, who are, however, not there. From this notification, the depths of reflection into which "the present age" has fallen are pierced. They announce to themselves, over and over, "police." The futility of this undertaking knows no limits: no *communicatio idiomatum* could be more idiotic or more idiomatic.

But the notification of the "police" to themselves is not without its own peculiar force. For each such notification enforces the reflection that it would seemingly seek to oppose. It feeds the swamp as it drains words of their hitherto established meanings. The prophetic character of Kierkegaard's statement lies in its ability to put *itself*, and not "the self" understood as the subject, into action, into the action that does not oppose reflection, the shattering or "chattering" of language. And the first word to be so "chattered" is precisely "police." For as Kierkegaard hastens to point out when the issue of "authority and revelation" is raised, the very notion of a police force includes that of authority, regardless of "whether a policeman be a rogue or an honest man."[45]

But a police force without authority, a police force devoid of every claim to authority other than that of the ghostly "press," a police force therefore without the speech of law, without any possible jurisdiction, including even the diction of "Christendom"—what is that? Not a metaphorical police force, to be sure, for the idea of authority is what transfers in every metaphorical deployment of the word "police." Without the transfer of this idea, without even the "poetic" authority to make a transfer and to transport auditors into a region of pure possibility, a police force can do nothing but *defraud* "the public." And this is what it would do. "Secret agents" would thus incriminate themselves in the linguistic crime par excellence—defrauding "the public" of its public character, defrauding discourse of its publicity, of everything that secures the public access to itself, including subjectivity, objectivity, substance, value, and significance. The police force *would* thus incriminate themselves, if only there were a law by virtue of which this force could be judged illegal. But it is the very absence of the law—or the uncanny "presence" of a law that says "no more present tense!"—that gives rise to a "*literary* police force" in the first place: not a metaphorical police, not a figural police of any kind, not a police through whom anyone could secure a home, but the lawless, disruptive, interruptive force of what is called the "literary." Saying "the police," notifying the authorities with *any* word, shatters language: nothing is referred to, no act is undertaken, nothing is said or done—but an alarming word rings.

Regimes remain behind, and authors continue to claim authority over their books. Authenticity is everywhere proclaimed as origin and goal. Existence is understood to have its highest expression in silence. And yet a mode of reading, which is secret but never silent, removes again and again the intimate underpinning of each of these slogans: legality, authority, authenticity, existence, or, to invoke that which by enforcing itself enforces all these others, "police." Striking words into slogans, "chattering" language, depriving authorities of their publicity as well as their privacy, draining each notification of the authorities—"police!"—of its own authority to give notice: none of these changes a thing. Everything remains in its place, yet each thing, as soon as it is spoken, is altered, struck down, shattered, "chattered."

Speaking in anticipation of this alteration, throwing himself into the irregular cycle of its strokes, Kierkegaard notifies "the public" of itself, notifies himself of his complicity in such publicity, and he therefore divides himself from himself, without, however, making this division into a theme of "indirect" communication. Anticipation not only haunts this notification but strikes it into a "political" slogan: a police force without law, without having been legislated, without an established executive, without the very authority to be a police force, is nevertheless *out there*. The being of this force, more than the tension of "inwardness," deserves the title "existence." It, "with crossed bayonets," crosses out every stance, yet leaves everything standing as before. *En literair Anmeldese* constitutes a fraudulent notification of a fraud whereby the "literary"—the interruptive, the disruptive, the shattering and the "chattering" of language—deprives the "public" of its privacy, its publicity, its commonality, and its communication.

Conclusion: Negotiations

Bavarder est la honte du langage.
                    —Maurice Blanchot, "La parole vaine"

A story could easily be constructed out of Kierkegaard's altercation with "chatter": he began his life as an author trying to combat its effects on all fronts, wrote a series of incomparable works in which this battle was waged with a progressively clearer understanding of its complications, and ended by capitulating to its superior force. This capitulation, far from being a mere surrender to an opponent, was in its own way a triumph: in the anticipation of "essential" speech—and this defines "chatter"—*anticipation* is itself announced; in the suspension of the disjunction between speech and silence—this too defines the term—the conception of language and linguistic activity that drove Kierkegaard into the hands of "indirect communication" is likewise undone; and the single law capable of holding back "chatter" on all fronts—the law stipulating "No more present tense!" and therefore "No more presence!"—opens up a future no longer comprehensible according to the schema of the future tense and therefore no longer comprehended as a future-present at all. In the future anticipated by this unauthorized law, "the present" would be, as it were, a thing of the past. Such a future, anticipated in "chatter" if not articulated in any particular speech categorized by this term, would turn out to be an *authentic* one, a future that withdraws from the determination of the present, a future that has nothing to do with the now-points from which presence, and "the present age," is determined and defined. The sign and seal of its authenticity would be the mutual inclusion of silence in speech and speech in silence. Everything silent would thus speak, and all speech would amount to a certain silence. Undecidability on this score, neither-nor, would in turn define the character of the future.

But this story, which turns out to be a story about historicity, does not capture Kierkegaard's relation to "chatter." For it never was an *enemy*, nor was it ever a definite object of polemics. From the beginning, it was a matter of a very particular, even "secret" mode of reading: "chatter" suspends disjunctive judgment, the either-or in which decision is lodged, and this suspension is made accessible to reading once texts are recognized as performances of this very suspension, once they are all, in other words, consigned to the category of "chatter." The explication of the textual character of affective ciphers, dispositions and moods to which no perception can correspond and no object determine, animates and gives direction to Kierkegaard's "psychological" works. At the conclusion of his life as an author, in the final sentence of the "First and Last Declaration" that attests to and puts an end to his "authorship," Kierkegaard affirms that a generalized reading has been his task from the beginning: "once again to read through solo, if possible in a more inward way, the original text of individual existence-relationships."[1] The reading not precisely of the "original" text but of its textuality, which never belongs to an "individual" and has no claims to "originality," does not take place under the rubric of psychology, aesthetics, or even the religious but in the undefined space of the "literary." Without the suspensions of judgment and the delays of decision, no text could be read, certainly no text could be read over and over, each time confirming its original unreadability. Without these suspensions and delays, a transparent medium and a perspicuous moment of decision would wipe away the textuality of the "original text of the individual." Delaying decision, as its anticipation, and the suspension of opposition are, however, the traits of "chatter" as the nonobject and nonsubject of the "literary."

Delays of decision and suspensions of oppositions make the reading of textuality into a *solo* reading, reading sui generis, reading without the established codices and corresponding codes of decipherment that by giving support for decisions only serve to delay decision and to make this delay of decision appear a matter of choice. "Solo" reading precludes every conclusion, and without a conclusion, no story, certainly no life-story or "life-view." Kierkegaard's discovery of "chatter" may give rise to a story about historicity, but it likewise eludes narrative schematization: its future is not simply open but recedes from the provisional conclusiveness demanded by the very concept of storytelling. No one can speak of the future of "chatter" without delaying its future. Therefore, when the topic of discussion comes around to "chatter," anticipations and delays, thus a certain uneasiness, idleness, and, boredom, are not only to be expected; they are, as it were, the rule. Conclusions, however well intended, rely on a present tense or on a future-present and therefore break the rule of "chatter," transforming its idleness into work, its emptiness into fulfillment, its suspension into sublation.

But Kierkegaard does indeed capitulate to "chatter." The word "capitulate" did not at first designate mere resignation before the inevitable but the discussions and negotiations undertaken among "heads" *after* a decisive contest has been fought. In his final newspaper articles and in his own periodical, a periodical that bears the title *The Instant* (*Øieblikket*) and thus accentuates the paradox of its own periodicity, Kierkegaard negotiates with "Christendom." Although these last articles and reviews have been collected under the heading *Attack on "Christendom,"* the term "attack" is misleading. For the decisive battle, if there ever was one, is already over: "Christendom" has won. Under discussion in Kierkegaard's newly founded newspaper are the terms of its victory. *Now Christendom is chatter*: each word in this sentence deserves quotation marks in keeping with Kierkegaard's practice of distinguishing the talk of "Christendom" from the concepts of Christianity and the latter in turn from the thing itself, which is practice or "exercise" *simpliciter*: "The most dreadful sort of blasphemy is that of which 'Christendom' is guilty: driving the God of Spirit into—ludicrous drivel [*Vrøvl*]."[2]

What is worse, the very text of Christianity, Scripture itself, is useless in holding back and driving out this drivel: "But strangely enough the New Testament takes no account of the thing there is all-too-great a mass of in this world, which is the content and vehicle of the world [*Verdens Gehalt*]: drivel [*Vrøvl*], twattle, patter, smallness, mediocrity . . . transforming everything into mere modes of speaking [*Talesmaader*] and so forth. For this reason, there is the difficulty that it is almost impossible to strike at real life, the real world in which we live."[3] This "difficulty," as a massive, yet miniscule, unforeseen lacuna in Scripture, makes it almost impossible to strike at "reality." Scripture could even be seen to give up its claim to providence and reveal its roots not in foresight but in scripturality—in "anticipation." Under these circumstances, every attack is empty. For attacks only reach words, not "the real world in which we live." All talk of "attack" on Kierkegaard's part, on the part of his proponents, and on the part of his antagonists is misleading, unless each attack is presented as a strike at *words themselves*. This strike opens up the possibility of reaching "existence."

Striking at mere words "in the instant"—which is never simply presence—constitutes Kierkegaard's strategy of *negotiation*: he does not enter into a dialogue with "Christendom," nor does he converse with its representatives, but rather negates its *otium*, its "idleness." The negation of idle talk is "negotiation." But there is no negotiation without engaging in this *otium*, the idleness of talk itself, so each negation of the *otium* amounts to the suspension of the opposition between idleness and activity. Such is Kierkegaardian "negotiation," and it knows only one strategy: the modulation of *tone*. After capitulating, without authority, how is it possible to strike back? By altering the tone of speech so thoroughly that no one knows its putative source: "The movement is **Back!** And although it is done without 'authority,' there is, nevertheless, something in the tone [*Tonearten*] which recalls a policeman when he faces a riot and says, Back!"[4]

Striking the word "back" is Kierkegaard's way of striking back. The word can be struck from inside out—in its *Tonearten*, its tonal modes. Once generalized, Kierkegaard's negotiation with "Christendom" strikes at every word until each one becomes a "word," which cannot be distinguished from its "tone." The result of these tonal strikes is the historically and geographically demarcated region of the world called "Christendom" held in quotation marks: "Christendom" as a name, emptied of content; "Christendom" as an idle vehicle of speech, abstracted, made colloquial, turned into an *x*. Since Kierkegaard could not discover terms of negotiation with "chatter" in Scripture, since this strategy of tonal modulation "without authority" cannot be found in the texts from which "Christendom" receives its name, he had no choice but to find it in profane texts. And this finding could only be done in writing and reviewing this writing. The peculiar prophetics developed in his "solo" reading is as a result an altogether profane one. The future of "chatter," which is indissociable from an unauthorized order to go back, is likewise profane, so profane and so common that it cannot, with the authority of a "no!" distinguish itself from the sacred, the uncommon, and the uncommunicable.

~

If "chatter" were to pose an open question, it could perhaps play an effective role in a historical dialogue. The reception of Kierkegaard's writings would not necessarily be understood as a conversation with the author or even a discussion with his "authorship" but could instead be comprehended as a dialogue with the tradition in which his writings function both as significant response and as impetus to new modes of questioning. They would constitute an alteration of the question, and the ability to alter the question in this way would confirm the historical effectivity of Kierkegaard's writings. But "chatter" cannot be so easily incorporated into this schema. Not only is it impossible to draw it into a genuine discussion, but it corrodes every such discussion to the point where there is nothing—and certainly no serious questions—to discuss; there is not even a question of a "real" discussion. When this "nothing" takes over conversation, silence does not set in; rather, "chatter" sets out on its incalculable course. The corrosive character of "chatter" is doubtless an effect, but its effectiveness cannot be captured in a net, or a "not," woven by the intricate interlacing of questions and answers. The degree and scope of its effectiveness await determination. Even the specific effects of Kierkegaard's concept of "chatter" have yet to be explored. No talk of its "future" can neglect these issues. Although neither the effects nor the effectivity of these effects can be examined here, an indication of how such an examination might proceed is indispensable for even a provisional review of Kierkegaard's negotiations with "chatter."

Stated without reservation: Kierkegaard's dealings with "chatter" stamped the character of the most powerful and effective programs for the renewal of philosophy in the twentieth century. Wittgenstein, Benjamin, and Heidegger, each in his own way, attempted to track down the enigmatic origin of "chatter."[5] Kierkegaard has often been credited with contributing to the development of modern philosophy, even if the exact nature of his contribution has been difficult to assess. Indicative of this difficulty is the attempt to make him—of all men!—into the "father" of this or that philosophical movement. But in the programs of Wittgenstein, Benjamin, and Heidegger, "chatter" survives not so much as a problem as the source of the very problematic of philosophy, a problematic each one of them wished, in unique ways and in line with Kierkegaard, to emancipate from "philosophy."

Language goes "on a holiday" . . . and philosophical problems emerge (Wittgenstein). The workplace, locus of significance, is abandoned . . . and "talk" takes over (Heidegger). The language of names, as the language of language, falls into judgment . . . and the abyss of "empty talk" opens up (Benjamin). Each of these motifs deserves a study of its own, and each one would be indebted to "chatter" in the Kierkegaardian sense. The terms of this debt are, however, so thoroughly implicated in "chatter" that they cannot be determined according to the schemata of spontaneous-receptive understanding, schemata whose aim is always the discovery of a continuous, substantial tradition through which understanding learns to understand itself. "Chatter" in the Kierkegaardian sense does not found or promote a tradition; it is closer to a swamp than a source. Its "origin" is an enigma whose solution—for Wittgenstein, Benjamin, and Heidegger—would be the very dissolution of philosophy as it has hitherto been thought and practiced. Kierkegaard insisted that even Scripture, which still had the glow of revelation to protect it, gave him no help in this one regard. Those who could read his "solo reading" are, by contrast, in a more favorable position.

Reference Matter

Notes

For complete author names, titles, and publication data for the works cited here in short form, see the Bibliography, pp. 295–308.

Introduction

1. Thematic discussions of "chatter" usually take place under the heading of "gossip," since the latter implies more highly developed social and psychological dimensions than does the former. Research into the uses, functions, and consequences of gossip has been undertaken in a variety of disciplines: in the field of psychology, see Thiel-Dohrmann, *Unter dem Siegel der Verschwiegenheit*; in sociology, see Rosnow and Fine, *Rumor and Gossip*; in anthropology, see Haviland, *Gossip, Reputation, and Knowledge in Zinacantan*; in media studies, see Kapferer, *Rumeurs*, and Lewin, *Gossip*; in philosophy, see Bok, *Secrets*; in literary studies, see Drew, *The Literature of Gossip* and especially Spacks, *Gossip*. Each of these studies presents and evaluates gossip according to its ambivalent social function: it can be an instrument of social control as well as a means of resistance to authority. For instance, anecdotes (Greek *an-ekdotē*, stories that are not to be given out, not authorized for publication, as yet unedited) can challenge authority at the very least through their denial of ascertainable authorship, but anecdotes can also solidify authority insofar as they put their subject in his or her place. The pressure to treat "chatter" as gossip and thereby to disclose purposes for its communicative performances is at least in part due to disciplinary obligations. No discipline can account for the nonpurposive, the random, or the aleatory—not even

the customary discipline of last resort, aesthetics, as long as the objects of aesthetic reflection are defined by the famous phrase "purposiveness without purpose." Whereas decoding gossip and disclosing its various social and psychological functions supply more than one discipline with an explicit goal, reading "chatter" cannot belong unambiguously to any established disciplinary practice. Deciphering the polemical drift of anecdotes cannot be its primary concern.

2. On the relation of "chatter" (*Geschwätz*), as Kierkegaard understood this word, to translation, see Benjamin, "Ueber die Sprache überhaupt und über die Sprache des Menschen," in *Gesammelte Schriften*, 2, 1:152–54; "On Language as Such and on the Language of Man," in *Reflections*, 326–28.

3. See the rather uncertain etymological suggestions in *The Oxford English Dictionary*, ed. J. A. Simpson and E. S. C. Weiner, 3:60.

4. See the famous remark of Ludwig Wittgenstein: "For philosophical problems arise when language *goes on holiday* [*wenn die Sprache* feiert]" (*Philosophical Investigations*, 19, sec. 38). The exact character of Wittgenstein's defense of language from the "vacations" it habitually takes and the relation of this defense to his reading of Kierkegaard has yet to be determined in the vast literature on his work. Preliminary to this exploration would be an understanding of the eruption of *celebration* in language as the source of philosophical problems. "Language on a Holiday" will be the title of the second part of this (necessarily incomplete) book.

5. See, for example, the accusations of *lēros* that interrupt both Socrates' and Hippias's attempts to define the nature of *to kalon* (the beautiful) in the *Hippias Major*, esp. 298 B. Hippias concludes with Socrates' words: "He [who wants to know what *to kalon*, the beautiful, means] should give up and abandon all that small talking [*smikrologias*] so he won't be thought a complete fool for applying himself, as he is now, to babbling nonsense [*lērous kai phluarias*]" (304 B; Ion—*Hippias Major*, 79). A reading of Plato's "small talk" cannot, of course, be undertaken here, but such a reading could perhaps begin with the quotation from the *Hippias Major* that serves as the epigraph for Kierkegaard's *Concluding Unscientific Postscript* and explicates the title of the text it appends, namely *Philosophical Fragments*: "But Socrates, really, what do you think of all that? It's flakings and clippings of speeches, as I told you before, divided up into little bits" (304 A; 78, translation modified). See Chapter 3.

6. See Schleiermacher, *Hermeneutik und Kritik*, 82–83: "Es wird gere-

det, weil die Sprache sich nur in der Kontinuität der Wiederholung erhält. Was nur schon vorhanden Gewesenes wiederholt, ist an sich nichts. Wettergespräche." (Things are said, because language maintains itself only in the continuity of its repetition. But whatever repeats only things that have already been around is nothing in itself. Talk of the weather.)

7. Schleiermacher, *Hermeneutik und Kritik*, 83.

8. The explication and examination of this thesis would itself demand a book, the prolegomenon for this one. Instead of this prolegomenon, an inadequate series of references to certain ground-breaking writings on romanticism, hermeneutics, and Hegel will have to suffice. For a reading of romantic irony in which it is connected to the catastrophe of an always inauthentic selfhood, see de Man, "The Rhetoric of Temporality," in *Blindness and Insight*, 187–228. On the problematic character of the "other" to whom, according to Schleiermacher, every hermeneutical endeavor is addressed, see Hamacher, "Hermeneutic Ellipses," 177–210. On the relation of speculative dialectics to dramatic discourse, see Lacoue-Labarthe, "The Caesura of the Speculative," in *Typography*. On Hegel's theory of the sign, see Derrida, "The Pit and the Pyramid," in *Margins of Philosophy*, 69–108. One further point of reference: the intricate reading of Kierkegaard's apartness—and of what sets Kierkegaard apart—that is undertaken with remarkable precision by Agacinski in *Aparté*.

9. See Kierkegaard, *Fear and Trembling*, 54: "Is There a Teleological Suspension of the Ethical?" (where the ethical, against a massive tradition, is defined as the suspension of teleological principles).

10. See *Fear and Trembling*, 123.

11. Kierkegaard, *Two Ages*, 77; see Chapter 5.

12. *Two Ages*, 97, translation modified.

13. On the relation of fate to the self-fulfilling prophecy, see Cohen, *Ethik*, 362; Benjamin, "Zur Kritik der Gewalt," in *Gesammelte Schriften*, 2, 1:197–99, and "Critique of Violence," in *Reflections*, 295–96. Cf. Fenves, *Peculiar Fate*, 184–88.

14. *Two Ages*, 97, translation modified.

15. The Hebrew Bible, the Christian Bible, and the Koran condemn and seek to eradicate defamation, rumor, gossip, hearsay, idle speech, and the like. The fundamental injunction from which this effort draws its strength is the prohibition against false witness in the Decalogue (Exod. 20:13). But the denunciation of loose talk casts a much wider net. In

Proverbs Solomon warns against association with gossips (Prov. 20:19), and certain sections of Job could be considered illustrations of this warning. In Amos the price of associating with those who engage in empty conversation is spelled out: "For He that forms the mountains and creates the wind [*ruach*: inspirational breath] reports to man his chatter [*sicho*: light, insipid conversation]" (Amos 4:13). Since this report takes place on the day of judgment, how and why one speaks is as decisive as how and why one acts. Further injunctions against defamation and gossip can be found in Paul's admonition to the Ephesians (Eph. 4:29) and, more graphically, in James's description of the tongue as a flame that ignites "the cycle of nature" and is "set on fire by hell" (James 3:6). Similar injunctions can be found in the Koran, especially when it is a question of defaming innocent women; see, for instance, *The Koran*, 246–48 (24:11–24).

Scriptural injunctions against loose talk lend authority and rigor to those who wish to define and suppress its manifestations. Moralizing condemnations of gossip and hearsay can never reach the heights of ingenuity and resolve that are to be found in condemnations based on scriptural exegesis. Talmudic and rabbinic literature, for instance, often denounces *loshon hora* (evil tongue, hearsay, gossip). Of the many rabbinic commentators who make the denunciation of "chatter" into a fundamental principle of life and learning, none is more persistent and more thorough than Rabbi Israel Meier Kagan, the Chafetz Chaim (1839–1933). His Talmudic commentaries never tire of stressing the harm done by *loshon hora*, and he even sees in this debasement of language (*loshon*) the first, if not the "original" or inherited sin: "The Chafetz Chaim points out that the first sin ever committed was a result of *loshon hora*. The serpent spoke *loshon hora* when he told Chavah that Hashem was deceiving her when he said He would punish her if she ate from the Tree of Knowledge" (Menachem Moshe Oppen, *A Twist of the Tongue*, 13). Hence, the supreme edict against spreading loose talk: "Refraining from *loshon hora* is not a simple *chessed* [kindness]; it is the highest form of *chessed* possible" (ibid., 19). Since purity depends on keeping speech to a minimum, it is important to alienate oneself from everyday discourse. No one should be too intimate with language; each word worth speaking comes from a distance: "One should use speech tersely, as in sending a telegram" (Israel Meir, *Middos*, 200). The justification for the injunction against *loshon hora* remains constant: once God entered into human language, he sanctified it, and so its only altogether legitimate use lies in the preservation, remembrance, and study of divinely sanctioned speech. Every other use, even those that are not blasphemous or otherwise *ra* (evil, wicked), amounts to illegitimate intrusions into a domain made holy by the divine presence.

16. On "empty" and "full" speech in relation to reference, self-reference, and illocution, see Jacques Lacan, "The Function and Field of Speech and Language in Psychoanalysis," in *Ecrits*, esp. 40–56. Cf. Mikkel Borch-Jacobsen, "How to Do Nothing with Words," in *Lacan*, 123–67.

17. The teleological premises of "speech act theory"—premises that alone guarantee the theoretical character of this theory—are admirably explicated by Jacques Derrida, *Limited, Inc.*, esp. 66–77.

18. Exemplary instances of these movements can be found in the following texts: Buber, *I and Thou*; Bakhtin, *Dostoevsky's Poetics*; Oakeshott, *Rationalism in Politics*; Rorty, *Philosophy and the Mirror*; Jauss, *Questions and Answers*. The *only* link among all these vastly different programs—and each of them is in its own way programmatic—is the more or less explicit model of conversation to which each one appeals against a supposedly "traditional" emphasis on monological presentations. Given these appeals, it would be worthwhile to reconsider the status of monologue in the strict sense of the word. See, for instance, the "Monolog" of Novalis (*Werke*, 426–27), which opens with the statement "Genuine dialogue is merely wordplay." For another instance, consider the "monological art" of Nietzsche, which is the only mode of logos that survives the death of God (see Nietzsche, *Sämtliche Werke*, 3:616; *Gay Science*, 324). Or Kafka: "One means of evil is dialogue."

19. Gadamer, *Wahrheit und Methode*, 361; *Truth and Method*, 383, translation modified.

20. See Gadamer, *Truth and Method*, 362.

21. Ibid., 367, translation modified.

22. Ibid., 366.

23. See the poem of Hölderlin, "Friedensfeier" (Celebration of peace), where the "since" of *Seit ein Gespräch* (since a conversation) takes its measure from a *Gesang* (song) that we are "soon" to be. The "conversation" is therefore always preliminary; "we" never "are" a "conversation" except on the condition that "we" not yet "be," a condition that Hölderlin calls *Ein Zeichen* (a sign). For a rendering of this poem into English, see Hölderlin, *Poems and Fragments*, 432–45.

24. Gadamer, *Truth and Method*, 363, translation modified. On the

difficulties and dilemmas of the rhetorical question, see the famous analysis of de Man, *Allegories of Reading*, 9–12. It is unfortunate that Gadamer, who acknowledges his acquaintance with de Man, does not respond to this not altogether disguised attack on the "principle" of hermeneutics; see "Hermeneutics and Logocentrism," 114. In Gadamer's discussion with Jürgen Habermas, he insists upon a certain unavoidability of rhetoric but does not see this insistence as altering the conception of authentic questioning, as our "existence," developed in *Truth and Method*; see Habermas, "Hermeneutic Claim," 247–48; Gadamer, "Reply to My Critics," 292–93.

Of note in this context is de Man's "response" to the conception of literary hermeneutics and "reception aesthetics" that Hans Robert Jauss has developed in close parallel with the philosophical hermeneutics of Gadamer. In his program for an aesthetics of reception, Jauss claims that "the open, indeterminate structure makes a new interpretation possible, whereas on the other hand the historical communication of question and answer limits the arbitrariness of interpretation. . . . In the historical tradition of art, a past work survives not through eternal questions, nor through permanent answers, but through the more or less dynamic interrelationship between question and answer, between problem and solution, which can stimulate a new understanding and can allow the resumption of the dialogue between past and future" (Jauss, *Aesthetic of Reception*, 69–70). De Man diagnoses a symptomatic ellipsis operating in the "logic" of question and answer: "Characteristic of such omissions is Jauss's lack of interest, bordering on outright dismissal, in any consideration derived from what has, somewhat misleadingly, come to be known as the 'play' of the signifier, semantic effects produced on the level of the letter rather than of the word or the sentence and which therefore escape the network of hermeneutic questions and answers" (introduction to *Aesthetic of Reception*, xix). To be sure, Jauss tries to distinguish himself from Gadamer and indeed claims in his "Response to Paul de Man" that he has left Gadamer behind, but the scale of this distance is never clearly articulated (see Jauss's contribution to Waters and Godzich, *Reading de Man Reading*, 202–8). The scale is evidently supposed to lie in Jauss's less "classical" and therefore more inclusive "horizon," and thus in his greater openness to an "other" whom the interpreter is supposed to "receive." But the essays collected into *Aesthetische Erfahrung* make such a claim doubtful. In one of these essays Jauss launches his most emphatic challenge to de Man. The essay, entitled "A Questioning Adam: On the

History and Functions of Questions and Answers," like another prominent essay in the collection, takes its point of departure from the Hebrew Bible, which is quoted in either Latin or German and is neatly submerged into the hermetic history of the Christian West (what Kierkegaard derisively called "Christendom" precisely because of its illusory continuity). After delineating de Man's presentation of the relation of grammar to rhetoric in the "rhetorical question," Jauss proceeds to discuss a few examples of how rhetorical questions have previously been treated. This brief history, if it even deserves the title "history," lightly touches on Quintilian, Cicero, Longinus, Abbé Sieyés, and ends up, quite naturally, with Goebbels: " 'Do you want total war?' [is a question] which pretends that one still has the freedom to choose in order more easily to steer the already inflamed crowd toward an unconditional 'Yes!' " (*Questions and Answers*, 84–85). De Man is effectively paired with Goebbels. The mechanism of this comparison, which is supposed to invalidate de Man's argument without further discussion, should not be overlooked: Jauss, simply stated, cannot think of Goebbels's question as anything but a rhetorical one; it cannot under any condition be a "real" question. Why? Because he has decided that the "inflamed crowd"—why are they inflamed?—has altogether lost its freedom, its ability to respond, and therefore its responsibility: the freedom, therefore, to say "no" and the responsibility that attends upon a "yes." Jauss thus absolves this "inflamed crowd," who after all have been made mad with rhetoric, of all responsibility for the total war that ensued. But the inflamed crowd could have cooled down and said no. Such things do happen, and even if they did not, it would make no difference. Not only is Jauss's "response" to de Man utterly inadequate, citing a couple of historical sources, drawing on the most banal psychology of the emotions and then proceeding to cite an incontrovertible authority ("Hugo Friedrich has clearly demonstrated the difference between the rhetorical and poetic functions of the question," *Questions and Answers*, 85); the entire "response," which is supposed to recognize the "other," undertaken in a chapter called "A Questioning Adam," sees in the Hebraic Bible, mistitled "The Old Testament," a text that "opens the field of play to questions and answers in the occidental, Christian tradition" (*Questions and Answers*, 52). That this "occidental, Christian tradition" is founded upon a denial of the "other"—and in this case, an "other" that wrote the texts in question—does not concern Jauss; in fact, he welcomes it since he can then proceed to cite, without question, a "tradition" from Quintilian to Goebbels.

Unfortunately, all this is not uncommon among those who make a profession of professing to "fuse horizons" and to "listen to the other."

25. See Heidegger, *Sein und Zeit,* 167–70. For a remarkable and perhaps even unique critique of this section of *Sein und Zeit,* see Maurice Blanchot, "La parole vaine," esp. 177–79.

26. See Emil Staiger, "Ein Briefwechsel mit Martin Heidegger," in *Kunst der Interpretation,* 28–42.

27. See, for instance, Gadamer, *Truth and Method,* 127–28, 572–73.

Chapter 1

1. Kierkegaard, *Af en endnu Levendes Papirer* (From the papers of one still living), in *Søren Kierkegaarde Samlede Værker,* 13:50; *Early Polemical Writings,* 60. All references in this chapter, unless otherwise indicated, are to *Early Polemical Writings,* which includes the pagination from the Danish edition in the margins. The novel Kierkegaard reviews is Hans Christian Andersen's *Kun en Spillemand*; an anonymous translation appeared in America under the title *Only a Fiddler.* For a view of Danish literary history that is far more congenial to Andersen as a novelist than that of the young Kierkegaard, see Fenger, *Kierkegaard,* 138–42; cf. Kreisberg and Jansen, "H. C. Andersen," 9:121–26. For an overview of Kierkegaard as reviewer, see Aage Henricksen, "Kierkegaard's Reviews."

2. See the articles on various topics, including those against the development of women's rights, which are collected in the opening pages of *Early Polemical Writings,* 3–34.

3. Kierkegaard's remarks on "the whole newer development" anticipate not only Nietzsche's second "untimely meditation," "The Use and Disadvantage of History for Life," but Nietzsche's general watchword "active forgetfulness" (see *Untimely Meditations,* 57–124). Similar conceptions and ever more similar formulations can be found in Charles Baudelaire, "The Painter of Modern Life," in *Painter and Modern Life,* 1–40.

4. The extent of scholarship on the relation of Kierkegaard to Hegel has by now grown vastly beyond the grasp of a note. Of particular importance for *Papers of One Still Living* is the scholarly excavation of Niels Thulstrup, *Kierkegaard's Relation to Hegel*; cf. the critique of Thulstrup found in Fenger, *Kierkegaard,* 132–49. As Fenger notes in his splendid work, Thulstrup minimizes the role of *Papers* in his account of Kierkegaard's philosophical "development." But Fenger fails to make a case for his assertion that "the very structure of [*Papers*] is Hegelian"

(141), nor does he even try to substantiate his assertion that Kierkegaard "thoroughly studied" (140) the Hegelian manifesto of Johan Ludvig Heiberg before setting out on his review, and indeed the quotation of Heiberg he adduces runs counter to the thesis and structure of *Papers*. Most other overviews of the Hegel-Kierkegaard relation simply ignore *Papers*. Influential interpretations of Hegel's relation to Kierkegaard can be found in Wahl, *Etudes kierkegaardiennes*; Hannay, *Kierkegaard*; Kroner, "Kierkegaards Hegelverständnis"; Crites, *Twilight of Christendom*; and Taylor, *Journeys to Selfhood*. See also the incisive readings of Sussman, *Hegelian Aftermath*, and Newmark, "Between Hegel and Kierkegaard." Attempts have also been made to comprehend the relation of Kierkegaard to Hegel by way of more or less disguised Marxian categories; see, in particular, Georg Lukàcs, *Destruction of Reason*, 243–308; Theodor W. Adorno, *Kierkegaard: Construction of the Aesthetic*; Schweppenhäuser, *Kierkegaards Angriff*.

5. For Kierkegaard's lecture notes on Schelling's "positive philosophy," which quickly turns into a "philosophy of mythology," see *Concept of Irony*, 335–410; the clearest definition of a "positive philosophy" is recorded on 364–65; cf. Schelling, *Philosophie der Offenbarung*. For an account of Kierkegaard's early enthusiasm for, and later disappointment with, Schelling, see Howard Hong's introduction in *Concept of Irony*, xviii–xxv; cf. Thulstrup, "Kierkegaard and Schelling's Philosophy." For a wider account of the general enthusiasm that greeted Schelling's attempt to overcome Hegel's "negativity," see *Philosophie der Offenbarung*, 419–503. It is remarkable how Kierkegaard expresses the disappointment that almost all the auditors of Schelling's lectures felt: "Schelling talks endless nonsense both in an extensive and intensive sense" (xxiv). Such "nonsense," like the "chatter" discussed in *Papers*, proves impossible to dissociate from any talk of "positivity."

6. The author of "En Hverdags-Historie" (A story of everyday life), Thomasine Gyllembourg-Ehrensvärd, was the mother of Johan Ludvig Heiberg, who in turn served as the "editor" of his mother's anonymous publications. "En Hverdags-Historie" appeared in 1828 and was followed by a cycle of stories, each one more or less an "everyday story." Kierkegaard refers to her as a "he," thereby protecting her from possible "identification," but it is not unlikely that he knew who wrote the stories of "everyday life." In 1846, Kierkegaard published *Two Ages [A Literary Review]*, which is an extended review of Thomasine Gyllembourg's *To Tidsalder* (Two ages); see the extensive analysis of the review in Chapter 5.

By the time Kierkegaard wrote *A Literary Review* (1846), almost ten years after having finished *Papers*, he doubtless knew who wrote "A Story of Everyday Life." Although he continues to use the masculine personal pronoun, he also speaks of the author's "almost feminine resignation" (*Two Ages* [*A Literary Review*], 16. On the question whether Kierkegaard knew that Thomasine Gyllembourg was the "author of the 'Story of Everyday Life,'" see Howard Hong's note to *Two Ages*, 166).

7. Poul Martin Møller's review of Thomasine Gyllembourg's novella *Extremerne* was first published in *Maanedsskrift for Litteratur* in 1836, republished in *Efterladte Skrifter*, 2:115–55. For Kierkegaard's brief comment on this review, see the review of Johan Ludvig Heiberg's transcription of Scribe's *First Love*, which he published in the first part of *Either/Or* (an essay that was very likely written in close connection with *Papers*): "I know no other way to conclude than in an incomparable laconic manner in which I see that Professor Poul Møller concludes the introduction of his excellent review of *Extremerne*: With this the introduction is concluded" (*Either/Or*, 1:240; see Chapter 5).

On Kierkegaard's relation to his former teacher, see Henningsen, *Poul Martin Møller*; Rohde, "Poul Møller"; Jones, "Søren Kierkegaard"; Vergote, "Poul Martin Moeller."

8. Møller, *Efterladte Skrifter*, 2:131. The background for Møller's concept of the critical review, as he admits, is Friedrich Schlegel's reflections on the task of the reviewer. But Schlegel's writings constitute a negative background since Møller wants to set his concept of reviewing as far apart from Schlegel as Kierkegaard wishes to set his concept of irony from that of his romantic predecessor (see *Concept of Irony*, 286–301). Kierkegaard and Møller attack Schlegel on the same point, "lawlessness" (*Lovløshed*), not only in praxis but even in theory; the end result of this lawlessness according to Møller can be found in Schlegel's doctrine that "a good review about a poem, as a consequence of the nature of poetry itself, was a new poem," for the consequence of this doctrine is that "poetry could give up its connection with the rest of life [*det øvrige Liv*]; it will arrive at such independence and self-sufficiency that it can continually reproduce itself merely from itself and, like a snake, which is a symbol of eternity, uphold life by consuming its own tail" (*Efterladte Skrifter*, 2:132). Møller equally rejects an "aesthetic review" which would be based on Hegel's *Phenomenology of Spirit* and whose aim would consist in showing how a work corresponds to a particular stage of a philosophical system: "As a result, the art of reviewing here remains one of comple-

tion in which one reads the poet's incomplete cipher [*ufuldkomne Ciffre*] and transposes it into the scientist's universally valid discourse" (*Efterladte Skrifter*, 2:133). By contrast, Møller argues for reviewing as an *art* that is nevertheless not *art alone*, and the word on which he draws in order to present the relation of art to life is, as it will be with Kierkegaard, "subjectivity" (*Efterladte Skrifter*, 2:137). Without a subjective appropriation of the work, Møller asserts in the conclusion to his reflections on the art of reviewing, aesthetic reflection is given over to "one or another fragment," and the reader is left with "a mass of dismembered limbs from an unfamiliar aesthetic corpus" (*Efterladte Skrifter*, 2:137). Since Kierkegaard devotes his review of Andersen to dismembering the text and in the end to fragmenting his own reflections on the method of reviewing, his review would perhaps not have pleased his recently deceased teacher. But Kierkegaard does not then follow the procedure Møller attributes to Schlegel; he does not aim for "the literary absolute" but like his teacher seeks to relate, and therefore to relativize, literature to "life." For an instructive instance of Schlegel's procedure as a reviewer, see his review of Schiller's *Die Horen*, in Schlegel, *Kritische Schriften*, 238–49; for a reconstruction of Schlegel's idea of art criticism, see Benjamin, *Der Begriff der Kunstkritik in der deutschen Romantik* in *Gesammelte Schriften*, 1, 1:87–109. *Papers* constitutes an attempt by Kierkegaard to write a review that does not subscribe to Schlegel's theory of art, still less to a Hegelian one, but nevertheless avoids the syncretism, empiricism, and hedonism of Møller's procedure: "The reviewer tries to explain why a poet pleases him or displeases him" (*Efterladte Skrifter*, 2:134); for a recent attempt to rescue the concept of the critical review that in a curious manner repeats the problematic elaborated in Schlegel, Møller, and the young Kierkegaard, see Hartman, *Minor Prophecies*.

9. Møller, *Efterladte Skrifter*, 2:150.

10. See Møller, *Efterladte Skrifter*, 2: 151.

11. Translation altered. In the brief "Postscript" to *Prefaces*, which may indeed constitute the entire "text" of this strange book, Kierkegaard again cites this saying and adds, "The one who hits back begins the strife—the strife, not with 'The Prefaces,' but with all experience and concepts" (*Prefaces*, 99). As McDonald points out, the common saying "Forord bryder ingen Trætte" is "ambiguous, depending on whether 'Forord' or 'Trætte' is taken as the subject" (99).

12. Møller, *Efterladte Skrifter*, 2:141.

13. See the remarks of Rohde, *Gaadefulde Stadier*, 39–41; cf. Julia

Watkin's informative note to her translation (247). Rohde traces the title back to the strange works of Hermann Pückler-Muskau, published under the title "Letters from One Dead" (*Briefe eines Verstorbenen*); Hans Christian Andersen referred to these "letters" in *Kun en Spillemand*, so Kierkegaard would clearly have known of them.

14. *Early Polemical Writings*, 76. The translation of *Empirie* from "experience" to "lived experience" (*Erleben, opleve*) has been altered to capture a distinction among "experiences," which can open up a space for something like a "deeper experience." This early quotation should acquit Kierkegaard of any internal relation to the development of *Lebensphilosophie* and its cult of "lived" experience (*Erlebnis*).

15. By means of this formula and its variations, Kierkegaard attempts not only to capture but to forestall the conceptualization of irony in his master's thesis, "On the Concept of Irony." This formula is first articulated in the eighth and central thesis of *Concept of Irony*, 5; thereafter, this thesis disrupts Kierkegaard's discussion at more or less regular intervals.

16. Kierkegaard's earliest confrontation with the Cartesian phrases *cogito ergo sum* and *de omnibus disputandum* takes place in the theatrical as well as polemical setting of *The Battle Between the Old and the New Soap-Cellars*: "words that in every well-ordered speculative state really ought to be learned in confirmation instruction . . . as the state's scholarly order of the day, as a palladium that will eliminate all heresy, as words that, like the word 'Adam,' will remind us of the creation of our intellectual life" (*Early Polemical Writings*, 117). This battle is an allegory of the coming into being of modernity; it repeats the "quarrel between the ancients and the moderns" by turning each contestant into the very figures that they once were. Not without reason does the figure Phrase— "an adventurer, member of several learned societies and contributor to numerous journals" (106)—emerge as a decisive factor when he performs the movement wherein all other characters turn into vestigial figurations of a past: "I have gone beyond Hegel" (122).

17. In an important work on Kierkegaard's relation to his Danish contemporaries, Bruce Kirmmse has demonstrated how the entire "Golden Age" of Denmark was dominated by the idea of a culture (*Dannelse*) guarded by a few chosen individuals; see *Kierkegaard*, esp. 86–135 (on the romantic poet Adam Oehlenschläger and his affinity with Bishop Mynster). Unfortunately, in this huge book Kirmmse does not investigate Kierkegaard's early relations to the principal luminaries of the Golden Age—the circle centered around Johan Ludvig Heiberg, which included

his mother, Thomasine Gyllembourg, who wrote "The Story of Everyday Life"—so the book passes over the question whether Kierkegaard *ever* subscribed to the cultural elitism of the Heiberg circle, even if he originally wrote *Papers* for Heiberg's journal of speculative aesthetics and praised Thomasine Gyllembourg to the skies. Since the central issue around which Kierkegaard's critique of Andersen is organized—that "genius" not only does not need a sheltering atmosphere in order to flourish but indeed needs to resist such an atmosphere—flies in the face of the cultural elitism Kirmmse so well documents, it cannot be maintained, as Kirmmse implicitly does, that Kierkegaard turned away from Heiberg's gospel of the "few" when he first sought to destroy "Christendom."

18. *Early Polemical Writings*, 61–62. Immanuel Hirsch suggests that Kierkegaard is here referring to the speculative theologian Carl Daub (1765–1836). Julia Watkin considers it likely that this passage refers to Johann Georg Hamann (for both attributions, see *Early Polemical Writings*, 250). The latter suggestion is far more justifiable, especially when one considers Hegel's highly ambivalent review of the first edition of Hamann's complete writings, a review that could easily have led Kierkegaard to have contrasted him with Hegel (see Hegel, "Hamanns Schriften," in *Werke*, 11:275–352). In a brief sketch entitled "Something about Hamann," Kierkegaard refers to "the agility of Simeon Stylites," whose function Hamann had at one time fulfilled (see *Either/Or*, 1:472). But as "Something About Hamann" makes clear, the identification of Hamann with Simeon Stylites reinforces the self-referential character of the allusion since Kierkegaard's presentation of Hamann begins with a justification of his own "polemical" relation to "the present age" (*Either/Or*, 1:472)—and also presumably his polemical relation to Hans Christian Andersen. On the relation of Kierkegaard to Hamann, see Smith, "Hamann and Kierkegaard."

19. Luther put particular emphasis on the dogmatic notion of *communicatio idiomatum*; it refers to the "communication" between the two natures of Christ, divine and human. Outside of this reference—and a book review is most decisively outside every traditional Christology—its invocation must be considered learned blasphemy. On the history of *communicatio idiomatum*, see Berkof, *Systematic Theology*, 323–27; for a critique of this notion, see Schleiermacher, *Christian Faith*, 411–13. Although she does not mention this term, much of Sylviana Agacinski's *Aparté* could be seen as an exposition of *communicatio idiomatum*.

20. The vast field of the telegraphic, which could perhaps function as

the trope of Kierkegaard's entire "authorship," has been explored with great wit and cunning by Avital Ronell in her *Telephone Book*. The aptness of the term "telegraph" can be judged from Kierkegaard's "First and Last Declaration" of his responsibility for, and irresponsibility with regard to, the pseudonyms: "The importance [of the pseudonyms] . . . unconditionally does not consist in making any new proposal, some unheard-of discovery, or in founding a new party and wanting to go further, but precisely in the opposite, in wanting to have no importance, in wanting, *at a remove that is the distance of double-reflection,* once again to read solo . . . the original text of human existence-relationships" (*Concluding Unscientific Postscript,* 629–30, italics added). Reading at a distance, which will have amounted to insignificant writing—this is telegraphism at its extreme.

21. See John 19:22.

Chapter 2

1. See Kierkegaard, *Concept of Irony,* 198–218.

2. Kierkegaard, *Concept of Anxiety,* 8. All references in this chapter will be to this edition of *Concept of Anxiety,* which includes the pagination to the fourth volume of the Danish edition.

3. On the relation of conceptuality to anxiety, see the detailed analysis of *Concept of Anxiety* in Wahl, *Etudes kierkegaardiennes,* 210–56; cf. Sartre, "Singular Universal."

4. The English translation, oddly enough, consistently translates *Problem* as "issue." Since there is no reason not to translate it as "problem," all the translations in the text will be so altered. It should also be remembered that the word "science" (*videnskab,* cf. German *Wissenschaft*) means any methodical discipline, the results of which count for that particular discipline as knowledge. Since Kant's first *Critique, the* scientific problem has been that of science itself, its place, measure, and limit; from Fichte's *Wissenschaftslehre* (doctrine of science) to Hegel's *Wissenschaft der Logik* (science of logic), German philosophy has not only claimed the title of science but has proclaimed itself as the science of science: the unique science that can respond to the problem of science.

5. See Kant, *Critique of Practical Reason,* 43.

6. See *Concept of Anxiety,* 111–13. Kierkegaard's skeptical comments with regard to Hegel's claim to have overcome Kantian "skepticism" are reiterated in the *Concluding Unscientific Postscript*: "A skepticism that

confiscates thinking itself cannot be halted by being thought through. . . . It must be broken off. To answer Kant within the fantastic *Schattenspiel* of pure thinking is precisely not to answer him" (*Concluding Unscientific Postscript*, 292, translation modified). See Chapter 4.

7. See, in particular, Arthur Schopenhauer's 1841 prize essay "Ueber die Freiheit des menschlichen Willens," translated as *On the Freedom of the Will.* Late in life Kierkegaard recognized a certain affinity between himself and Schopenhauer, although an affinity mediated by "total disagreement" concerning the character of morality; see *Søren Kierkegaard's Journals and Papers*, 4:25–35. Cf. Holm, "Schopenhauer und Kierkegaard."

8. See, for example, the preface to Kant, *Foundations of the Metaphysics of Morals*, 5.

9. See Kant, *Anthropology from a Pragmatic Point of View.*

10. On Kant's thesis of "radical evil," see Kant, *Religion Within the Limits of Reason Alone*, 15–39.

11. See Kant, *Foundations of the Metaphysics of Morals*, 67–72. On Kierkegaard, Kant, and the problem of interest, see Schmidinger, *Interesse und die Philosophie Kierkegaards*, esp. 330–39. See the more extensive discussion in Chapter 4.

12. It has long been noted than Poul Møller, to whom *Concept of Anxiety* is dedicated, gave Kierkegaard the concept of "interest" through which he carried out his critique of metaphysical foundations; see the remarks "On the Concept of *esse* and *inter-esse*" in *Søren Kierkegaards Papirer*, 4 C:100; cf. *Concluding Unscientific Postscript*, 314. On Poul Møller's influence on Kierkegaard's concept of interest, see Malantschuk, *Frihed og Eksistens*, esp. 103–13; cf. Deuser, *Kierkegaard*, 6–14.

For Jacobi's conception of faith (*Glauben*), see Jacobi, *David Hume.* Kierkegaard's critique of Jacobi, including the terms by which one can distinguish the "leap of faith" from Jacobi's *salto mortale*, can be found in the *Concluding Unscientific Postscript*, 93–106. For Hegel's relation to Jacobi, see Hegel, *Faith and Knowledge*, 97–152; Hegel, *Logic*, 95–112.

13. See Chapter 1, 37–39.

14. Although it has rarely been recognized, *The Concept of Anxiety* is Kierkegaard's contribution to the "origin of language" debate made famous through Herder's prize essay (see Herder, *Ueber den Ursprung der Sprache*). The mediating link between this debate and Kierkegaard is, of course, Hamann, whom Kierkegaard cites at the close of the treatise and whose many "responses" to Herder constitute a severe challenge to any

identification of language with the power to concentrate thought (*Besonnenheit*) and thus to fashion and employ concepts (see the compilation in Hamann, *Schriften zur Sprache*). As the last quotation clearly suggests, Kierkegaard put no more trust in a "divine" origin of language than in a human one. For this reason, Bejerholm's survey of Kierkegaard's remarks on the origin of language, which tries to show it as a "gift of God," is unconvincing; see *Meddelelsens Dialektik*, 39–48.

15. For an analysis of the presuppositions of this conception, see Derrida, *La voix et le phénomène*, esp. 78–97.

16. See Kierkegaard, ("Anti-Climacus") *Sickness unto Death*, 96; cf. Schelling, *Ueber das Wesen*, 70–71. More than any other work, *The Concept of Anxiety* reveals its debt to Schelling. Not only does it refer to Schelling's work in numerous occasions; it could be read as an explication of the following line, which it does not cite: "Die Angst des Lebens selbst treibt den Menschen aus dem Zentrum, in das er erschaffen worden; denn dieses als das lauterste Wesen alles Willens ist für jeden besondern Willen verzehrendes Feuer; um in ihm leben zu können, muß der Mensch aller Eigenheit absterben, weshalb es ein fast notwendiger Versuch ist, aus diesem in die Peripherie herauszutreten, um da eine Ruhe seiner Selbstheit zu suchen." (The anxiety of life itself drives man from the center in which he was created; for this, as the purest essence of all willing is, for every particular will, a consuming fire; and in order for him to live in it, man must let all peculiarities die off. For this reason, it is necessary to try to go beyond this into the periphery in order to seek there a rest from selfhood) (74). Kierkegaard is distinguished from Schelling on two points: he does not draw on an original "selfhood" that has to be protected *from* anxiety, and the "temptation" to which the self is drawn, for Schelling, has nothing to do with language and is not related, as it is in Franz von Baader, to the allurement of the prohibitory word itself; cf. McCarthy, "Schelling and Kierkegaard."

17. On the relation of drive, instinct, and anxiety, cf. the famous analysis of Freud, *Three Essays*, 33–35, 90. An extensive comparison of Kierkegaard to Freud has been undertaken by Nordentoft in *Kierkegaard's Psychology*, esp. 142–65. Freud's concept of anxiety is analyzed with great precision by Weber, *Legend of Freud*, 48–60; on Lacan's "displacement" of the Freudian concept of anxiety and its relation to Kierkegaard's *Concept of Anxiety*, see Weber, "The Witch's Letter" in *Return to Freud*, 152–67.

18. On the etymology of "algebra," see Ernest Klein, *A Comprehensive Etymological Dictionary of the English Dictionary*, 48. The term arose from the title of the enormously influential work of Mohammed ibn Musa al-Khowarizmi (whose name gave rise to the word "algorithm"). From this work, Arabic numbers reached Europe and were then called "Arabic numbers." Not without reason does the very structure of *The Concept of Anxiety* rest on the conflict between Arabic and Roman numerals.

In a different context, Adorno makes much of Kierkegaard's constant deployment of "mathematical" figures in the explication of spirit. Of particular concern to Adorno are the figures of the "sphere" (as in "spheres of existence") and the point (which is a "paradoxical" figure): "It is no accident that Kierkegaard is fond of using mathematical metaphors in his doctrine of Christian paradox. . . . Kierkegaard's paradoxy is here compared to the mathematical-rational paradox of a point that has 'no extension,' just as, in fact, the point serves as the model of every Kierke-gaardian paradox from the *Journal of a Seducer* on" (Adorno, *Kierkegaard: Construction of the Aesthetic*, 114; cf. Fenves, "Image and Chatter," 104–6).

19. On the relation of spirit to quotation marks (in the case of Heidegger's appeals to "science"), see the exemplary analysis by Derrida, *De l'esprit: Heidegger et la question*, esp. 43–54.

20. "Algebraic" modes of speech, as the following quotation from *Philosophical Fragments* seems to suggest, are merely meant to exclude history from the formulation of "dialectical" contradictions: "Opposites show up most strongly when placed together, and therefore we choose here the first generation of secondary followers and the latest (the boundary of the given *spatium*, the eighteen hundred and forty-three years), and we shall be as brief as possible, for we are speaking not historically but algebraically." (Kierkegaard, *Philosophical Fragments—Johannes Climacus*, 91). Algebra would seem to oppose itself to history and doubtless does in those cases where historical modes of speech go without saying. In the quotation from *Philosophical Fragments*, however, an algebraic mode of speech not only does *not* oppose itself to history but is the only one in which the historical, as generational difference, makes itself manifest. In "algebraic naming" historicity comes to speech, and what it bespeaks is, as this quotation emphasizes, the loss of the present age, of presence, even of *parousia*. Everywhere this presence, as presentless, attracts an algebraic mode of speech, as the even more

algebraic counterpart to *The Concept of Anxiety*—namely *The Sickness unto Death*—makes clear. See Kierkegaard, *The Sickness unto Death*, esp. 42–47 (where *The Concept of Anxiety* is recited and rewritten).

21. See Kierkegaard, *Two Ages* [*A Literary Review*], 90. See Chapter 5, esp. 218–21.

22. The connection between spirit and spirit (*aand* and *spøgelse*) is even more closely drawn in one of the *Christian Discourses*: "Just as ghosts [*Spøgelser*] flee before the dawn, and apparitions [*Gjenfærd*] collapse when their name is uttered, and enchantment ceases when the magic word is spoken—so to thee does the world and what the world calls 'all' become nothing. . . . The world must hate a deceased man; there is nothing contemporaries more hardly endure in a contemporary than that he lives like a departed spirit. . . . In a company it is disturbing when a deaf man is present who cannot hear what the others say and nevertheless takes part in the conversation, inasmuch as he is to be heard transforming the talk of the others into nonsense [*forvandlende de Andres Tale til Meningsløshed*]; but a believer is likewise a deaf man" (*Christian Discourses*, 152).

The inability to distinguish the language of spirit from that of spiritlessness becomes, for Kierkegaard's last writings, the defining feature of language in general: all language of spirit is said to be "metaphorical" because it transforms what is proper to spirit into the improper space of mere language. Such, at least, is the defining doctrine of *Works of Love*, the doctrine that divides and separates the first part of this "work" from the second: "All human language about the spiritual, yes, even the divine language of Holy Scripture, is essentially transferred or metaphorical language. . . . Transferred language is, then, not a brand new language; it is rather the language already at hand" (*Works of Love*, 199). The *total* metaphoricity of language, divine as well as human, implies, however, that language can be saved for spirit, that spirit can inhabit language without *itself* being "transferred" or transformed, in any case transfigured into "spirits." Because of its *total* metaphoricity, spirit can "use" language and get away unharmed: "Just as spirit is invisible, so also is its language a secret, and the secret rests precisely in this, that it uses the same language as the simple man and the child but uses it as transferred. Thereby the spirit denies . . . that it is the sensuous or sensuous-psychic" (*Works of Love*, 199–200). As long as language is altogether metaphorical, spirit can use it to deny its negation (in psycho-sensuous relations) without this denial having anything to do with the positivity of spirit. If, by contrast, language is not *altogether* metaphorical, if metaphoricity does not distinguish language, then spirit cannot remain altogether itself when it ventures into this alien space. A language that is not altogether metaphorical when it comes to spirit would be a *material* one, but the word "material" is doubtless misleading and perhaps even metaphorical.

23. On Kierkegaard's presentation of spiritlessness and its relation to Hegel's evaluation of modernity, see Taylor, *Journeys to Selfhood,* 52–61.

24. For Kierkegaard's interpretation of Socrates' daimon, see *Concept of Irony,* 157–67.

25. On the relation of spirit to "legion," see the remarkable reading of the passages Kierkegaard cites in Jean Starobinski, "Le combat avec Légion," in *Trois fureurs,* 73–126; cf. Warminski, *Readings in Interpretation,* 171–73.

26. Mark 7:15, 20. Citations of the Greek biblical text are from A. Souter's edition of *Novum Testamentvm Graece*; citations of the Latin biblical text are from St. Jerome's *Novum Testamentum Latine*; translations are modifications of the abridged edition of *The New Testament of the Jerusalem Bible,* ed. Alexander Jones.

27. Matthew 15:11. Both the passage from Mark and the one from Matthew are, of course, concerned with the status of the *kashrut* laws. What passes into a mouth does not, according to Jesus, reach "the heart," but what passes out of the mouth, what is spoken, originates from there. In both Gospels the disciples ask how the metaphorical language of this "parable" is to be understood, and they are told in both cases that the key to the comprehension of the dictum lies in the knowledge that "the dialectical designs, the evils [*oi dialogismoi oi kakoi*]" take the place of "the heart" (Mark 7:21). On the multivocity of *koinos* (common), *koinōnos* (participant), *koinōnia* (fellowship), *koinōneō* (to share, to make common, to defile), see Hauck, 789–809. On the Latin word "communication" in Kierkegaard, see the brief notice of Bejerholm, "Communication"; cf. Deuser, *Kierkegaard,* 75–83.

On the concept and inconceivability of "communication," both of which play decisive if nevertheless resolutely undecidable roles in the pages that follow, these texts are indispensable: Benjamin, "Ueber die Sprache überhaupt und über die Sprache des Menschen," in *Gesammelte Schriften,* 2, 1:142 ("On Language as Such and on the Language of Man," in Benjamin, *Reflections,* 315–16); Blanchot, *L'Entretien infini,* ix–xxvi; Nancy, *Le Partage* and *Inoperative Community*; Hamacher, "Die Sekunde," esp. 99–100. Cf. also Fenves, *Peculiar Fate,* 263–66 (where

Kant's attempt to present a communicability of sympathy without the threat of emotional communicability is explored at length).

28. See Fenves, "Antonomasia."

29. This famous phrase appears for the first time in the first edition of the Transcendental Deduction; see Kant, *Critique of Pure Reason*, 137 (= A, 109).

Chapter 3

1. *Philosophical Fragments—Johannes Climacus*, 8. All references in this chapter, unless otherwise indicated, are to this volume; references to *Philosophiske Smuler*, which would be better translated as "Crumbs of Philosophy," can as usual be found on the margins of the English edition.

2. *Concept of Irony*, trans. Capel, 258, translation modified. On this remarkable passage, see the incisive comments of Baldwin in "Irony." See also Newmark, "Taking Kierkegaard Apart."

3. Aristotle, *De Interpretatione*, 17a1–8; cf. *Metaphysics* (theta, 10), 1051b3. *Philosophical Fragments* revises the Aristotelian *Organon* and in particular *De Interpretatione* on one essential point: truth will not be at the disposal of propositions. Given this (entirely negative) determination, it becomes necessary for Climacus to revise the relationship between apophantic discourse and time as Aristotle elaborates it with the help of a famous example of a future contingency—a sea battle will take place tomorrow, or it will not take place. These revisions take place in the "Interlude: Is the Past More Necessary Than the Future? Or Has the Possible, by Having Become Actual, Become More Necessary Than It Was?" (72–88). Aristotle's attribution of necessity to that which has come into existence is not, however, the most important point of contrast between *De Interpretatione* and *Philosophical Fragments*; it serves, rather, to show how the problem of future contingencies rests upon a prior decision concerning the veritative character of language. In keeping with the concentration on apophansis, Aristotle writes: "It makes no difference whether people have or have not made the contradictory statements. For it is manifest that things are *thus* whether or not the affirmation or denial has been uttered. For it is not because of the affirmation or denial that something happens" (18b36–39). Another understanding of this "thus"—or a suspension of its comprehensibility—is considered later in this chapter.

4. It might then be supposed that Climacus, like so many other scholars, has taken the opening of the Gospel of John as his starting point. But this is not necessarily the case. When Anti-Climacus reworks Climacus's "Project of Thought" in *Training in Christianity*, Christ does not figure as logos (John 1:1) but as *semeion antilegomenon* (sign of a contradiction) (Luke 2:34). All of Kierkegaard's "religious" writing could doubtless be read as the interaction between these two passages. In the "sign of a contradiction," the "autopsy of faith" is doubly mirrored—mirrored, no doubt, to make faith into the opposite of doubt: "A communication which is the unity of jest and earnest is such a sign of contradiction. . . . When one sees into [the sign] as in a mirror and one gets to see oneself, or the sign of contradiction, see into the depths of one's heart while one is gazing into the contradiction" (*Samlede Værker*, 12:116–117; *Training in Christianity*, 125–26).

5. *Oeuvres de Descartes*, 7:25; *Meditations on First Philosophy*, 17. The statement "I do not exist" is, of course, the counterpart to the Cartesian cogito, the subject of the incomplete and unpublished *Johannes Climacus eller De Omnibus Dubitandum Est* (in *Søren Kierkegaards Papirer*, 4 [B 1]: 103–50). The relationship between this work and *Philosophical Fragments* is extremely complex, but two points are worth noting here: (1) both texts undertake to tell how one learns language, but whereas *Philosophical Fragments* inquires into how one learns to say "I do not exist," *Johannes Climacus* retells the story of how Johannes comes to say *cogito, sum* (and it breaks off just before he is able to utter this momentous statement); (2) *Johannes Climacus* is the mirror image of *Philosophical Fragments* since "the absolute fact," wherein the eternal meets the temporal, is not posed as the God-Man but as the articulation of the cogito. Universal doubt is in modern philosophy the event of decisive significance, but in seeking to *repeat* it, the follower, Johannes himself, recedes into complete insignificance (and once again, at the moment of repetition, *Johannes Climacus* breaks off).

6. See *Concept of Anxiety*, 14–15. The reciprocal concepts of seriousness and jest are explored with great ingenuity in Michael Theunissen, *Begriff Ernst*. Theunissen shows how seriousness and jest determine, or over-determine, every one of Kierkegaard's "concepts" and do so because they themselves are never entirely conceptual but always indicate a relation to "reality" (*virksomhed, Wirklichkeit*); and "reality," according to Theunissen's analysis, constitutes the "object" of seriousness. Another work,

which has unfortunately not benefited from Theunissen's superb treatise, locates the difficulty of *Concept of Irony* in an analogous problematic of "workplay" (see Smyth, *Question of Eros*, esp. 118–45).

7. The relationship between Climacus's *sorg* and Heidegger's *Sorge* has not been explored; see *Sein und Zeit*, 191–200. Kierkegaard, who wanted at one point to write a *Faust* drama (see Lowrie, *Kierkgaard*, 1:77), may have drawn on Goethe's presentation of *Sorge* in the second part of *Faust* (see *Faust*, 331–33; 2, act 5).

8. *De Interpretatione*, 2:16a30–34. One should keep in mind another manifestation of the "not human" that seems always in the background: Odysseus responds to the monster Polyphemos with the famous words *outis emoi g'onoma* (my name is *no one*); see Homer, *Odyssey*, bk. 9, l. 366.

9. Many commentators, including Howard Hong, have noted that the word *Guden* (the god) is "an extraordinary Danish expression," and they quite rightly point toward its Socratic and Platonic provenance. But the historical reference does not make the name-concept "the god" any more meaningful since the *function* of this pseudo-name cannot be integrated into the teloi that Socrates and Plato assign "the god." This discontinuity is, of course, a theme of the text itself. See the preface to *Philosophical Fragments*, trans. Swenson, ix–xii.

10. The precedent of Lessing's "Education of the Human Race" perhaps plays as important a role in this passage as his essay on the "proof of spirit" plays in the *Concluding Unscientific Postscript*: "Even though the first man was furnished at once with a conception of the One God; yet it was not possible that this conception, freely imparted and not won by experience, should subsist long in its clearness. As soon as human reason, left to itself, began to elaborate it, it broke up from one immeasurable into many measurables, and gave distinguishing marks to every one of these parts" (*Lessing's Theological Writings*, 83, sec. 6).

11. Climacus invokes the distinction elaborated by Kant between *Denken* (thinking) and *Erkennen* (cognition), a distinction that for Hegel would have an entirely different function since all thought is, in the end, knowing (*Wissen*). For both Climacus and Kant, by contrast, it is possible to think an object even if the thought has no reference to phenomena and cannot therefore claim to cognize anything: "Thought is free to occupy itself therewith as with the strangest proposal possible," so long as it does not "contain a self-contradiction" (101). Thus, Kant can think (that is, conceptualize) an object that has absolutely no relationship (*Beziehung*) to our sensibility, but he cannot claim to know such an

object. The clearest explanation of this distinction can perhaps be found in the Transcendental Deduction in the second edition of the *Critique of Pure Reason* (sec. 22; B 146–48). It is clear that the distinction between *Erkennen* and *Denken* depends upon the retention of the principle of noncontradiction, for it is the principle of conceptualization itself. On the relation of Kant to Kierkegaard, see the detailed remarks in Chapter 4.

12. Climacus occasionally returns to the word "autopsy" in the *Postscript* when he discusses Lessing's wonderful capacities as a scholar: "Honor be to learning and knowledge; praised be the one who masters the material with the certainty of knowledge, with the reliability of autopsy. But the dialectical is nevertheless the vital power of the problem" (*Concluding Unscientific Postscript*, 11, translation modified). One should note that on the one hand, "autopsy" is here opposed to *vitality* and that on the other, autopsy *alone* (without the help of "the dialectical") names a self-examination—or solo examination, or both—of dead objects of knowledge, including the lifeless "text" of one's life. Whether "autopsy" is interpreted as "see for yourself," or more specifically "see a dead body for yourself," or finally "see yourself dead by yourself" cannot be decided by the context since each contextualization involves a vitalization that "autopsy" on its own excludes. But it cannot be ruled out that the medical sense of the word enters into Kierkegaard's "therapeutic" writings. The course of "autopsy" from "seeing for oneself" to "examining the body" and finally to "necropsy" is not well charted, but a short history can be found in Skinner, *Origin*, 45.

13. See the explication of relation of faith to remembrance in terms of backwardness and forwardness undertaken in Müller, *Meddelelsesdialektikken*, 52–56.

14. On the perhaps unfortunate translation of *Philosophiske Smuler* as "Philosophical Fragments," see the discussion between Swenson and Lowrie reprinted in Swenson, *Something About Kierkegaard*, 207–9. In German translations of Kierkegaard, the word *smuler* is rendered by *Brocken*; in French ones, by *miette*.

15. See, in particular, Schlegel, "Kritische Fragmente," in *Kritische Schriften*, 5–24; cf. the analysis of Lacoue-Labarthe and Nancy, "The Fragmentary Exigency," in *Literary Absolute*, 39–59.

16. Plato, *Ion—Hippias Major*, 78, translation modified; *Concluding Unscientific Postscript*, 3.

17. Plato, *Ion—Hippias Major*, 79, translation modified.

18. One might compare Climacus's snack with Hegel's onetime and repetitive ingestion of the philosophical meal as it is explored with great precision by Hamacher in "Pleroma," esp. 70–71.

19. It is not insignificant that Climacus's closure of the question finds a significant precursor in St. Augustine. The discussion between Augustine and Evodius in the dialogue *De libero arbitrio* abruptly ends when the question of sin and with it the question of the question—anxiety before sin—makes an appearance. In the section devoted to the demonstration that "The Will Is the Radical Cause of All Evil," Augustine turns to Evodius, who seems to be unaware of the concept of will altogether, and he then raises the last question of the dialogue, a question, however, that Evodius does not answer and a question that concludes the *dialogue* but does not put an end to the *treatise*: "Will there be any end to your questions, when you really should want no more than to know the root of the question?" (*Free Choice*, 125).

20. On the highly ambiguous motif of echo in Kierkegaard, see Viallaneix, *Ecoute, Kierkegaard*, esp. 1:73–87.

Chapter 4

1. For an inquiry into "avoidance" and its relation to "negative theology," see Derrida, "Comment ne parler pas: dénégations," in *Psyché*, 335–97. On Kierkegaard and the "thesis" of noncommunicability, see Hügli, "Gibt es Dinge."

2. See *Concluding Unscientific Postscript*, 76n.

3. Of the many remarks on Kierkegaard's "indirect communication," none are as accurate or as succinct as those of Blanchot; see "Le 'journal' de Kierkegaard," in *Faux Pas*, 27–33; cf. the remarks on this essay by Agacinski, *Aparté*, 189–91, and Newmark, "Taking Kierkegaard Apart," which serves as an introduction to his translation of *Aparté*, 7–10. See also the remarks of Nordentoft on "indirect communication": "What constitutes the style is the breach of style, the unprepared shift from soporific circumlocution to a stringent lapidary style, from pathos to mockery, from spoken language to narration, from sublime rhetoric to vulgarisms, etc." (*Kierkegaard's Psychology*, 347).

4. See Kierkegaard's story of Hegel's concession on his deathbed that "no one understood him except one person, who misunderstood him" (*Concluding Unscientific Postscript*, 70n).

5. See the "First and Last Declaration" appended to the conclusion of

Concluding Unscientific Postscript, 625–30. A strong case for "nonsense" as the argumentative core and conclusive "position" (or nonposition) of the *Concluding Unscientific Postscript* can be found in Allison, "Christianity and Nonsense."

6. Kierkegaard, *Concluding Unscientific Postscript*, 69.

7. See Kant, "On a Newly Arisen Superior Tone in Philosophy" (1796), in Fenves, *Raising the Tone of Philosophy*, 68. For Kierkegaard's similarly motivated attack on elevation in tone, see *Concluding Unscientific Postscript*, esp. 566–70.

8. On few matters would ethical philosophies as divergent as those of Aristotle and Kant prove more closely aligned. Aristotle's ethics has often been championed over that of Kant because it fosters something like "moral education": the child is supposed to learn how to integrate moral choices into his character (*ēthos*). But as is equally well known but perhaps not sufficiently analyzed, Aristotle also ejects from his lecture hall (and from the reading of his treatises on ethics) those "young men" who would not in any case understand what he had to say (see *Nicomachean Ethics*, 3–4; 1095 A 2–13). Only those who already act "in accordance with a rational principle" (*kata logon*) can profit from hearing a lecture about ethics, but these people are, of course, the ones who least need the lectures: they are already educated; they already have "character." The difficulties to which Kant was exposed when he considered "moral education" are apparent in the section of *Critique of Practical Reason* devoted to the "Doctrine of Method" and even more so in his unhappy lectures on education; see Kant, *Education*.

9. Kierkegaard, *Concept of Anxiety*, 124; see Chapter 2.

10. Kierkegaard, *Concluding Unscientific Postscript*, 328, translation modified.

11. Ibid., 328. On the "breach of thinking" in Kierkegaard, see Bigelow, *Kierkegaard*, 55–58.

12. See Kant, *Critique of Practical Reason*, 124–26; Akademie ed. 5:119–21.

13. As it is spelled out in *Concluding Unscientific Postscript*, the difference between "religiosity A" and "religiosity B," both of which have distanced themselves from Hegelianism, could be made to resemble that between Kant's concession that reason must give up a place to incomprehensibility and the presentation of its collapsing ground as it is shown in *Fear and Trembling*. But filling in the algebraic names A and B with the nonalgebraic names Kant and Kierkegaard would doubtless be

misleading and would foreclose a reading of A and B in the term of their arbitrary sequentiality.

14. Kierkegaard, *Concluding Unscientific Postscript*, 328.

15. Ibid., 568.

16. The relation of Kant to Kierkegaard has not been explored with the same degree of thoroughness as the relation of Hegel to Kierkegaard, but much has nevertheless been written on this topic. See the ground-breaking essay of Brunner, "Grundproblem der Philosophie"; cf. Gill, "Kant, Kierkegaard"; Ricoeur, "Philosophie après Kierkegaard." On the relation of Kantian ethics to Kierkegaard, see the fine essay by Fahren-bach, "Kierkegaards ethische Existenzanalyse." Fahrenbach is doubtless correct when he asserts that "Kierkegaards Fragestellung zielt auf die Voraussetzung der Kantischen Moralphilosophie, das Pflichtbewußtsein, dessen Faktizität und Präsenz im sittlichen Bewußtsein der moralphilo-sophischen Auslegung vorausliegt und doch als solche konkret unaufge-klärt bleibt" (219), but Fahrenbach does not sufficiently place the *problem* of a "concrete" clarification (i.e., presentation) in relation to the possible "suspension" of the ethical. Only in this relation, however, does Kierke-gaard expose the Kantian "presupposition," as this chapter seeks to show. Other incisive clarifications of Kierkegaard's "corrective" to Kantian ethical thought can be found in Schrader, "Kant and Kierkegaard"; Hausschildt, *Ethik Søren Kierkegaards*, 41–43, 111–16. See also Hannay, *Kierkegaard*, 224–40; Deuser, *Kierkegaard*, 136–38. That Kierkegaard was familiar with most of Kant's writings can be verified by his personal library; see *Søren Kierkegaards Bibliotek*, 51, 89.

17. On the complex historical background for Kant's principle, see Schneewind, "Use of Autonomy"; cf. Schmucker, *Ursprünge*; Schilpp, *Kant's Pre-Critical Ethics*. For an analysis of the *Grundlegung* in relation to reading, see Miller, *Ethics of Reading*. Miller's opening affirmation that Kant "ends up reaffirming *the* morality of his country, class, religion and time" (15, italics added) can hardly go unchallenged, not least because of the extraordinary challenge it poses to Kant. To pull it off would be an astounding feat. If Kant were indeed to reaffirm the morality of his country (Prussia sometimes, Russia at others), he would contradict the morality of class (house servant at times, state-bureaucratic at others); and since precisely what religion Kant accepted is in question, it would be as difficult to ascertain what its morality was as to determine the morality of *the* time (presumably 1785). Miller, moreover, elides precisely that moment in the *Grundlegung* to which the analysis undertaken here is

directed—the moment, that is, in which a maxim (a word that never appears in the text, although it names the linguistic moment in the law) undergoes a test. When Miller says that the reader of the *Grundlegung* is betrayed since the "text has not given him what it seemed to promise, a clear understanding of the ethics of reading" (39), the reader can only wonder where the text made any such promise. On the relation of promising to interpretation in Kant, see Hamacher, "Das Versprechen der Auslegung," in Bolz and Hübener, *Spiegel und Gleichnis*, 252–73. On "the ethics of reading" in Kierkegaard and de Man, see Norris, "De Man Unfair?"; it is doubtful whether Norris can describe the problem confronted in *Fear and Trembling* as "appalling" (97) yet count on Kierkegaard to support a concept of ethics that stands as a decisive alternative to de Man's "anti-humanism."

18. Kant, *Grundlegung zur Metaphysik der Sitten*, in *Kants Gesammelte Schriften*, 4:463. All translations are my own; references to Kant are to the Akademie edition (volume: page). English translations refer to the pagination for the Akademie edition, which are reproduced on the side of every available English version.

19. On this passage, see the remarks of Heidegger, *Schellings Abhandlung*, 195–96; see also the countercurrents to these remarks developed by Nancy, *L'Expérience de la liberté*, esp. 65–83. From an elaboration of Schelling's relation to Kant, a reading of his relation to Kierkegaard could be undertaken. Heidegger, however, tries to preclude this reading (see, for example, *Schellings Abhandlung*, 225).

20. On the motif of war and peace in Kantian thought, see the thorough compilation of Saner, *Kant's Political Philosophy*. Jean-François Lyotard has considered in many different ways and with divergent means of presentation how Kant "comes to terms" with the interminable; see, in particular, Lyotard, *The Differend: Phrases in Dispute*.

21. On the alteration from the goal of *Grundlegung*, a critique of pure practical reason, to the *Critique of Practical Reason*, see the preface to the latter (Akademie edition, 5:3). Kant does not rule out the possibility of subjecting pure practical reason to critique, but in a critique of practical reason it is altogether superfluous: "So bedarf [die Kritik] das reine Vermögen selbst nicht zu kritisieren" (thus critique does not need to criticize the pure capacity itself), *Critique of Practical Reason*, 4; Akademie edition, 5:3. Only one conclusion can be drawn: the need for such a critique is rooted neither in "practice" nor in "speculation," neither in praxis nor in theory; the space of such critical necessity, as the critique of

purity itself, appears under an altogether different rubric. On the function of this fact (*Faktum, Tat-sache*) of reason in Kant's overall project of grounding and justifying autonomy, see Allison, *Kant's Theory of Freedom*, esp. 230–38; cf. Nancy, *L'Expérience de la liberté*, 27–39; Fenves, *Peculiar Fate*, 218–21.

22. The discussion of Kant's use of "maxim" has been vigorously pursued in recent years. For the history of the concept, see Bittner, "Maximen." The work of Onora O'Neill has largely been responsible for the renewed interest in the problem of formulating maxims; see *Acting on Principle*.

23. The relation between maxims of conduct and maxims found in schoolbooks is "illustrated" in the second volume of Kierkegaard's *Either/ Or*. As a child, the author had the duty of reading Balle's *Lesson-Book*, the book in which the duties of children were spelled out. But the duty to read the book in which maxims of conduct were written was not itself written in the book, nor could the maxims be learned without reading the book: "It seemed to me that heaven and earth would tumble down if I did not do my homework, and on the other hand it seemed to me that if heaven and earth did tumble down this upheaval would in no way excuse me from doing what had once been set before me—doing my homework. At that age I knew very little about my duties; I had not yet become acquainted with them in Balle's 'Lesson Book.' I had but one duty, to do my homework, and yet I can derive my whole ethical view of life from this impression" (*Either/Or*, 2:267, translation modified; on the relation of *Either/Or* to Kantian moral philosophy, see Stack, *Kierkegaard's Existential Ethics*, 167–70). The original duty is to read, even if the whole world, including the book that has to be read, disappears; to read, therefore, *nothing* but the empty space of inscription to which the force of duty, and therefore ethics in general, refers. The force of "original" reading is the "impressive" character of reading, its power to inscribe before any comprehension of particular inscriptions. This passage so impressed Wittgenstein that it could give him as idea of immortality: "A great writer said that, when he was a boy, his father set him a task, and he suddenly felt that nothing, not even death, could take away the responsibility [in doing this task]; this was his duty to do, and that even death couldn't stop it being his duty. He said that this was, in a way, a proof of the immortality of the soul—because if this lives on [the responsibility won't die]. The idea is given by what we call the proof" (Wittgenstein, *Lectures and Conversations*, 70).

24. On interest and *inter-esse*, see *Concluding Unscientific Postscript*, esp. 314–15; see Chapter 2, esp. 70–71.

25. On the theological and political background for Kant's invocation of dictatorial commands, see Schmitt, *Die Diktatur*, 1–25. After Schmitt notes the contrast between Kant's invocation of *dictamina rationis* and Rousseau's dictates of the heart, he characteristically finds a dissolution in the further (romantic) development of the latter: "The phrase finally dissolved; feeling, enthusiasm, everything possible can dictate" (11). That "dictation" is indissociable from "feeling" escapes him here as it does elsewhere; romanticism can then only be seen as degradation. Quite a different conception of the relation of "dictation" to "feeling" is found in those sections of Benjamin's *Ursprung des deutschen Trauerspiels* (*Origin*) explicitly concerned with Schmitt's conception of the dictator or tyrant.

26. On the universal voice in which pleasure is spoken, see Kant, *Critique of Judgment*, sec. 8: "We can see that nothing is postulated in a judgment of taste except such a *universal voice* [*allgemeine Stimme*] about a liking unmediated by concepts" (*Critique of Judgment*, 60). The universality of this voice consists in neither "privacy" nor "publicity" but in attunement with the power of subjectivity to generate cognitive judgments—and therefore to propose publicizable propositions—in general.

27. See Kant's discussion of the binding of Isaac in *Der Streit der Fakultäten*, his last philosophical work and indeed a work whose overall aim is to defend the autonomy of philosophy against the incursions of the so-called higher faculties as well as the state (*Conflict of the Faculties*, 115; Akademie ed. 7:63). Cf. Derrida, "Mochlos ou le conflit des facultés," in *Du Droit*, 397–429. On this passage of *Conflict of the Faculties* and Kierkegaard, see Perkins, "For Sanity's Sake."

28. The alteration of criticism on the basis of Kant's concept of critique was accomplished by German romanticism. For an account of how *Kunstkritik*, understood precisely as a medium (of reflection), emerged out of Kantian critique, see Benjamin, *Begriff der Kunstkritik*, in *Gesammelte Schriften*, 1, 1:26–40. Benjamin himself distills every heteronomous element—every trace of the irrational other than that of mystical sobriety, *ponderación misterioso*—out of German romanticism and thus not only describes but above all enacts its principle.

29. "Was Tarquinius Superbus in seinem Garten mit den Mohnköpfen sprach, verstand der Sohn, aber nicht der Bote" (*Fear and Trembling*, 3). All further quotations in this chapter, unless otherwise indi-

cated, will be to this edition of *Fear and Trembling*, which has the Danish pagination on the side.

30. The discussion of the meaning and significance of pseudonymous authorship will never come to an end. An exceptional account of the function of the pseudonyms, which is exceptional since it does not capitulate to Kierkegaard's own reconstruction, can be found in Agacinski, *Aparté*, esp. 235–44. A broad and vigorous defense of Kierkegaard's own understanding of the function of pseudonymous authorship, as recounted in *The Point of View for My Work as an Author* and applied to *Fear and Trembling*, can be found in Hartshorne, *Kierkegaard*, esp. 7–12. Hartshorne does not resolve the difficulty of reading Kierkegaard's "irony" with the tools of Kierkegaard's self-interpretation; on the contrary, he simply dissolves the difficulty of reading: "There is the preposterous (and terrifying) assumption of the teleological suspension of the ethical, which would open the door to legitimizing anything a fanatic might want to do, provided only he could persuade himself that God had spoken to him and to him alone. What Kierkegaard is doing in *Fear and Trembling* is ironically showing the ultimate absurdity of attempting to reach faith by a mighty effort. Good Lutheran that he was, he believed that faith is a matter of grace, not of spiritual heroics. . . . The biblical witness is clear: God spoke to Abraham, and Abraham believed" (10–11). But God's "speech" is not at all clear since it bids Abraham to sacrifice his son. The "spiritual heroics" of which Hartshorne writes involve acts of reading that cannot be hushed aside through an appeal to interpretative authority. How "good" a Lutheran Kierkegaard is can be found only in reading his texts, and doubtless not even there.

31. Of the many interpretations of the surname de Silentio, at least three deserve mention; see Louis Mackey, "View from Pisgah"; Newmark, "Between Hegel and Kierkegaard"; Taylor, "Sounds of Silence."

32. See Kant, *Critique of Judgment*, 119–23; 5:260–64. On the relation of "sublime" trembling to the collapse of presentation, see Nancy, "L'Offrande sublime"; cf. Hamacher, "Beben der Darstellung."

33. See Hume, *Treatise of Human Nature*, 517.

34. On Kant and lying, see Fenves, "Testing Right."

35. The counterpart to *Fear and Trembling* is an "unfinished" text called *Repetition* in which the concept of repetition no longer lets itself be understood as a repetition of Platonic *anamnesis* and Hegelian *Erinnerung* but is the "foundering of metaphysics" (see *Fear and Trembling— Repetition*, 149). On the structuring event of repetition (iterability) and

its relation to the ideality of conceptual thought, see Derrida, *Limited Inc.*

36. The fourth presentation is by no means a conclusive one: "Thus and in many similar ways did the man of whom we speak ponder this event." Supplementary presentations could be found in one who also "pondered" this event, although not necessarily in "similar ways"; see Kafka, *Briefe*, 333–34. The first Abraham Kafka ponders is one who is "as willing as a waiter" to sacrifice Isaac but unfortunately cannot find the time to abandon his business. Abraham, in other words, no longer goes out: "Er [kann] nicht fort" (333). Each of Kafka's versions takes place at home: no sublimity, no "pedestrian sublime," no coming down the mountain, no going out again and again.

37. The inability of a negation, once negated, to end up with—or rise into, *aufheben*—a determination has always marked off Kierkegaard's "dialectic" from that of Hegel, and it has since given rise to a "negative dialectics" that from its inception must radically distinguish itself from Kierkegaard. On Kierkegaard and allegory, as it is presented in Benjamin's *Origin*, see Adorno, *Kierkegaard: Construction of the Aesthetic*, 97; on the relation of Kierkegaard's dialectics to Adorno's "negative dialectics," see the massive work of Deuser, *Dialektische Theologie*; cf. Fenves, "Image and Chatter," esp. 110–14.

38. Galatians 4:1–26; on the editions and translation of the biblical texts, see 271*n*26 above. For the dominant interpretation of Isaac's binding under the term "figure" (*schēma*), see Hebrews 11:17–19. From these two passages the tradition of Christian "typological" has its origin; on the relation of "allegory" to "typology," see Lubac, " 'Typologie' et 'allégorisme.' " For a discussion of *Fear and Trembling*'s presentation of Abraham in terms of typology, see Mackey, *Kierkegaard*, 222–23. Mackey, who quotes from Hebrews and Romans (4:20–25), does not take the passage from Galatians into account and like many commentators, leaves out the many mothers in favor of the one father.

39. See Johannes Chrysostom, *In Epistolam ad Galatas*, 662. St. Augustine, as a Roman rhetorician, was also troubled by Paul's use of *allegoroumena* and considered it a misuse, if not, as Chrysostom did, an abuse. Outstanding discussions of this perennial topic of controversy can be found in Hartmut Freytag, "*Quae sunt*"; cf. Whitman, "Textual to the Temporal." Luther, whom Kierkegaard (and indeed, if he had been so interested, Kant) would have consulted more readily than Chrysostom or Augustine, was just as uneasy with Paul's use of "allegory." For not only is

allegory in general related more closely to "beauty" than "persuasion" and thus unfit for serious study, "I durst not have been so bold to handle the allegory after this manner. . . . Wherefore it is not for every man to use allegories at his pleasure; for a goodly outward show may deceive a man, and cause him to err" (*Commentary on St. Paul's Epistle to the Galatians*, 501). On the *divertissement* of allegory in the context of Lutheranism, see Benjamin, *Ursprung des deutschen Trauerspiels*, in *Gesammelte Schriften*, 1, 1:361–65.

40. On the relation of catachresis to philosophical discourse, see Derrida, "The White Mythology," in *Margins of Philosophy*, 255–57.

41. See Hamann, "Metakritik über den Purismum der Vernunft," in *Schriften zur Sprache*, 213–18.

Chapter 5

1. *Either/Or*, 1:234. Fenger surmises that the section of "First Love," from which these lines are drawn, "is an old item, perhaps the oldest of the layers in *Either/Or*" (*Kierkegaard*, 11). According to Fenger, it belongs to a group of literary-critical writings that includes *From the Papers of One Still Living*.

2. *Either/Or*, 1:236.

3. See Luke 2:34; Kierkegaard, *Training in Christianity*, 125–26; *Samlede Værker*, 12:106–10.

4. *Either/Or*, 1:236.

5. Ibid., 234.

6. Ibid., 235.

7. Ibid., 239–40; Poul Møller's review of the story "Extremerne," by Thomasine Gyllembourg (mother of Johan Ludvig Heiberg and author of "A Story of Everyday Life"), is discussed in Chapter 1; see above, 35–39.

8. Kierkegaard, *Two Ages* [*A Literary Review*], 12. All further references in this chapter, unless otherwise indicated, are to this volume, which includes the references to the Danish edition in the margins.

On the relation of *A Literary Review* to *From the Papers of One Still Living*, see Kirmmse, *Kierkegaard*, 265–66. Although Kirmmse, a very careful scholar, notes the similarity between the two works and the symmetry of their publication, he regards *Papers* as a pseudonymous work: "Near the beginning and the conclusion of the *Review* there are direct references to SK's very first book, *From the Papers of One Still*

Living, a pseudonymous work, the one work which SK had not acknowl-
edged in his afterword to the just-completed *Postscript* and which he
finally acknowledges here in the *Review*. . . . SK sees *A Literary Review* as
the concluding work of his literary production. Thus, his literary work
began with a lengthy and pseudonymous book review that concerned
itself with ethical questions, and it concludes—with the symbolic symmetry that SK loved so well—with another lengthy ethical-political book
review which is, significantly, not pseudonymous but in SK's own name"
(265–66). Such "symmetry" is both sharpened and distended when it is
recognized that the first work is not pseudonymous and that Kierkegaard
recognizes himself, as empty and unrecognizable, in the "anonymity" to
which *A Literary Review* directs its attack.

9. Peder L. Møller, "A Visit to Sorø," first published in *Gæa*, December
1846; quoted from Kierkegaard, *Corsair Affair*, 9. To the accusation that
he acted "exactly *à la* Andersen," Kierkegaard insists that since he never
uses the word "I." He acted, rather, "a little Socratically, in order teasingly
to thrust people away" (*Corsair Affair*, 44). Kierkegaard, under the guise
of Father Taciturnus, proceeds to explain why "existential dialectic,
especially in the form of double-reflection, cannot be communicated
directly." The ghostly double of Andersen hovers over this "double-
reflection."

On the battle of reviews that makes up this "affair," see the meticu-
lously documented presentation of the Hongs, *Corsair Affair*, vii–xxxviii.
A lucid and succinct account of the famous controversy can be found
in Josiah Thompson, *Kierkegaard: A Critical Biography*, 188–94. P. L.
Møller's review of Kierkegaard's *oeuvre* is extraordinarily penetrating, far
more so than the review by Johan Frederik Hagan of *Philosophical
Fragments* that Kierkegaard discusses at length in the *Concluding Unscientific Postscript* (see 274–77n; for the review itself, see Theunissen and
Greve, *Materialien zur Philosophie Søren Kierkegaards*, 132–35). P. L.
Møller, not related (by birth) to Poul Møller, was as clearly stamped by
the latter's style as Kierkegaard himself. Nowhere is this more apparent
than in his review of Kierkegaard, for it is presented as a "conversation,"
precisely the mode of presentation that Poul Møller had recommended
for the form of the review in his review of Thomasine Gyllembourg (see
262–63n8). From a certain perspective, P. L. Møller appears to be a better "son" of Poul Møller than Kierkegaard himself. But the situation is
even more complicated. Just as Kierkegaard accuses P. L. Møller of not
having understood the "indirectness" of his conversation, Møller accuses

Kierkegaard of having attributed to a certain Professor Hauch words that he had placed in the mouth of a pseudonym: "Not a single one of the persons in the conversation is mentioned by name, which would have been difficult, since the conversation did not actually take place . . . but is only a fictional form for some critical observations" (see *Corsair Affair*, 105). Of course, Kierkegaard could have used exactly the same words in response to almost every one of the literary reviews of his work that he encountered. "Indirection" is turned against him. P. L. Møller, incidentally, has often been viewed as the prototype for the "seducer" whose diary appears in *Either/Or*. His accusations against Kierkegaard would therefore be all the more biting; it is as though a pseudonym were to step out of character and "review" Kierkegaard back. For an analysis of the relationship between these two sons of Møller, see Poole, "Søren Kierkegaard."

10. *Corsair Affair*, 102. Kierkegaard responds to this accusation in a lengthy footnote to his "Activity of a Traveling Esthetician and How He Still Happened to Pay for the Dinner" (*Corsair Affair*, 39–40n), but he does not refer to the specific "experiment" to which P. L. Møller draws attention—the torturing of his former fiancée. In their "Historical Introduction" to *Fear and Trembling* and *Repetition*, Howard and Edna Hong discuss the "misunderstanding" that lies at the root of Møller's presentation of Kierkegaard's concept of *experimentere* (see xxvii). It is, however, unfortunate that the Hongs do not similarly undertake an investigation of misunderstanding itself, especially since it is the outstanding difficulty encountered in, for instance, *Fear and Trembling*. P. L. Møller may have indeed "misunderstood" Kierkegaard, but such misunderstanding is not to be dismissed with the healthy assurance that "Regine herself" understood him, especially when Regine herself, a half century later, is not allowed to speak but is *told* what she thinks: "It must be said and positively maintained that S. Kierkegaard has never misused your love in order to torment you or to conduct mental experiments with you, as has been commonly and erroneously assumed," she is told (see *Fear and Trembling*, xxviii). The misunderstanding, like all misunderstandings, lies in a certain prior understanding whose "correctness" cannot be judged. Fenger has tried to show that Kierkegaard's relation to Regine does indeed parallel the playful cruelty of Johannes the Seducer; see *Kierkegaard*, 207–12. Whether "Diary of the Seducer" refers to the "lived" experience of P. L. Møller or Kierkegaard himself is of little importance; that one cannot refrain from demanding reference is, however, significant: it shows the extent to which "chatter" is implied in reading.

11. *Stages on Life's Way* already marks out a space in which *A Literary Review* could emerge. The diarist of its final section, entitled "Guilty/ Not Guilty," plans to write a flattering review of a work rumored to be written by a woman and at the same time denigrates the work of reviewing as well as the novel under review: "But still one must have a little something to hold on to. It will be a long while before I run after anonymous novels again—the last one made me really feel the ridiculousness of my fancy. If I have not learned anything else from it, I have gained some idea of how reviews come about. I have never been able to take seriously the idea of the work of a reviewer, but merely on the vaguest suspicion that she could be the writer (for rumor had it that it was by a woman), I set myself in motion to convince people that it was something superlative" (*Stages on Life's Way*, 244). The parallel passage in "The Seducer's Diary," *Either/Or*, 1:374: a "book has the remarkable characteristic that it can be interpreted as one pleases."

12. Kierkegaard, *Corsair Affair*, 47. "The Dialectical Result of a Literary Police Action," published in *Fædrelandet* on January 10, 1846, was Kierkegaard's last direct publication on the matter, although it too was signed by a pseudonym. On the relation of the *Corsair* to "public prostitution," see 47.

13. Gyllembourg, *To Tidsaldre* (1845), reprinted in *Samlede Skrifter*, 12:1; for the prefatory review, see *Two Ages*, 153–54. Bretall has noted that the concept of reflection is the "principal category" in *A Literary Review*; see *Kierkegaard Anthology*, 260; cf. the Hongs' discussion in the "Historical Introduction" to *Two Ages*, ix. Neither Bretall nor the Hongs consider in any detail the question of reflection, even though it is of course a constant preoccupation Kierkegaard inherited from Schelling and Hegel. An indispensable guide to the history and significance of the reflection can be found in Gasché, *Tain of the Mirror*.

14. See *To Tidsaldre*, preface; *Two Ages*, 153.

15. Ferdinand's first poetic venture concerns the passion of Jeanne d'Arc (see *To Tidsaldre*, 17–18). Claudine exclaims, "A poem about Jeanne d'Arc! My own heroine!" (17); although certain that his father will disapprove of his poetry, Ferdinand publishes the volume under his own name and even translates it into French (see *To Tidsaldre*, 52).

16. According to Thomasine Gyllembourg, Kierkegaard misunderstood the character of Ferdinand Bergland. For she insists in her glowing letter to Kierkegaard of April 26, 1846, that Ferdinand ought to be defended against Kierkegaard's interpretation: "It is not 'out of fear of financial difficulties' that he leaves his beloved, but on account of his

love, owing to his pity for her unfortunate situation, which he despairs of ever altering. He believes that a man whom he honors and at whose side he regards her fate as assured is offering her a happiness to which he must not become an obstacle, and he breaks the bond that ties her to him out of a misunderstood sense of duty, which I, by the way, think is in agreement with the thought of our own day, as Lusard also accusingly remarks in her first conversation" (Kierkegaard, *Letters and Documents*, 198). Kierkegaard's "alteration" is the cornerstone of his "survey," the transposition of the novel into a literary review.

17. See Kierkegaard, *From the Papers of One Still Living*, 77; cf. Chapter 1, esp. 44–46.

18. On the complicated movements of P. A. Heiberg, Thomasine Gyllembourg, and J. L. Heiberg, see the excellent presentation of Fenger, *Heibergs*, esp. 23–37. On the intricate relation between Kierkegaard and the Heibergs, see Fenger, *Kierkegaard*, 15–18, 135–49. Fenger shies away from the consequences of his overall thesis, namely, that Kierkegaard's huge production of 1843–46 is a "gigantic reaction against the Heiberg circle and its ecclesiastical, philosophical and literary adepts" (148). Like numerous other commentators, Fenger emphasizes the importance Kierkegaard attached to J. L. Heiberg's review of *Either/Or* and his disappointment at its brevity ("It was Heiberg's review of March 1, 1843, which set Kierkegaard off," 147). Kierkegaard's later attacks on Goethe and Hegel would then have no antecedents in the complex strategy of *Concept of Irony*. Rather, "with the years, Kierkegaard's admiration and longing were transformed into neurotic hatred and bitterness" (65). Fenger, however, does not thereafter draw the inevitable conclusion: *A Literary Review* and *The Crisis and a Crisis in the Life of an Actress* are utterly ironic in their appraisal of two central figures in Heiberg's circle (mother and wife). What is clear, however, is that Fenger has made it impossible to understand Kierkegaard's praise of Thomasine Gyllembourg and Johanne Luise Heiberg as clear and unambiguous expressions of admiration.

19. On the two heroines of *Two Ages*, see Cutting, "Interpersonal Relationships." Cutting does not see how Kierkegaard undermines Gyllembourg's presentation of resignation (repetition), and the concluding remarks on the projected "age of genuine relationships with others" (83) makes Kierkegaard into a Hegelian historian of world progress (thesis, antithesis, synthesis). For an incisive analysis of the relation between Kierkegaard's critique of the novel and his presentation of history, which

does not rule out the possibility of a "synthesis" and yet does not project it onto Kierkegaard's text, see Bové, "Penitentiary of Reflection." It is doubtful, however, that Bové's categories, drawn for the most part from Foucault, furnish the material for a meta-commentary on Kierkegaard's critical practice.

20. See *Repetition*, 204, 228. For a superb reading of *Repetition* in relation to the issue of textuality, see Melberg, "*Repetition*." It is by no means coincidental that Melberg's reading of de Man in relation to Kierkegaard's *Repetition* ends with the term *stutter*. For stuttering is closely linked to chatter (involuntary movement of the mouth), but Melberg's analysis of stuttering is far from satisfactory: "Stuttering has no 'point'—and perhaps de Man associates it with 'prosaic materiality' since it seems free from visuality. Stuttering is in any case devoid of anything like 'intention' and definitely has no 'existential' pathos" (86). On the contrary: stuttering, unlike chatter, has both "intention" and *extraordinary* pathos, the pathos of being struck dumb.

21. See *Urania Aarbog for 1844*, ed. J. L. Heiberg (1843), 101, cited from the Hong translation of *Fear and Trembling—Repetition*, 382.

22. *Urania Aarbog*, 101; *Fear and Trembling—Repetition*, 382.

23. *Urania Aarbog*, 106; *Fear and Trembling—Repetition*, 383.

24. See the unpublished review of Heiberg's review, "Little Contribution by Constantin Constantius," *Papirer*, 4 (B 117):293; *Fear and Trembling—Repetition*, 312.

25. One of Kierkegaard's counterreviews was, however, published as the second "Preface" to *Prefaces*. According to the "Preface," the "logic" of reviewing is that of scapegoating: authors are exposed to a public that vilifies them for its own satisfaction: "With this I have finished. I have in readiness the straw man, which I will throw deftly into the barrel while I myself stand outside and enjoy the fun. To stop the violence is not within my power. I could at most suggest that a committee be appointed to inquire how one could interrupt the critical proceedings. . . . The critique should not be a bandit who attacks a published book, not a gossipmonger who clings fast to a work in order to get a place of hearing for his observations, not a haughty beggar-king who of a published book 'takes the opportunity' [Heiberg's words] to say something himself. A reviewer is and ought to be, ought to place his honor in being, a serving spirit" (Kierkegaard, *Prefaces*, 40–41). Neither *Papers* nor *Literary Review* corresponds to this definition of the reviewer. Whereas the writer of the first "attacks" a published book, the writer of the second "takes the oppor-

tunity" to say something himself. The "service" Kierkegaard renders Thomasine Gyllembourg compares with the disservice he does to Hans Christian Andersen: he does not enshrine her book but presses his "observations" of "the present age" onto a literary world.

26. Gyllembourg, *To Tidsaldre*, 242; cf. *Two Ages*, 156.

27. Kierkegaard practices a type of reading that has been pursued under the rubric of "typography"; see Lacoue-Labarthe, *Typography*.

28. *Literary Review* first became widely known in the partial translation of Theodor Haecker under the title *Kritik der Gegenwart*. This translation was then the basis for Alexander Dru's 1940 translation, *The Present Age*. On the reception of Kierkegaard's text in the German-speaking world of the early twentieth century, see the excellent essay of Janik, "Haecker, Kierkegaard."

29. See the opening scene in "The Diary of the Seducer" (*Either/Or*, 1:313–15).

30. On spiritlessness, see in particular Kierkegaard's succinct words in *Sickness unto Death*, 42–47; see Chapter 2.

31. See Adorno, *Kierkegaard*, 63.

32. Peder L. Møller, "A Visit in Sorø," in Kierkegaard, *Corsair Affair*, 103–4.

33. See *Concluding Unscientific Postscript*, 387–555.

34. Peder L. Møller, "A Visit to Sorø," in Kierkegaard, *Corsair Affair*, 104.

35. In the section of the "Dionysian Dithyrambs" entitled "Among the Daughters of the Desert," Nietzsche writes: "Die Wüste wächst: weh dem, der Wüsten birgt." (The desert grows: woe to anyone who conceals deserts.) See *Sämtliche Werke*, 6:382. *Literary Review* has often been compared with Nietzsche's writings; an evaluation of this effort at comparison can be found in Walter Kaufmann's introduction to Kierkegaard, *The Present Age*, 9–29. When Nietzsche said "the desert grows," it is impossible to understand the desert as anything but a figure of nihilism, "the uncanniest guest of all." But the image of the swamp in *Literary Review*, which could be compared fruitfully with the nonfigure "disaster" in Maurice Blanchot's *Writing of the Disaster*, is not so easy to decipher. For it is not simply an image of "nothing" but constitutes, inversely, the nothingness of image and figure in speech: it is therefore closer to the slogan "God is dead" than to the death itself. The threat of this slogan is briefly indicated in Heidegger's well-known discussion of the growing desert, but it quickly disappears into the event of nihilism itself: "What

once was a scream: 'the desert grows . . .' threatens to turn into chatter [*Geschwätz*]. The threat of this perversion [*Verkehrung*] belongs to that which gives us cause to think. This threat consists in this: that perhaps that which has been thought the most [*Gedachteste*] today and tomorrow and even overnight is still only a mode of discourse [*Redensart*], going around and spreading in the form of a mode of discourse" (*Was heißt Denken?*, 19–20). It is scarcely an accident that the perversion (*Verkehrung*) of the "word" into chatter has already taken place *in the text*. For the mother who cries out that she will teach precisely *authority*—"Ich werde dich lehren, was gehorchen heißt" (I will teach you what it means to obey) (19)—turns into a Nietzsche whose "teaching" consists in a screaming. This turning constitutes, for Heidegger, not a turn of speech but a perversion of language, and this perversion, which he has not been able to distinguish from turns of speech, makes it impossible to say who turns into whom and whose "turn" it is when the word *Kehre* (turning) is in play. The "confusion" of Nietzsche and Heidegger in the very text of *Nietzsche-Heidegger*, which serves to mark a certain *Kehre*, is thus bound up with the perversion of "word" in chatter, mother into Nietzsche, Nietzsche into the language, if not the "cry," of Heidegger.

Not without reason does the beginning of this chain of substitutions— the cry of mother to child—present itself as an *Anzeige*, a "notification" to the authorities. Its end point consists of a language altogether without authority, indeed so devoid of self-legitimizing power that authorship itself is put into question. Without the name of Kierkegaard ever making an appearance in the text, Heidegger determines the "desert" as the place of perversion pure and simple, the indomitable domain in which "the saying" (*die Sage*) turns into "discourse" (*die Rede*). And yet Kierkegaard, unnamed if not anonymous, is not completely absent from this lecture on learning. As a ghostly presence, he inhabits the exchange of letters through which Nietzsche comes into public discussion. For "the Dane Georg Brandes" (*Was heißt Denken?*, 22), the same Dane who made Kierkegaard famous and who suggested Nietzsche read Kierkegaard, makes Nietzsche's apothegm a public matter, at least according to Heidegger. On Heidegger and the call of the mother, see the extraordinary intertextual network of Ronell, *Telephone Book*; cf. her essay on Benjamin, Kierkegaard, and Heidegger, "Street Talk."

36. In the section entitled "The Tragic in Ancient Drama," those on the edge of the dead (*sumparanekromenoi*) make every writing into papers from one still living because the distinction of life from death

suspends itself in the "still living"—or still life—of writing: "Our society requires a renewal and rebirth at every single meeting and to that end requires that its intrinsic activity be rejuvenated by a new description of its productivity. Let us, then, designate our intention as a venture in fragmentary endeavor or the art of writing posthumous [*efterladt*] papers. . . . Unfinished papers are like a ruin, and what place of resort could be more natural for the buried? The art, then, is to produce skillfully the same effect, the same carelessness and fortuitousness, the same anacoluthic [*anakoluthisk*] thought process; the art is to evoke an enjoyment that is never present tense but always has an element of the past and thus is present in the past" (1:152). On anacoluthon, see the concluding pages of de Man, *Allegories of Reading*, esp. 300–301.

37. On the extensiveness of Kierkegaard's antagonism to the press, see the introduction and compilation of Kjær-Hansen, *Søren Kierkegaards Pressepolemik*.

38. On hearing oneself speak, see, of course, Derrida, *La voix et le phénomène*, esp. 34–52. On Kierkegaard's obsession with listening to echoes, see the voluminous documentation in Viallaneix, *Ecoute, Kierkegaard*.

39. See *Concept of Anxiety*, 128.

40. On the law, anonymity, and the people, see Weber, "In the Name of the Law."

41. See *From the Papers of One Still Living*, 56; cf. Chapter 1.

42. *Either/Or*, 1:19.

43. See *Concept of Anxiety*, 118.

44. On Mrs. Waller's recitation of the word "demonic," see the first footnote to the "Esthetic Interpretation," 33–34, which refers to Thomasine Gyllembourg, *To Tidsaldre*, 177–78.

45. See Kierkegaard, *Authority and Revelation*, III. This book was also originally entitled *A Literary Review* (see *Two Ages*, 149); cf. Schleifer and Manckley, "Writing Without Authority."

Conclusion

1. See *Concluding Unscientific Postscript*, 629–30.

2. See Kierkegaard, *Attack on "Christendom"*, 110, translation modified.

3. See ibid., 108, translation modified.

4. Kierkegaard, *Point of View of My Work as an Author*, 75. Kierkegaard notes that "more than one of the pseudonyms applies this expression to

himself, saying that he is a policeman [*Betjent*], a member of the detective force" (75). On "tone" in philosophy, see Fenves, *Raising the Tone*, esp. 30–39.

  5. Wittgenstein, Heidegger, and Benjamin do not exhaust the list of those who, having read Kierkegaard, articulate the altercation with "chatter." Blanchot, for instance, stated the terms of this altercation with exceptional clarity in his writings on Kierkegaard, Wittgenstein, and Heidegger, as well as in his remarkable essay "La parole vaine," where one finds the memorable sentence: "Chatter is the shame of language"—a shame that conceals itself in active, worklike, and upright communication.

Bibliography

Works by Kierkegaard

Attack on "Christendom," trans. and intro. Walter Lowrie. Princeton: Princeton University Press, 1968.

Christian Discourses, trans. Walter Lowrie. Princeton: Princeton University Press, 1940.

The Concept of Anxiety, ed. and trans. Reider Thomte and Albert B. Anderson. Princeton: Princeton University Press, 1980.

The Concept of Irony, trans. and intro. Lee M. Capel. Bloomington: Indiana University Press, 1965.

The Concept of Irony, trans. and ed. Howard V. Hong and Edna H. Hong. Princeton: Princeton University Press, 1989.

Concluding Unscientific Postscript, trans. and ed. Howard V. Hong and Edna H. Hong. Princeton: Princeton University Press, 1992.

The Corsair Affair, trans. and ed. Howard V. Hong and Edna H. Hong. Princeton: Princeton University Press, 1982.

Crisis in the Life of an Actress and Other Essays on Drama, trans. and intro. Stephen D. Crites. New York: Harper & Row, 1967.

Early Polemical Writings, trans. and ed. Julia Watkin. Princeton: Princeton University Press, 1990.

Either/Or, trans. and ed. Howard V. Hong and Edna H. Hong. Princeton: Princeton University Press, 1987.

Fear and Trembling—Repetition, trans. and ed. Howard V. Hong and Edna H. Hong. Princeton: Princeton University Press, 1983.

A Kierkegaard Anthology, trans. and ed. R. Bretall. Princeton: Princeton University Press, 1947.

"Kritik der Gegenwart" (Critique of the present), trans. Theodor Haecker. *Der Brenner* 4 (1914): 815–49, 869–908.

Letters and Documents, trans. Henrik Rosenmeier. Princeton: Princeton University Press, 1978.

On Authority and Revelation (the book on Adler), trans. Walter Lowrie. New York: Harper & Row, 1966.

Philosophical Fragments. trans. David Swenson, intro. Niels Thulstrup, rev. trans. Howard Hong. Princeton: Princeton University Press, 1967.

Philosophical Fragments—Johannes Climacus, trans. and ed. Howard V. Hong and Edna H. Hong. Princeton: Princeton University Press, 1985.

The Point of View of My Work as an Author, trans. Walter Lowrie, ed. Benjamin Nelson. New York: Harper & Row, 1962.

Prefaces, trans. and ed. William McDonald. Tallahassee: Florida State University Press, 1989.

The Present Age, trans. Alexander Dru, intro. Walter Kaufmann. New York: Harper & Row, 1962 [1940].

The Sickness unto Death, trans. Howard V. Hong and Edna H. Hong. Princeton: Princeton University Press, 1980.

Søren Kierkegaards Bibliotek, ed. Niels Thulstrup. Copenhagen: Munksgaard, 1957.

Søren Kierkegaard's Journals and Papers, trans. and ed. Howard V. Hong and Edna H. Hong. Bloomington: Indiana University Press, 1975.

Søren Kierkegaards Papirer, ed. P. A. Heiberg, V. Kuhr, and E. Torsting. Copenhagen: Gyldendal, 1909–48. Rev. ed.: ed. N. Thulstrup. Copenhagen: Gyldendal, 1968–70.

Søren Kierkegaards Samlede Værker, ed. A. B. Drachmann, J. L. Heiberg, and H. O. Lange. Copenhagen: Gyldendal, 1920–36. Rev. ed.: ed. P. P. Rohde. Copenhagen: Gyldendal, 1962–64.

Stages on Life's Way, trans. Howard V. Hong and Edna H. Hong. Princeton: Princeton University Press, 1940.

Training in Christianity, trans. W. Lowrie. Princeton: Princeton University Press, 1972.

Two Ages [*A Literary Review*], trans. and ed. Howard V. Hong and Edna H. Hong. Princeton: Princeton University Press, 1978.

Works of Love, trans. and ed. Howard Hong and Edna Hong. New York: Harper & Row, 1962.

Other Works

Adorno, Theodor W. *Kierkegaard: Construction of the Aesthetic*, trans. Robert Hullot-Kentor. Minneapolis: University of Minnesota Press, 1989.

Agacinski, Sylviana. *Aparté: Conceptions and Deaths of Søren Kierkegaard*, trans. and intro. K. Newmark. Tallahassee: Florida State University Press, 1988.

Allison, Henry A. "Christianity and Nonsense," in *Kierkegaard: A Collection of Critical Essays*, ed. J. Thompson (see below), 289–323.

———. *Kant's Theory of Freedom*. Cambridge, Eng.: Cambridge University Press, 1990.

Andersen, Hans Christian. *Kun en Spillemand*. Copenhagen: Reitzel, 1837.

———. *Only a Fiddler*, translator anonymous. New York: Hurd and Houghton, 1845.

Aristotle. *The Nicomachean Ethics*, trans. D. Ross, J. L. Ackrill, and J. O. Urmson. Oxford: Oxford University Press, 1980.

Augustine. *On Free Choice of the Will*, trans. A. S. Benjamin and L. H. Hackstaff. Indianapolis: Bobbs-Merrill, 1964.

Bakhtin, Mikhail. *Problems of Dostoevsky's Poetics*, trans. R. W. Rotsel. New York: Ardis, 1973.

Baldwin, Birgit. "Irony, That 'Little, Invisible Personage': Reading Kierkegaard's Ghosts." *Modern Language Notes* 104 (1989): 1124–41.

Baudelaire, Charles. *The Painter and Modern Life and Other Essays*, trans. and ed. Jonathan Mayne. London: Phaidon, 1964.

Bejerholm, Lars. "Communication," in *Bibliotheca Kierkegaardiana*, ed. N. Thulstrup and M. M. Thulstrup (see below), 3:52–59.

———. *Meddelelsens Dialektik*. Copenhagen: Munksgaard, 1962.

Benjamin, Walter. *Gesammelte Schriften*, ed. Rolf Tiedemann and Hermann Schweppenhäuser. Frankfurt am Main: Suhrkamp, 1977–85.

———. *The Origin of German Tragic Drama* (The Origin of the German Mourning-Play), trans. John Osborne. New York: Verso, 1985.

———. *Reflections*, trans. Edmund Jephcott. New York: Schocken, 1986.

Berkof, L. *Systematic Theology*. Grand Rapids, Mich.: Eerdman, 1959.

Bertung, Birgit, ed. *Kierkegaard—Poet of Existence*. Copenhagen: Reitzel, 1989.

Bigelow, Pat. *Kierkegaard and the Problem of Writing*. Tallahassee: Florida State University Press, 1987.

Bittner, Rüdiger. "Maximen," in *Akten des Kongresses*, ed. G. Funke and J. Kopper (see below), 485–98.

Blanchot, Maurice. *L'Entretien infini*. Paris: Gallimard, 1969.

———. *Faux pas*. Paris: Gallimard, 1943.

———. "La parole vaine," in Louis-René Forêts, *Le Bavard*. Paris: Union Générale d'Editions, 1963.

———. *The Writing of the Disaster*, trans. Ann Smock. Lincoln: University of Nebraska Press, 1986.

Bok, Sissela. *Secrets*. New York: Pantheon, 1983.

Bolz, N. W., and W. Hübener, eds. *Spiegel und Gleichnis*. Würzburg: Königshausen und Neumann, 1983.

Borch-Jacobsen, Mikkel. *Lacan: The Absolute Master*, trans. D. Brick. Stanford, Calif.: Stanford University Press, 1991.

Bové, Paul. "The Penitentiary of Reflection: Sören Kierkegaard and Critical Activity," in *Kierkegaard and Literature*, ed. Ronald Schleifer and Robert Manckley (see below), 25–57.

Brunner, Emil. "Das Grundproblem der Philosophie bei Kant und Kierkegaard." *Zwischen den Zeiten* 2 (1924): 31–44.

Buber, Martin. *I and Thou*, trans. Walter Kaufmann. New York: Scribner, 1970.

Chrysostom, Iohannes. *In Epistolam ad Galatas*, vol. 16, *Patrologiae cursus completus*, Greek series, ed. P. Migne. Paris: Migne, 1857–87.

Cohen, Hermann. *Ethik des reinen Willens*, 2d ed. Berlin: Cassirer, 1907.

Courtine, J.-F. et al., ed. *Du sublime*. Paris: Editions Belin, 1988.

Crites, Stephen. *In the Twilight of Christendom*. Chambersburg, Pa.: American Academy of Religion, 1971.

Cutting, Pat. "The Levels of Interpersonal Relationships in Kierkegaard's *Two Ages*," in *International Kierkegaard Commentary: "Two Ages,"* ed. Robert L. Perkins (see below), 73–86.

de Man, Paul. *Allegories of Reading*. New Haven, Conn.: Yale University Press, 1979.

———. *Blindness and Insight*, 2d rev. ed. Minneapolis: University of Minnesota Press, 1983.

———. Introduction to Hans Robert Jauss, *Toward an Aesthetic of Reception* (see below), vii–xxv.

Derrida, Jacques. *De l'esprit: Heidegger et la question*. Paris: Galilée, 1987.

———. *Du Droit à la philosophie*. Paris: Galilée, 1990.

———. *Limited Inc*, trans. Sam Weber. Evanston, Ill.: Northwestern University Press, 1988.

———. *Margins of Philosophy*, trans. Alan Bass. Chicago: University of Chicago Press, 1982.

———. *Psyché*. Paris: Galilée, 1987.

———. *La voix et le phénomène*. Paris: Presses Universitaires de France, 1967.

Descartes, René. *Meditations on First Philosophy*, trans. Donald A. Cress. Indianapolis: Hackett, 1979.

———. *Oeuvres de Descartes*, ed. Charles Adams and Paul Tannery. Paris: Vrin, 1964.

Deuser, Hermann. *Dialektische Theologie: Studien zu Adornos Metaphysik und zum Spätwerk Kierkegaards*. Munich: Grünewald, 1980.

———. *Kierkegaard: Die Philosophie des religiösen Schriftstellers*. Darmstadt: Wissenschaftliche Buchgesellschaft, 1985.

Drew, Elizabeth A. *The Literature of Gossip: Nine English Letterwriters*. New York: Norton, 1964.

Fahrenbach, Helmut. "Kierkegaards ethische Existenzanalyse (als 'Korrektiv' der Kantisch-idealistischen Moralphilosophie)," in *Materialien zur Philosophie Søren Kierkegaards*, ed. M. Theunissen and W. Greve (see below), 216–40.

Fenger, Henning. *The Heibergs*, trans. F. J. Marker. New York: Twayne, 1971.

———. *Kierkegaard: The Myths and Their Origin*, trans. George C. Schoolfield. New Haven, Conn.: Yale University Press, 1980.

Fenves, Peter. "Antonomasia: Leibniz and the Baroque." *Modern Language Notes* 105 (1990): 432–52.

———. "Image and Chatter: Adorno's Construction of Kierkegaard." *Diacritics* 22 (1992): 100–114.

———. *A Peculiar Fate: Metaphysics and World-History in Kant*. Ithaca, N.Y.: Cornell University Press, 1991.

———. "Testing Right—Lying in View of Justice," *On the Necessity of Violence for Any Possibility of Justice*, special edition of the *Cardozo Law Review* 13 (1991): 1081–1113.

———, ed. *Raising the Tone of Philosophy: Late Essays by Kant, Transformative Critique by Derrida*, trans. P. Fenves and John Leavey, Jr. Baltimore: Johns Hopkins University Press, 1993.

Freud, Sigmund. *Three Essays on the Theory of Sexuality*, trans. James Strachey. New York: Basic Books, 1962.

Freytag, Hartmut. "*Quae sunt per allegoriam dicta*: Das theologische Verständnis der Allegorie in der frühchristlichen und mittelalterlichen

Exegese von Galater 4,21–31," in *Verbum et Signum*, ed. Hans Fromm, Wolfgang Harms, and Uwe Ruberg (see below), 1:32–35.

Fromm, Hans, Wolfgang Harms, and Uwe Ruberg, eds. *Verbum et Signum*. Munich: Fink, 1975.

Funke, G., and J. Kopper, eds. *Akten des Kongresses*. Berlin: de Gruyter, 1974.

Gadamer, Hans-Georg. "Hermeneutics and Logocentrism," in *Dialogue and Deconstruction*, ed. D. P. Michelfelder and R. E. Palmer (see below), 112–20.

———. "Reply to My Critics," in *The Hermeneutic Tradition*, ed. G. L. Ormiston and A. D. Schrift (see below), 273–97.

———. *Truth and Method*, trans. J. Weinsheimer and D. G. Marshall. New York: Crossroads, 1989.

———. *Wahrheit und Methode*. Tübingen: Mohr, 1972.

Gasché, Rodolphe. *The Tain of the Mirror*. Cambridge, Mass.: Harvard University Press, 1987.

Gill, Jerry H. "Kant, Kierkegaard and Religious Knowledge," in *Essays on Kierkegaard*, ed. J. H. Gill (see below), 58–73.

———, ed. *Essays on Kierkegaard*. Minneapolis: Burgess, 1969.

Goethe, Johann Wolfgang. *Faust*, ed. Günther Fetzer. Munich: Artemis, 1977.

Gyllembourg, Thomasine. *Samlede Skrifter*. Copenhagen: Reitzel, 1867.

Jones, Alexander, ed. *The New Testament of the Jerusalem Bible*, abridged ed. Garden City, N.Y.: Doubleday, 1969.

Habermas, Jürgen. "The Hermeneutic Claim to Universality," in *The Hermeneutic Tradition*, ed. G. L. Ormiston and A. D. Schrift (see below), 245–72.

Hamacher, Werner. "Das Beben der Darstellung," in *Positionen der Literaturwissenschaft*, ed. David Wellbery (see below), 150–92.

———. "Hermeneutic Ellipses: Writing the Hermeneutic Circle in Schleiermacher," trans. Timothy Bahti, in *Transforming the Hermeneutic Context*, ed. G. L. Ormiston and A. D. Schrift (see below), 177–210.

———. "*Pleroma*—zu Genesis und Struktur einer dialektischen Hermeneutik bei Hegel," in *Der Geist des Christentums*, ed. W. Hamacher. Frankfurt am Main: Ullstein, 1978.

———. "Die Sekunde der Inversion: Bewegungen einer Figur durch Celans Gedichte," in *Paul Celan*, ed. W. Hamacher and W. Menninghaus (see below), 81–126.

———. "Das Versprechen der Auslegung," in *Spiegel und Gleichnis*, ed. N. W. Bolz and W. Hüber (see above), 252–53.

Hamacher, Werner, and W. Menninghaus, eds. *Paul Celan*. Frankfurt am Main: Suhrkamp, 1988.

Hamann, Johann Georg. *Schriften zur Sprache*, intro. and ed. Joseph Simon. Frankfurt am Main: Suhrkamp, 1967.

Hannay, Alastair. *Kierkegaard*. London: Routledge & Kegan Paul, 1982.

Hartman, Geoffrey H. *Minor Prophecies*. Cambridge, Mass.: Harvard University Press, 1991.

Hartshorne, M. Holmes. *Kierkegaard, Godly Deceiver*. New York: Columbia University Press, 1990.

Hauck, Friedrich. "*Koinos*," in *Theological Dictionary of the New Testament*, ed. G. Kittel (see below), 3:789–809.

Hausschildt, Friedrich. *Die Ethik Søren Kierkegaards*. Gütersloh: Mohn, 1982.

Haviland, John B. *Gossip, Reputation, and Knowledge in Zinacantan*. Chicago: University of Chicago Press, 1977.

Hegel, G. W. F. *Faith and Knowledge*, trans. Walter Cerf and H. S. Harris. Albany: State University of New York Press, 1977.

———. *Logic*, trans. William Wallace. Oxford: Clarendon Press, 1975.

———. *Werke*, ed. E. Moldenhauer and K. M. Michel. Frankfurt am Main: Suhrkamp, 1986.

Heidegger, Martin. *Sein und Zeit*. Tübingen: Niemeyer, 1979.

———. *Schellings Abhandlung über das Wesen der menschlichen Freiheit*. Tübingen: Niemeyer, 1971.

———. *Was heißt Denken?* Tübingen: Niemeyer, 1971.

Heller, T. C., M. Sosna, and D. Wellbery, eds. *Reconstructing Individualism*. Stanford, Calif.: Stanford University Press, 1986.

Henningsen, Bernd. *Poul Martin Møller oder die dänische Erziehung des Søren Kierkegaard*. Frankfurt am Main: Akademische Verlagsgesellschaft, 1973.

Henricksen, Aage. "Kierkegaard's Reviews of Literature." *Orbis Litterarum* 10 (1955): 75–83.

Herder, Johann Gottfried. *Ueber den Ursprung der Sprache*, ed. Klaus Träger. Berlin: Akademie, 1959.

Hölderlin, Friedrich. *Poems and Fragments*, trans. and intro. Michael Hamburger. Cambridge, Eng.: Cambridge University Press, 1980.

Holm, Søren. "Schopenhauer und Kierkegaard." *Schopenhauer-Jahrbuch* 43 (1962): 5–14.

Hügli, Anton. "Gibt es Dinge, die sich nicht mitteilen lassen? Kierke-gaard und die Nicht-Mitteilbarkeits-These." *Liber Academiae Kierke-gaardiensis Annuaris* 2–4 (1979–81): 70–84.

Hume, David. *A Treatise of Human Nature*, ed. L. A. Selby-Bigge, rev. P. H. Nidditch. Oxford: Clarendon, 1978.

Israel Meir, ha-Kohen. *Middos: The Measure of Man.* Jerusalem: S.ll., 1987.

Jacobi, F. H. *David Hume über den Glauben, oder Idealismus und Realis-mus, ein Gespräch.* Breslau: Löwe, 1785.

Janik, Allan. "Haecker, Kierkegaard, and the early *Brenner*," in *Interna-tional Kierkegaard Commentary: "Two Ages,"* ed. R. L. Perkins (see below), 189–222.

Jauss, Hans Robert. *Aesthetische Erfahrung und literarische Hermeneutik.* Frankfurt am Main: Suhrkamp, 1982.

———. *Questions and Answers*, ed. and trans. Michael Hays. Minneapolis: University of Minnesota Press, 1989.

———. *Toward an Aesthetic of Reception*, trans. Timothy Bahti, intro. Paul de Man. Minneapolis: University of Minnesota Press, 1982.

Jones, Glyn W. "Søren Kierkegaard and Poul Martin Møller." *Modern Language Review* 60 (1965): 73–82.

Kafka, Franz. *Briefe*, ed. Max Brod. Frankfurt am Main: Fischer, 1983.

Kant, Immanuel. *Anthropology from a Pragmatic Point of View*, trans. Mary J. Gregor. The Hague: Nijhoff, 1974.

———. *Conflict of the Faculties*, trans. Mary Gregor and Robert E. An-chor. New York: Abaris, 1979.

———. *The Critique of Judgment*, trans. W. Pluhar. Indianapolis: Hackett, 1987.

———. *Critique of Practical Reason*, trans. Lewis White Beck. Indi-anapolis: Bobbs-Merrill, 1956.

———. *The Critique of Pure Reason*, trans. Norman Kemp Smith. New York: St. Martin's Press, 1965.

———. *Education*, trans. Annette Churton. Ann Arbor: University of Michigan Press, 1960.

———. *Foundations of the Metaphysics of Morals*, trans. and intro. Lewis White Beck. Indianapolis: Bobbs-Merrill, 1959.

———. *Kants Gesammelte Schriften*, ed. Königliche Preussische (later, Deutsche) Akademie der Wissenschaften. Berlin and Leipzig: Walter de Gruyter, 1902–.

———. *On History*, ed. Lewis White Beck, trans. L. W. Beck, R. E. Anchor, and E. L. Fackenheim. Indianapolis: Bobbs-Merrill, 1963.

———. *Religion Within the Limits of Reason Alone*, trans. Theodore M. Greene and Hoyte H. Hudson. New York: Harper & Row, 1960.

Kapferer, Jean-Noel. *Rumeurs: le plus vieux média du monde*. Paris: Editions du Seuil, 1987.

Kirmmse, Bruce. *Kierkegaard in Golden Age Denmark*. Bloomington: Indiana University Press, 1990.

Kittel, Gerhard, ed. *Theological Dictionary of the New Testament*, trans. and ed. Geoffrey W. Bromily. Grand Rapids, Mich.: Eerdmans, 1965.

Kjaer-Hansen, Ulf. *Søren Kierkegaards Pressepolemick*. Copenhagen: Berlingske, 1955.

The Koran, trans. N. J. Dawood. Harmondsworth, Eng.: Penguin, 1990.

Kreisberg, Ove, and F. J. Billeskov Jansen. "H. C. Andersen," in *Bibliotheca Kierkegaardiana*, ed. N. Thulstrup and M. M. Thulstrup (see below), 9:121–26.

Kroner, Richard. "Kierkegaards Hegelverständnis," in *Materialien zur Philosophie Søren Kierkegaards*, ed. Michael Theunissen and Wilfried Greve (see below), 425–36.

Lacan, Jacques. *Ecrits*, trans. A. Sheridan. New York: Norton, 1977.

Lacoue-Labarthe, Philippe. *Typography*, ed. and trans. Christopher Fynsk. Cambridge, Mass.: Harvard University Press, 1989.

Lacoue-Labarthe, Philippe, and Jean-Luc Nancy. *The Literary Absolute*, trans. P. Barnard and C. Lester. Albany: State University of New York Press, 1988.

Lessing, Gotthold Ephraim. *Lessing's Theological Writings*, ed. and trans. Henry Chadwick. Stanford, Calif.: Stanford University Press, 1956.

Lewin, Jack. *Gossip: The Inside Story*. New York: Plenum, 1987.

Lowrie, Walter. *Kierkegaard*. New York: Harper, 1962.

Lubac, Henri de. " 'Typologie' et 'allégorisme.' " *Recherches de science religieuse* 34 (1947): 180–226.

Lukàcs, Georg. *The Destruction of Reason*, trans. Peter Palmer. Atlantic Highlands, N.J.: Humanities Press, 1981.

Luther, Martin. *Commentary on St. Paul's Epistle to the Galatians*, translator anonymous. Philadelphia: Quaker City, 1972.

Lyotard, Jean-François. *The Differend: Phrases in Dispute*, trans. Georges Van Den Abbeele. Minneapolis: University of Minnesota Press, 1988.

McCarthy, Vincent A. "Schelling and Kierkegaard on Freedom and the Fall," in *International Kierkegaard Commentary: "The Concept of Anxiety,"* ed. R. L. Perkins (see below), 89–109.

Mackey, Louis. *Kierkegaard: A Kind of Poet.* Philadelphia: University of Pennsylvania Press, 1971.

———. "The View from Pisgah," in *Kierkegaard: A Collection of Essays,* ed. J. Thompson (see below), 395–97.

Malantschuk, Gregor. *Frihed og Eksistens: Studier i Søren Kierkegaards tænking,* ed. N. J. Cappeldørn and P. Müller. Copenhagen: Reitzel, 1980.

Melberg, Arne. "*Repetition* (in the Kierkegaardian Sense of the Term)." *Diacritics* 20 (1990): 71–87.

Michelfelder, D. P., and R. E. Palmer, eds. *Dialogue and Deconstruction.* Albany: State University of New York Press, 1989.

Miller, J. Hillis. *The Ethics of Reading.* New York: Columbia University Press, 1989.

Møller, Poul M. *Efterladte Skrifter.* Copenhagen: Bianco Lunos, 1839–43.

Müller, Paul. *Meddelelsesdialektikken i Søren Kierkegaard's "Philosophiske Smuler."* Copenhagen: Reitzel, 1979.

Nägele, Rainer, ed. *Benjamin's Ground.* Detroit: Wayne State University Press, 1986.

Nancy, Jean-Luc. *L'Expérience de la liberté.* Paris: Galilée, 1988.

———. *The Inoperative Community,* ed. Peter Connor, foreword Christopher Fynsk. Minneapolis: University of Minnesota Press, 1991.

———. "L'Offrande sublime," in *Du sublime,* ed. J.-F. Courtine et al. (see above), 37–75.

———. *Le Partage des voix.* Paris: Galilée, 1982.

Newmark, Kevin. "Between Hegel and Kierkegaard: The Space of Translation." *Genre* 16 (1983): 373–88.

———. "Taking Kierkegaard Apart," in Sylviana Agacinski, *Aparté: Conceptions and Deaths of Søren Kierkegaard* (see above), 3–30.

Nietzsche, Friedrich. *The Gay Science,* trans. Walter Kaufmann. New York: Vintage, 1974.

———. *Sämtliche Werke,* ed. Giorgi Colli and Mazzino Montinari. Berlin: de Gryter, 1967–77.

———. *Untimely Meditations,* trans. R. J. Hollingdale. Cambridge, Eng.: Cambridge University Press, 1983.

Nordentoft, Kresten. *Kierkegaard's Psychology,* trans. Bruce Kirmmse. Pittsburgh: Duquesne University Press, 1978.

Norris, Christopher. "De Man Unfair to Kierkegaard? An allegory of (non)-reading," in *Kierkegaard—Poet of Existence,* ed. Birgit Bertung (see above), 89–107.

Novalis. *Werke*, ed. Gerhard Schulz. Munich: Beck, 1969.

Oakeshott, Michael. *Rationalism in Politics*. London: Methuen, 1977.

O'Neill, Onora. *Acting on Principle: An Essay in Kantian Ethics*. New York: Columbia University Press, 1975.

Oppen, Menachem Moshe. *A Twist of the Tongue: Insights and Stories About the Power of Words Based on the Parshah of the Week, Beraishis*. Baltimore: M'chon Harbotzas Torah, 1987.

Ormiston, G. L., and A. D. Schrift, eds. *The Hermeneutic Tradition*. Albany: State University of New York Press, 1990.

———, eds. *Transforming the Hermeneutic Context*. Albany: State University of New York Press, 1990.

Perkins, Robert L. "For Sanity's Sake: Kant, Kierkegaard, and Father Abraham," in *Kierkegaard's "Fear and Trembling": Critical Appraisals*, ed. R. L. Perkins (see below), 43–61.

———, ed. *International Kierkegaard Commentary: "The Concept of Anxiety."* Macon, Ga.: Mercer University Press, 1985.

———, ed. *International Kierkegaard Commentary: "The Corsair Affair."* Macon, Ga.: Mercer University Press, 1990.

———, ed. *International Kierkegaard Commentary: "Two Ages."* Macon, Ga.: Mercer University Press, 1984.

———, ed. *Kierkegaard's "Fear and Trembling": Critical Appraisals*. University: Alabama University Press, 1981.

Plato. *Ion—Hippias Major*, trans. Paul Woodruff. Indianapolis: Hackett, 1983.

———. *Platonis Opera*, ed. John Burnet. Oxford: Clarendon Press, 1903.

Poole, Roger. "Søren Kierkegaard and P. L. Møller: Erotic Space Shattered," in *International Kierkegaard Commentary: "The Corsair Affair,"* ed. R. L. Perkins (see above), 141–62.

Rickels, Laurence A., ed. *Looking After Nietzsche*. Albany: State University of New York Press, 1990.

Ricoeur, Paul. "Philosophie après Kierkegaard." *Revue de théologie et de philosophie* 3 (1963): 303–16.

Rohde, H. P. *Gaadefulde Stadier paa Kierkegaards Vej*. Copenhagen: Rosenkilde og Bagger, 1974.

———. "Poul Møller," in *Bibliotheca Kierkegaardiana*, ed. N. Thulstrup and M. M. Thulstrup (see below), 10:89–109.

Ronell, Avital. "Street Talk," in *Benjamin's Ground*, ed. Rainer Nägele (see above), 119–46.

———. *The Telephone Book*. Lincoln: University of Nebraska Press, 1989.

Rorty, Richard. *Philosophy and the Mirror of Nature.* Princeton: Princeton University Press, 1979.

Rosnow, Ralph L., and Gary A. Fine. *Rumor and Gossip: The Social Psychology of Hearsay.* New York: Elsevier, 1976.

Saner, Hans. *Kant's Political Philosophy: Its Origins and Development,* trans. E. B. Ashton. Chicago: University of Chicago Press, 1967.

Sartre, Jean-Paul. "The Singular Universal," in *Kierkegaard: A Collection of Essays,* ed. Josiah Thompson (see below), 230–65.

Schelling, F. W. J. *Philosophie der Offenbarung,* ed. Manfred Frank. Frankfurt am Main: Suhrkamp, 1977.

———. *The Philosophy of Art,* ed. and trans. Douglas W. Stott. Minneapolis: University of Minnesota Press, 1989.

———. *Ueber das Wesen der menschlichen Freiheit.* Frankfurt am Main: Suhrkamp, 1975.

Schilpp, Paul. *Kant's Pre-Critical Ethics.* Evanston, Ill.: Northwestern University Press, 1938.

Schlegel, Friedrich. *Kritische Schriften,* ed. Wolfdietrich Rasch. Munich: Hansen, 1964.

Schleiermacher, Friedrich. *The Christian Faith,* trans. H. R. Mackintosh and J. S. Stewart. Edinburgh: T & T Clark, 1928.

———. *Hermeneutik und Kritik,* ed. Manfred Frank. Frankfurt am Main: Suhrkamp, 1977.

Schleifer, Ronald, and Robert Manckley. "Writing Without Authority and the Reading of Kierkegaard," in *Kierkegaard and Literature,* ed. authors (see below), 3–22.

———, eds. *Kierkegaard and Literature.* Norman: University of Oklahoma Press, 1984.

Schmidinger, Heinrich D. *Das Problem des Interesse und die Philosophie Kierkegaards.* Freiburg: Alber, 1983.

Schmitt, Carl. *Die Diktatur.* Berlin: Duncker & Humblot, 1928.

Schmucker, Joseph. *Die Ursprünge der Ethik Kants.* Meisenheim: Anton Hain, 1961.

Schneewind, J. B. "The Use of Autonomy in Ethical Theory," in *Reconstructing Individualism,* ed. T. C. Heller, M. Sosna, and D. Wellbery (see above), 64–75.

Schopenhauer, Arthur. *On the Freedom of the Will,* trans. Konstantin Koldenda. Oxford: Blackwell, 1985.

Schrader, George. "Kant and Kierkegaard on Duty and Inclination," in

Kierkegaard: A Collection of Critical Essays, ed. Josiah Thompson (see below), 324–41.

Schweppenhäuser, Hermann. *Kierkegaards Angriff auf die Spekulation*. Frankfurt am Main: Suhrkamp, 1967.

Skinner, Henry Alan. *The Origin of Medical Terms*. Baltimore: William & Wilkins, 1949.

Smith, Ronald G. "Hamann and Kierkegaard." *Kierkegaardiana* 5 (1964): 52–67.

Smyth, John Vignaux. *The Question of Eros*. Tallahassee: Florida State University Press, 1986.

Souter, A., ed. *Novum Testamentvm Graece*. Oxford: Clarendon, 1950.

Spacks, Patricia Meyer. *Gossip*. New York: Knopf, 1985.

Stack, George. *Kirkegaard's Existential Ethics*. University: University of Alabama Press, 1977.

Staiger, Emil. *Die Kunst der Interpretation*. Nördlingen: Beck, 1971.

Starobinski, Jean. *Trois fureurs*. Paris: Gallimard, 1974.

Sussman, Henry. *The Hegelian Aftermath*. Baltimore: Johns Hopkins University Press, 1982.

Swenson, David F. *Something About Kierkegaard*, ed. Lilian M. Swenson. Minneapolis: Augsburg, 1945.

Taylor, Mark. *Journeys to Selfhood*. Berkeley: University of California Press, 1980.

——. "Sounds of Silence," in *Kierkegaard's "Fear and Trembling": Critical Appraisals*, ed. R. L. Perkins (see above), 43–61.

Theunissen, Michael. *Der Begriff Ernst bei Kierkegaard*. Freiburg: Alber, 1958.

Theunissen, Michael, and Wilfried Greve, eds. *Materialien zur Philosophie Søren Kierkegaards*. Frankfurt am Main: Suhrkamp, 1979.

Thiele-Dohrmann, Klaus. *Unter dem Siegel der Verschwiegenheit: Die Psychologie des Klatsches*. Düsseldorf: Claassen, 1975.

Thompson, Josiah. *Kierkegaard: A Critical Biography*. New York: Knopf, 1974.

——, ed. *Kierkegaard: A Collection of Essays*. Garden City, N.Y.: Doubleday, 1972.

Thulstrup, Niels. "Kierkegaard and Schelling's Philosophy of Revelation," in *Bibliotheca Kierkegaardiana*, ed. N. Thulstrup and M. M. Thulstrup (see below), 4:144–59.

——. *Kierkegaard's Relation to Hegel*, trans. George L. Stengren. Princeton: Princeton University Press, 1980.

Thulstrup, Niels, and M. N. Thulstrup, eds. *Bibliotheca Kierkegaardiana.* Copenhagen: Reitzel, 1975–.

Vergote, Henri-Bernard. "Poul Martin Moeller et Soeren Kierkegaard." *Revue de métaphysique et de morale* 75 (1970): 452–76.

Viallaneix, Nelly. *Ecoute, Kierkegaard.* Paris: Editions du Cerf, 1979.

Wahl, Jean. *Etudes kierkegaardiennes.* Paris: Aubier, 1938.

Warminski, Andrzej. *Readings in Interpretation.* Minneapolis: University of Minnesota Press, 1987.

Waters, Lindsay, and Wlad Godzich, eds. *Reading de Man Reading.* Minneapolis: University of Minnesota Press, 1989.

Weber, Samuel. "In the Name of the Law." *Cardozo Law Review* 11 (1990): 1515–38.

———. *The Legend of Freud.* Minneapolis: University of Minnesota Press, 1982.

———. *Return to Freud.* Cambridge, Eng.: Cambridge University Press, 1991.

Wellbery, David, ed. *Positionen der Literaturwissenschaft.* Munich: Beck, 1985.

Whitman, Jon. "From the Textual to the Temporal: Early Christian 'Allegory' and Early Romantic 'Symbol.'" *New Literary History* 22 (1991): 161–76.

Wittgenstein, Ludwig. *Lectures and Conversations,* ed. Cyril Barrett. Berkeley: University of California Press, n.d.

———. *Philosophical Investigations,* trans. G. E. M. Anscombe. New York: Macmillan, 1958.

Index of Names

In this index an "f" after a number indicates a separate reference on the next page, and an "ff" indicates separate references on the next two pages. A continuous discussion over two or more pages is indicated by a span of page numbers, e.g., "57–59." *Passim* is used for a cluster of references in close but not consecutive sequence.

Adorno, Theodor Wiesengrund, 269n18, 283n37
Agacinski, Sylviana, 255n8, 265n19, 276n3, 282n30
al-Khowarizmi, Mohammed ibn Musa, 269n18
Allison, Henry, 277n5
Andersen, Hans Christian, 29–63 *passim*, 197, 235, 260n1, 264n13, 290n25
Archimedes, 216
Aristotle, 117, 125, 130–33 *passim*, 272n3, 277n8
Augustine, 276n19, 283n39

Baader, Franz von, 268n16
Bakhtin, Mikhail, 257n18
Baudelaire, Charles, 260n3
Bejerholm, Lars, 268n14
Benjamin, Walter, 248–49, 254n2, 255n13, 263n8, 271n27, 281n25, 281n28, 284n39, 293n5

Bible, *see* Hebrew Bible, Christian Bible
Blanchot, Maurice, 243, 260n25, 271n27, 276n3, 290n35, 293n5
Bok, Sissela, 253
Borch-Jacobsen, Mikkel, 257n16
Bové, Paul, 289n19
Brandes, Georg, 291n35
Bretall, Robert, 287n13
Buber, Martin, 257n18

Chafetz Chaim, the (Israel Meier Kagan), 256–57n15
Christian Bible, 61, 102–3, 271n26, 273n4; meaning of "communication" in, 106–7, 271n27; allegory in, 184–86, 283n38, 283–84n39; and "chatter," 246–47, 255–56n15. *See also* Hebrew Bible
Chystostom, Johannes, 185
Cohen, Hermann, 255n13
Cutting, Pat, 288–89n19

de Man, Paul, 255n8, 258–59,
    279n17, 289n20, 292n36
Derrida, Jacques, 255n8, 257n17,
    268n15, 269n19, 276n1, 282–
    83n35, 284n40
Descartes, Réne, 50, 121, 273n5
Drew, Elizabeth A., 253

Fahrenbach, Helmut, 278n16
Fenger, Henning, 260n1, 260–61n4,
    284n1, 286n10, 288n18
Freud, Sigmund, 268n17

Gadamer, Hans-Georg, 19–26 *pas-
    sim*, 257–58n24
Gasché, Rodolphe, 287n13
Goebbels, Josef, 259
Goethe, Johann Wolfgang von, 208,
    274n7, 288n18
Gyllembourg-Ehrensvärd, Thoma-
    sine, 194, 261–62n6, 265n17;
    anonymous author of "A Story of
    Everyday Life," 35ff, 55, 195–96,
    199–200; anonymous author of
    Two Ages, 200–214 *passim*, 223,
    232–37 *passim*, 287n15, 287–
    88n16, 288n18, 290n25

Habermas, Jürgen, 258
Haecker, Theodor, 290n28
Hamacher, Werner, 255n8, 271n27,
    276n18, 279n17
Hamann, Johann Georg, 164, 172,
    186, 265n18, 267–68n14
Hartman, Geoffrey, 263n8
Hartshorne, M. Holmes, 282n30
Haviland, John, 253
Hebrew Bible, 255–56n15, 259; *Gen-
    esis* (Adam), 79–94 *passim*; (Isaac)
    162–90 *passim*. *See also* Christian
    Bible
Hegel, F. W. G., 9, 16, 19, 36, 77,

233–34, 262n8, 267n12; and mo-
    dernity, 31–33, 271n23; and nega-
    tivity, 33, 36, 68–70, 99–100, 223–
    24; and communication, 146–51,
    276n4; interpretations of Kierke-
    gaard's relation to, 260–61n4
Heiberg, Johan Ludvig, 191–95 *pas-
    sim*, 208–9, 217, 261n4, 262n7,
    264–65n17
Heiberg, Johanne Luise, 288n18
Heidegger, Martin, 23, 248–49,
    274n7, 279n19, 290–91n35, 293n5
Herder, Johann Gottfried, 267–
    68n14
Hölderlin, Friedrich, 21, 27, 257n23
Homer, 274n8
Hong, Howard, 274n9, 285n9,
    286n10, 287n13
Hume, David, 172–73

Jacobi, F. H., 71, 172, 267n12
Jauss, Hans Robert, 257n18, 258–59

Kafka, Franz, 1, 257n18, 283n36
Kant, Immanuel, 7, 9, 15, 69–71,
    149–51, 163–64, 173, 277n13; *Cri-
    tique of Practical Reason*, 158–59,
    277n8, 279–80n21; *Critique of
    Judgment*, 168–69, 281n26; *Cri-
    tique of Pure Reason*, 272n29,
    274–75n11; interpretations of
    Kierkegaard's relation to, 278n16;
    Conflict of the Faculties, 281n27
Kapferer, Jean-Noel, 253
Kaufmann, Walter, 290n35
Kierkegaard, Søren, 8–15, 19, 25–26
    —Works: *Attack on "Christendom,"*
    245–47; *Battle of the Old and
    New Soap-Cellars*, 39, 264n16;
    Christian Discourses, 270n22;
    Concept of Anxiety, 12, 64–112,
    124, 234, 236; *Concept of Irony*, 48,

64, 114, 262n8, 264n15, 271n24, 288n18; *Concluding Unscientific Postscript*, 139–40, 146–51, 209, 221, 244, 254n5, 266n20, 266–67n6, 267n12, 275n12, 276n4, 276–77n5, 277–78n13; "Corsair Affair," 198–99, 213–14, 285n9, 286n10, 287n12; *Crisis in the Life of an Actress*, 288n18; *Either/Or*, 113, 191–95, 225, 235–36, 262n7, 265n18, 280n23, 286n9, 287n11, 288n18, 291–92n36; *Fear and Trembling*, 12, 151, 164–90 passim, 255n9; *From the Papers of One Still Living*, 29–63 passim, 66, 75, 85, 196–97, 203, 213, 231, 284n1, 284–85n8; *Johannes Climacus*, 121, 273n5; *On Authority and Revelation*, 239, 292n45; *Philosophical Fragments*, 12, 113–44, 254n5, 269–70n20, 275n14; *Point of View*, 246, 293–94n4; *Prefaces*, 263n11, 289–90n25; *Repetition*, 207–11, 282n35, 289n20; *Sickness unto Death*, 86, 270n20; *Stages on Life's Way*, 197–99, 287n11; *Training in Christianity*, 192, 273n4; *Two Ages*, 13, 195–241 passim, 284–85n8; *Works of Love*, 270–71n22

Kirmmse, Bruce, 264–65n17, 284–85n8
Koran, the, 171, 255–56n15

Lacan, Jacques, 257n16, 268n17
Lacoue-Labarthe, Philippe, 255n8, 290n27
Lessing, Gotthold Ephraim, 274n10, 275n12
Lewin, Jack, 253
Luther, Martin, 265n19, 283–84n39
Lyotard, Jean-François, 279n20

Mackey, Louis, 282n31, 283n38
Melberg, Arne, 289n20
Miller, J. Hillis, 278–79n17
Møller, Peder L., 197–99, 285–86n9, 286n10
Møller, Poul, 37–39, 71, 194, 262–63, 267n12
Müller, Paul, 275n13

Nancy, Jean-Luc, 271n27, 279n19
Newmark, Kevin, 261n4, 276n3
Nietzsche, Friedrich, 221, 257n18, 260n3, 290–91n35
Nordentoft, Kresten, 276n3
Norris, Christopher, 279n17
Novalis, 1, 257n18

Oakeshott, Michael, 257n18
Olsen, Regine, 47, 286n10
O'Neill, Onora, 280n22

Pilate, Pontius, 61
Plato, 6, 17, 126, 139–40, 254n5, 274n9. *See also* Socrates
Pückler-Muskau, Hermann, 264n13

Ronell, Avital, 266n20, 291n35
Rorty, Richard, 257n18
Rosnow, Ralph, 253

Schelling, Friedrich, 35, 69–70, 261n5, 268n16
Schlegel, Friedrich, 262–63n8
Schleiermacher, Freidrich, 7–8, 19, 254–55n6, 265n19
Schmitt, Carl, 281n25
Schopenhauer, Arthur, 70, 267n7
Schrader, George, 278n16
Scribe, Augustin Eugène, 191–95 passim, 262n7
Simeon Stylites, 56–57, 265n18
Smyth, John Vignaux, 274n6

Socrates, 115–21 *passim*, 126, 139–40,
274n9. *See also* Plato
Spacks, Patricia Meyer, 253
Spinoza, Baruch, 7, 75
Starobinski, Jean, 271n25
Sussman, Henry, 261n4
Swenson, David, 275n14

Talleyrand, Charles Maurice, 101
Taylor, Mark, 271n23, 282n31
Theunissen, Michael, 273–74n6

Thiel-Dohrmann, Klaus, 253
Thompson, Josiah, 285n9
Thulstrup, Niels, 260n4

Viallaneix, Nelly, 292n38
Voltaire, 5–6

Watkin, Julia, 263–64n13, 265n18
Weber, Samuel, 268n17
Wittgenstein, Ludwig, 6, 248–49,
254n4, 280n23, 293n5

MERIDIAN

Crossing Aesthetics

Jean-François Lyotard, *On the Analytic of the Sublime*

Peter Fenves, *"Chatter": Language and History in Kierkegaard*

Jean-Luc Nancy, *The Experience of Freedom*

Jean-Joseph Goux, *Oedipus, Philosopher*

Haun Saussy, *The Problem of a Chinese Aesthetic*

Jean-Luc Nancy, *The Birth to Presence*

Library of Congress
Cataloging-in-Publication Data

Fenves, Peter D. (Peter David), 1960–
"Chatter" : language and history in Kierkegaard /
Peter Fenves.
p.   cm. — (Meridian)
Includes bibliographical references and index.
ISBN (invalid) 0-8047-1107-1 (alk. paper) —
ISBN 0-8047-2208-0 (pbk. : alk. paper):
1. Kierkegaard, Søren, 1813–1855—Language.
2. Language and languages—Philosophy.
3. History—Philosophy.   I. Title.
II. Series: Meridian (Stanford, Calif.)
B4378.L35F46   1993
198'.9—dc20
93-16347
CIP

⊗ This book is printed on acid-free paper.
It was typeset in Adobe Garamond and Lithos
by Keystone Typesetting, Inc.